Here's what reviewers said
about the first edition of

The
Essential Outdoor
Gear Manual

"The trouble with outdoor equipment is that everyone has an opinion—one usually based on advertising hype, personal bias, or hearsay. Finally, here's a book that gives you all the information necessary to make objective buying decisions. This book, with its sound advice, will save you money and make you a better backcountry traveler."

—Nancy Prichard, outdoor adventure journalist

"Think about something that we all need, yet we'd all hate to have to write a book about. After mouthwash, we'd probably settle on gear repair and maintenance. Thank goodness Annie Getchell came along with her artist's sensitivity for detail, a flair for language, and best of all, her wit. From repairing zippers to selecting 'green' adhesives, she nails it and keeps us smiling the entire distance."

—John Viehman, Publisher of *Backpacker* and
Executive Producer and Series Host of *Anyplace Wild*

"*The Essential Outdoor Gear Manual* has set a new standard for books about gear."

—*Backcountry*

"All of us should be grateful to Annie Getchell for creating what is the best book I have ever seen on caring for and repairing your outdoor gear. If you want to know how to make your gear last longer, you need this book. . . . This is the complete word on care and repair."

—*Adventure West*

"The big challenge with this sort of book is to make what is essentially an instruction manual into something that's pleasant to read, functional, and authoritative. Annie Getchell pulls it off."

—Alan Kesselheim, writer and noted long-distance paddler

THE
ESSENTIAL
OUTDOOR
GEAR
MANUAL

Second Edition

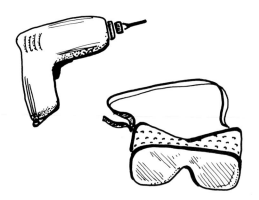

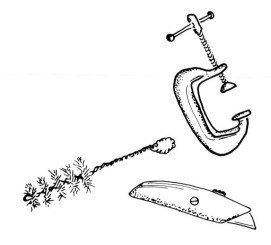

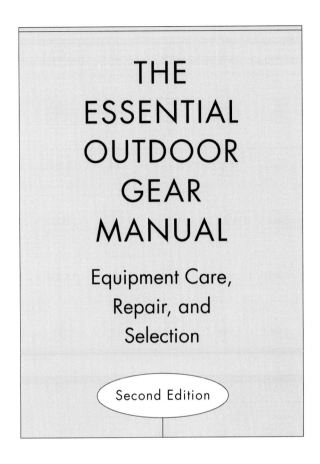

THE ESSENTIAL OUTDOOR GEAR MANUAL

Equipment Care, Repair, and Selection

Second Edition

Annie Getchell and Dave Getchell Jr.

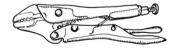

Ragged Mountain Press / McGraw-Hill

Camden, Maine • New York • San Francisco • Washington, D.C. • Auckland
Bogotá • Caracas • Lisbon • London • Madrid • Mexico City • Milan
Montreal • New Delhi • San Juan • Singapore • Sydney • Tokyo • Toronto

Ragged Mountain Press

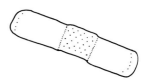

A Division of The McGraw·Hill Companies

10 9 8 7 6 5 4 3 2 1

Acknowledgments for chapter-opening quotations begin on page viii, which constitutes an extension of the copyright page.

Library of Congress Cataloging-in-Publication Data
Getchell, Annie.
  The essential outdoor gear manual / Annie Getchell and Dave Getchell Jr.—2nd ed.
      p.   cm.
  Includes bibliographical references and index.
  ISBN 0-07-135712-2
    1. Outdoor recreation—Equipment and supplies—Maintenance and repair—Handbooks, manuals, etc.   I. Getchell, Dave. II. Title.
  GV191.76.G48 2000
  688.7'6'0288—dc21   99-054850

Questions regarding the content of this book should be addressed to
Ragged Mountain Press
P.O. Box 220
Camden, ME 04843
http://www.raggedmountainpress.com

Questions regarding the ordering of this book should be addressed to
The McGraw-Hill Companies
Customer Service Department
P.O. Box 547
Blacklick, OH 43004
Retail customers: 1-800-262-4729
Bookstores: 1-800-722-4726

This book is printed on 70-lb. Citation

Printed by R. R. Donnelley & Sons, Crawfordsville, IN
Design by Carol Gillette, Communications Graphics
Production by Faith Hague and Dan Kirchoff
Illustrated by Annie Getchell
Photographs by Annie Getchell and Dave Getchell Jr.
Edited by Jon Eaton and Joanne Allen

The authors and publisher have made all effort to represent registered trademarks accurately.

To Dorcas Miller, with her keen sense of direction.
Thanks for pointing us down the path.

CONTENTS

ACKNOWLEDGMENTS

There's an old axiom, or should be one: something about how the more you know, the less you know you know. You know? Nearly every telephone call led us into some smart person's particular lair of expertise; several factory tours yielded enough material for as many books. The enthusiasm and willingness to educate from so many folks was heartening, occasionally overwhelming, and always appreciated. Thanks everyone for the interest, support, and patient guidance.

Dorcas Miller; Kristin Hostetter and the staff of *Backpacker* magazine; the *Anyplace Wild* film crew; Audrey Sutherland; Win Ellis; Randy Burnett, Brunton USA; Jerry Lloyd, Kitty Graham, Pete Haggerty, and Diana Eken, inveterate Cascade Designs folks; Rob Center, Kay Henry, Lili and Gordon Colby, plus the gang at the Confluence of Mad River Canoe; Colin Lantz and Charley Oliver, La Sportiva; Amy Fischer; Del Smith; Dan Hammill, McNett Corporation; John Abbenhouse and crew, Northwest Kayaks; Stuart and Marianne Smith, Maine Sport Outfitters; David "The Doctor" Goodman; Nantahala Outdoor Center; Mark Jenkins; the editors of *AMC Outdoors*; Paul Hebert, Ascension Enterprises; Paul Ramer, Ramer Products; Tom McCarthy, supportive rep; the folks at Feathered Friends; Karen T'Kint, Five Ten; Chris Townsend, token Scot; Mark Eckhart, Klepper Service Center; L.L. Bean Outdoor Discovery Program; John Harlin III; Doug Simpson, Feathercraft; Cathi "Petal" Buni; all the folks at Dagger and Headwaters; D'Arcy Marsh, gear wrecker and mentor nonpareil; Patrick Smith, Mountainsmith; the Cobblers: Steve Komito, Dave Page, David Yulan; Larry Edwards, Baidarka Boats; Greg Wozer, Leki Sport; Paul Farrow, Walden Paddlers; Kenyon Consumer Products; Scottie Simper, man of 10,000 talents; Steve and Mary Gorman; Trondak/Aquaseal; Ted Dishner and Pendra Legasse, Moss Tents; Martin Brown, Sunrise County Canoe Expeditions; Mike Patterson, Maine Guide; Steve "Cupcake" Howe; REI/MSR, Malden Mills, and Gore-Tex for the insider factory tours; Mike Sherer, Designer Emeritus; Peter "Allah" Cole; Bob Upton, Rainy Pass Repair; Sam and Susan Manning for their reality checks; Stowe Canoe and Snowshoe Company; Malcolm Daly, Trango USA; Paul Cleveland; Mike McCabe, ZRK Enterprises; Mike Curtis, Nikwax; editors Jon Eaton and Tom McCarthy at Ragged Mountain Press; plus all our folks for teaching us how to learn.

Further Note: This compendium of snippets, tips, and techniques spans myriad resources, including a zillion books and magazines. Those listed in appendix H, Recommended Reading, certainly guided the development of this project and are heartily recommended for a complete outdoor library. However, the real substance of research is contained in the countless product manuals, manufacturers' literature, and personal anecdotes from afield. Every attempt has been made to credit those contributions and make specific recommendations for further reading throughout the text.

Grateful acknowledgment is made to the publishers to reprint the following quotations.

The quotations on pages 1, 85, and 104 are reprinted from Felice Benuzzi, *No Picnic on Mount Kenya*, courtesy of The Lyons Press.

The quotation on page 25 is reprinted from James W. Davidson and John Rugge, *Complete Wilderness Paddler*, courtesy of Alfred A. Knopf, a Division of Random House, Inc.

The quotation on page 75 is reprinted from Samuel Beckett, *Waiting for Godot: With a Revised Text*, courtesy of Grove Press.

GROW A DEEPER SHADE OF GREEN

The subtitle reads "Care, Repair, and Selection," but this book is really about becoming a greener gearhead. While more and more outdoor equipment is marketed as "green," these lower-impact products amount to something of a mixed blessing that still promotes consumption. A better solution may be to look at what you already have in a new way. You can start by simply adopting a few new attitudes.

Use what you have. Outdoor gear can usually withstand a lot more abuse than weekend warriors dish out, and too many of us graduate to shinier, techier toys long before old ones wear out.

Maintain your equipment. Gear lasts longer and performs better given regular sessions of seam-sealing, waterproofing, cleaning, or tuning. Tinkering is fun and educational and ensures reliable service from your equipment when you most need it. A little time spent puttering can be relaxing and meditative—a sort of mental half-step to some windy place you'd rather be, even if there's no time to actually go there.

Repair rather than replace. Fixing up rather than buying up can save enough to pay the airfare for a dream adventure. And just how big is that box of stuff you've been meaning to mend? Our friend John moved his box from coast to coast without ever opening it, but he thinks the contents include torn rainpants, gored gaiters, bent ski bindings, a shorted-out headlamp, a bunch of tired boots, and assorted unknown stove parts. If you aren't going to fix stuff, give it to someone who will or enlist a reputable repair center for a first-rate job.

Almost any gear is worth the effort to restore. Not long ago Annie dropped a battered rucksack off at an outfitters for a repair estimate. Even though the shop offers a well-stocked preventive-maintenance department, the salesperson quickly dismissed the idea because major surgery would run nearly as much as a similar new pack. The price, maybe, but not the cost—the global cost of manufacturing, that is.

Keep old gear in circulation. The woods are crawling with incurable funhogs who windmill through equipment fads and trends. This accumulated, outmoded, outgrown stuff has more than sentimental value. Sell used hardware at an equipment swap or consignment shop; hold a cooperative gear sale with a gang of cronies, then take a trip with the ill-gotten cash. Churches, schools, and other charitable services do backflips for donations of warm, practical outerwear and usable sporting equipment. Once, with just a few phone calls, we assembled an entire family camping kit (packs, bags, tent, stove, boots, and more) for a neighbor whose home had been destroyed by fire—all with stuff from the attic.

Replace your gear with preowned models. This book helps you profit from others' ignorance and unwillingness to care for their equipment. We recently acquired yet another canoe, a really nice one, on the cheap; all it needed was attention to the wood trim and minor patching at the stern. Buying used gear is like buying a used car: someone else takes the depreciation.

Modify and innovate. Recycle odd parts into functional inventions all your own. Consider this guide a primer of sorts that will teach the basics of materials, glues, and fasteners, giving you the technical background to create custom gear.

Inquire about manufacturing practices and materials used in products you're considering

buying. This book may enlighten you about the petrochemical nature of our leisure-time toys.

Learn to appreciate lasting quality. The more you repair, the more you'll value good design. One well-made backpack might outlast three el cheapos. If you're going to use plastic gear, you owe it to the planet to use less. Besides, the people who dream up and build the best outdoor gear deserve our support.

NOTES ON THE SECOND EDITION

Annie knew she'd have to update the book sooner or later. Fortunately, the publisher called just about the time Dave had had enough of spending two hundred days a year in the bush, shooting outdoor-adventure TV shows. She cajoled him into lending his wisdom gained from countless gear failures toward beefing up the first edition.

For Dave, working on this book was the culmination of the last decade as a *Backpacker* magazine equipment editor, plus producing some seventy-odd outdoor adventure movies. We've taken countless trips together: portaging ancient trails, climbing stormy peaks, enduring airline jokes, and meeting all manner of outdoor savants happy to share their gear tales of terror.

As we worked through the text, we kept thinking, "Jeez, this is pretty good stuff!" The original premise still holds up: Take care of your gear, and it will take care of you.

The biggest change since the release of the first edition is the corporatization of the outdoor industry—and yes, it is indeed an industry. On the heels of this merge-and-acquisition binge, a remorseless marketing Darwinism has weeded out the schlock. What's left is remarkably good stuff, stuff that will last if you let it.

Niche marketing—women's gear, for instance—has given the consumer ever more bewildering choices of highly specialized equipment. Our time-tested tips will help you cut through the clutter.

And then you've got the Internet. Bill Gates may not be much of an outdoor guy, but he sure has made it easy for us dyed-in-the-woolly back-country geeks to find obscure gear, plan trips, and spew to all our friend about it (check the bibliography for our favorite research websites).

Finally, repair is no longer a four-letter word to retailers these days—and we'd like to take a little credit for this. The first edition helped detrivialize and professionalize equipment repair. Once outdoor retailers discovered that glues, screws, and goos could become a profit center, they happily obliged to supply you with all your needs, and then some. Check your local outfitters first—they may well have it.

What we've added are the latest developments in gear and repair, firsthand accounts of near disasters, and new illustrations and accompanying photos. You'll also find time-tested tips for finding and choosing the equipment that'll work best for you.

We're still out there somewhere—soaking wet, lounging in the sun, gritting our teeth, enjoying every minute. We can't think of a better place for you to be, either. The wide, wild outdoor world can be a harsh teacher, but you'll never forget what you bring home.

HOW TO NAVIGATE THIS TOME

In our golden age of sound bites, channel-surfing, and web navigating, the temptation to skim is nearly irresistible. Before barging straight into the table of contents in search of specific repair scenarios (like unclogging your stove), please take a moment to understand just how the book is organized.

First of all, we give you credit for being familiar enough with gear to have wrecked it in the first place; for having a functional brain; for grasping the universal dharma of duct tape.

Given that all-purpose field repair is rarely more exotic than a roll of silver tape and a little red knife, this book focuses primarily on preventive maintenance. Each section starts with the building blocks of materials, design, and construction, followed by inherent weaknesses and typical failures. You'll find pertinent suggestions for field-fixes before going over the broad brushstrokes of effecting permanent repairs at home. You'll also learn when to cut your losses and send the mess off to a professional.

To best apprehend the contents, begin with Essential Techniques, outlined in chapter 1, where you'll find the most generally useful and condensed information, on the likes of zipper repair, stain removal, or seamsealing tips. Then read the appendices. Otherwise, prepare to be sidetracked by cross-references to these sections throughout the text.

While looking for particulars, keep in mind that each section is designed to be read chronologically, so you first understand the materials at hand. This book is *not* designed to deliver the detailed beta, with exhaustive step-by-step repair directions for every conceivable broken widget. Rather, we offer a more conceptual treatment of techniques so you can apply what's needed to your unique situation.

This is by no means the last word on any of the topics discussed, but an opening to the world of outdoor-equipment self-reliance. As our novelist friend Marco says, "The book will never be finished—you just have to stop."

All puns are intentional.

PART 1

Soft Goods

*I cannot remember the number of needles I broke
in sewing the tent as I had to work in the quiet of the
night by the flickering light of an oil lamp, made from a
corned-beef tin. The thread I was compelled to use
proved to be so bad that I had to smear it with pitch.
Unlike thread and needles I did not need
to "acquire" the pitch, because we had it in plenty.*

Felice Benuzzi, *No Picnic on Mount Kenya*

What More Could You Possibly Need?

When preparing for a wilderness adventure, there are two general packing methods. One is to pack hours before departure, wildly grabbing and stuffing, then stopping here and there en route to the put-in or trailhead to pick up last-minute or forgotten items. Followers of this school often wind up with too much gear, yet missing essential components like matches or a tent.

A second system, advocated by those more disciplined, is to carefully list and lay out every available manifestation of outdoor technology, accounting for plausible panhandling by practitioners of the first methodology. While the person following this system may not forget anything, he or she will certainly be overburdened.

A happy medium? Consider the kit of our ancestors. Pioneers, trappers, and mountain men all carried less than an average woman does in her purse, but they were ready for anything the wilderness could dish out. Called a "possibles" bag, an adventurer's 14- by 17-inch kit ensured comfort as well as survival. A possibles bag generally contained a knife and whetstone, a tin cup for boiling water, tea, beeswax or lard for lubricating or waterproofing, an awl, a needle and waxed linen thread, several fish hooks and sinkers, and tinder, a striker, and a flint. A little grain and dried meat supplemented each journey.

Patrick Smith, modern man and frequent traveler, also employs a possibles bag. Smith, better known as the founder and designer of Mountainsmith Packs, was once a teacher of wilderness living and survival skills in his home state of Colorado.

Meticulous, Smith rarely leaves home without his signature lumbar pack, containing, among other things, his possibles bag. When asked, he'll enthusiastically review its contents, some of which have been in the kit for 20 years. "Someday I'll be in a plane wreck," he says, "and I'll be ready."

PATRICK SMITH'S POSSIBLES BAG

On his person:
- small notebook and mechanical pencil
- key chain with AAA Maglite
- wallet (which contains a spare AAA battery plus spare lead and an eraser for his pencil)
- Swiss Army "Tinker" knife
- lip grease
- butane lighter

Possible bag contents (in no particular order)
- compass
- lightweight gloves and hat
- Superglue
- wire saw
- nylon repair tape
- tiny tube of Urebond adhesive
- bandanna
- four spare AA batteries
- compact fluorescent light (uses AAs)
- several plastic Ziploc bags, large and small
- toilet paper and small package of baby towelettes
- assorted rubber bands
- fiberglass strapping tape
- Power Bar
- toothbrush
- tiny headlamp (uses AAs)
- spare headlamp bulb
- fire-starting kit: Trioxane fire-starter, lighter, metal match
- insect repellent

- tape measure (Smith's a designer, remember?)
- custom sewing kit with nylon thread (see pages 5–6)
- slice of adhesive-backed Velcro
- first-aid bag: gauze, butterfly bandages, antihistamine, Tums, Kaopectate, aspirin, prescription painkiller and muscle relaxant, burn ointment, antibiotic
- antifog cloth for glasses
- fluorescent orange tape
- tiny stuff sack used for pillow
- large baking-powder tin for melting snow or boiling water
- dental floss
- tiny whetstone
- tiny flask of baking powder for toothpaste

- ear plugs (for rushing streams and snoring companions)
- wire
- safety pins
- biodegradable soap
- tiny straw for sipping out of puddles or starting fires
- eyeglass screwdriver
- quarter-sized magnifying lens (for working with eyeglass screwdriver)
- bicycle valve core
- nail clippers
- tweezers
- tiny Peruvian worry doll

CHAPTER 1

Essential Techniques

See also appendix A, Adhesives

> "Open thy bundle!"
> It was the usual collection of
> small oddments: bits of cloth,
> quack medicines, cheap fairings,
> twists of down-country tobacco,
> tawdry pipe-stems and a packet
> of curry-stuff all wrapped
> in a quilt.
>
> Rudyard Kipling, *Kim*

Before you run off to fix all your broken outdoor gear, better to slow down and walk first: learn the fundamental skills of stitching, patching, gluing, seamsealing, and, of course, curing the myriad ills of the omnipresent zipper. That's the job of this chapter: to make sure that you are able to effect the most basic repairs in a way that'll last longer than halfway through your next trip.

You'll find coverage of more involved repairs and material-specific techniques later in the book; for now, keep it simple. One of Annie's earliest memories is learning to sew on a button using a little swatch of cloth her mother gave her. (If a toddler can, so can you.) Some of these essential techniques are almost biblical in their timelessness.

Sewing Basics

Stitching a makeshift patch or reattaching a pack strap is a pretty simple operation requiring only the most minimal skill with a needle. For those interested in more complex projects, such as replacing a zipper or even creating a custom garment, check out appendix G, beginning on page 236, for suppliers of notions and advice, or seek out a copy of Louise L. Sumner's *Sew and Repair Your Own Outdoor Gear.* Your local library houses many other books on this age-old craft. Methods discussed here are straightforward solutions to the most primitive sewing needs.

NEEDLES AND THREAD

- For packcloth and multiple layers of rugged fabric, heavy-duty nylon thread, carpet thread, waxed linen, and dental floss are all suitable.
- For finer fabrics, including nylon taffeta, ripstop, laminates, or coated materials, use cotton-polyester-blend thread that is not overly strong. Thread that's too strong (like a thick nylon thread or monofilament line) will slice right through lightweight fabrics.
- Unless sewing on a button, don't use doubled thread —you just make larger holes in the fabric.
- Use short lengths of thread—thread that is too long snarls easily and is weakened each time you tug it through the stitch hole.
- When removing stitches, use small scissors or tweezers to clip and pluck each thread. Don't be

CARDINAL RULES FOR ANY REPAIR

1. Allow twice as much time as you think you need.
2. Clear an adequate work surface and lay out supplies.
3. Measure twice, cut once.

Always sew with a short thread. Long thread will tangle & weaken from being pulled repeatedly.

tempted to use a razor knife—you risk creating more of a repair than you started with.

- Carry several sizes of needles—they weigh next to nothing and are invaluable, particularly as gifts in remote villages.
- Use embroidery needles, which have bigger eyes for easy threading in the bush.

TECHNIQUES
Backstitching
Backstitching is a strong, simple stitch for closing seam tears.

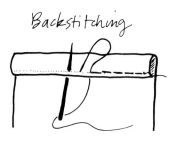

Backstitching

Hemming
Also called whipping or overhand stitch, the hem stitch is useful for attaching nonstructural patches and repairing garments. The long, slanting stitches

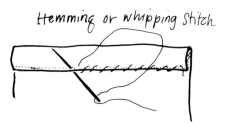

Hemming or whipping stitch

are visible on the working side; the finished side reveals little, since you catch just one or two fabric threads with each stitch.

Handmade Bar Tack
A bar tack can prevent further ripping at the end of a fly or pocket, or it can be used to reattach a belt loop or pack strap. Sewing a bar tack by hand is easy. Make several long stitches to form the length of the bar tack. Small overhand stitches across the threads strengthen the bar. Finish with tiny bar stitches at each end.

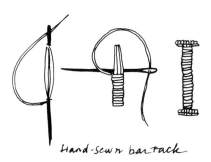

Hand-sewn bar tack

Darning
Darning mitts is a pleasant, meditative task ideally suited to transcontinental flights or waiting out storms in your tent. Reinforcing socks or mitts requires little more than understanding the concept of weaving. The real trick is to work in new yarn or threads so there are no hard, blister-causing ridges. Thick yarn makes the job quick, but the repair won't be as long-lasting; try to match the diameter of the original fibers.

If you're beefing up a sock, employ a rock or tennis ball as your darning form (hardcore Yankees use a special darning ball that looks like something from a croquet set). Make a running-stitch perimeter around the worn area. Then run parallel rows of stitching across the hole. Work back and forth until the hole or worn spot is covered with parallel threads. Turn the work and run the thread or yarn through the stitch lines as if weaving—over,

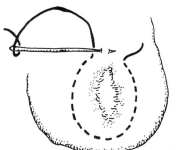

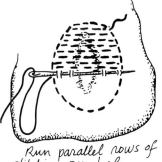

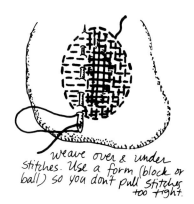

using thread or yarn to match original, run stitches around hole or worn area.

Run parallel rows of stitching over hole

weave over & under stitches. Use a form (block or ball) so you don't pull stitches too tight.

Splicing socks, a.k.a. darning.

under, over. Don't draw the threads taut, or the fabric will pucker.

SAILOR'S PALM

Basically a giant thimble, the palm protects the paws of salty dogs as they mend sails. The thick leather fits around your hand so you can stab away through multiple fabric layers with a heavy awl or needle and thread. Palms are convenient to carry in your pack.

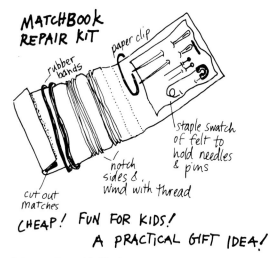

MATCHBOOK REPAIR KIT

paper clip

rubber bands

staple swatch of felt to hold needles & pins

notch sides & wind with thread

cut out matches

CHEAP! FUN FOR KIDS! A PRACTICAL GIFT IDEA!

Tiny but tough

tent tubing wrapped with thread & filled with needles.

Sailmaker's Palm lets you hand-sew heavy fabrics or use an awl with ease.

SEWING KITS

A useful kit can be made by filling a 35-mm film canister with safety pins, a half-dozen needles, a few buttons, some paper clips, plus several colors and thicknesses of thread.

Make a tiny, self-contained kit from a matchbook. Cut matches out of the folder; notch the sides and wrap with different threads. Staple or glue a piece of fabric to the top for holding needles and safety pins. (This is a great gift for kids to make.)

Mountainsmith Packs guru Patrick Smith used a small section of an old aluminum tent pole to create a nifty sewing kit. Rubber caps on each end hold needles inside; the tube is wrapped with heavy-duty nylon thread.

The best kit, formerly distributed by Chouinard/ Black Diamond Equipment, may still be found in outdoor stores or through Kenyon Consumer Products (see appendix G, beginning page 236). This tiny leather pouch includes the essentials plus the field lock-stitching assembly mentioned above. If you've lost or broken the needle to the ingenious mini-awl in this kit, replace it with a sewing machine needle (the kind with the hole in the pointy end), readily available at your nearby five and dime.

SEWING AWLS AND LOCK-STITCHERS

If you need an awl, you're working with rugged fabric or lots of layers, so be patient and focus so you don't punch a hole into a fingernail, as we've managed to do more than once. For leather, initiate holes before attempting to stitch—use the leather punch on your Swiss Army knife, a hammer and a finish nail, or an ice pick.

Some field kits include a collapsible awl that combines a sewing machine needle, cotter pin, and plastic joint. Lock-stitchers like the Speedy Stitcher (other brands are available) are "machine" versions of the basic awl and include a bobbin and tensioning post.

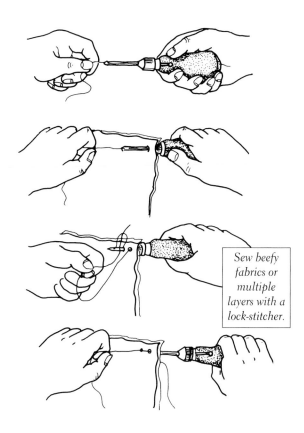

Sew beefy fabrics or multiple layers with a lock-stitcher.

Lock-Stitching

- Draw out enough thread to cover the repair area plus about 4 inches for tolerance. If the repair area is large, break the stitching up into several short sections so you're not encumbered with excess thread.
- Push the needle through the material, then draw the end of the thread through with your other hand. Pull the needle back out (leaving a long tail of thread).
- Push the needle through the material to make a stitch, then pull the needle halfway back, creating a loop of thread at the end of the needle.
- Thread the tail end of the thread through the loop, then fully withdraw the needle. Pull with equal tension on both awl and free thread so the stitching appears the same on each side of the

material. Don't pull so hard that the material puckers.
- Repeat the procedure, taking care not to pucker the material, and finish the row by tying the two ends of the thread together on one side of the fabric.

RETHREADING DRAWSTRINGS

Annie thought everybody knew how to rethread a drawstring, so she was astonished to stumble across poor Dave fumbling with his parka waistcord. Simply attach a cotter

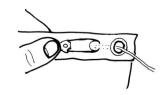

pin, paper clip, or safety pin to one end of the string. Insert the pin into the grommet or eyelet entrance to the drawcord channel and begin threading the drawstring through the casing. Move the pin along through the channel by feeling and feeding with your fingers. Don't forget to knot the drawstring so that it doesn't slip through again.

Fabric Patching

See also Seams and Seamsealing beginning on page 20; and appendix A, beginning on page 212

Patches are badges of honor in two ways: they identify those who get out and really *use* their gear while at the same time revealing the sort of respect folks give to their possessions. Admit it: a crusty old salt with faded, patched, and cobbled gear holds a certain cachet—especially when he's standing next to a young hyper-buck with the latest gadgets topped by a virgin Lord Mountbatten hat.

PREVENTION PATCHES
Regular inspection of all your gear alerts you to weaknesses and potential failures. Often you can reinforce a worn spot by sealing, taping, or patching, cover an abraded tent pole sleeve with matching nylon tape, or caulk tiny punctures in a gaiter with adhesive. Prevention patches *protect* the design integrity of any gear. Failure permanently weakens a structure, and a repair is often stronger than the material around it, causing further stress to the original (damaged and undamaged) areas.

Spare the Preparation and spoil the patch

FIELD FIX: THE DUCT TAPE OR NYLON ADHESIVE PATCH
Considered a *temporary* repair, a taped patch may actually cling for years. Annie always wants to rip

the dangling duct tape off friends' tattered gear and only occasionally manages to control this urge. She often ends up offering to fix the offending rent properly (clearly a Midwesternism).

Taped patches are best suited to puncture wounds in light nylon and other fabrics or to gear not often exposed to moisture. Taping does not work to hold stretched, stressed fabric together. The larger the tear, the less effective a taped patch will be.

Just like any other glue or patch job, a successfully taped patch requires a clean, dry, prepped surface. In the field these conditions are hard to control, so carry a few foil-sealed alcohol swabs in your repair kit. The alcohol will help your raingear or tent fly dry out enough for duct tape or nylon tape to stick. Remember to replace these packets periodically—they dry out quickly.

- Clean and prep fabric.
- Cut the patch at least ½ inch larger than the damaged area. Rounded edges on the patch are essential.

there's a reason why Band-Aids have rounded edges-- they stick better, longer.

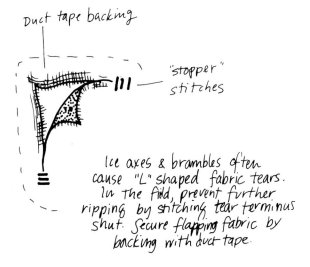

Duct tape backing

"stopper" stitches

Ice axes & brambles often cause "L" shaped fabric tears. In the field, prevent further ripping by stitching tear terminus shut. Secure flapping fabric by backing with duct tape.

- Join the two sides of the tear together so they meet but don't overlap. Don't trim ragged edges.
- Place the tape with the adhesive facing inside and burnish the patch edges with a blunt stick or spoon. Lay a paper or cloth barrier between the patch and your burnishing device so you don't agitate the edges of the patch and cause them to peel.
- Any straggling fibers can be burned back with a lighter or candle flame.

URETHANE ADHESIVE PATCHES

Punctures in single layers of fabric lend themselves to adhesive patches. Small tears in low-stress areas are also adhesive patch candidates—sometimes a combination of nylon tape with adhesive works well. Since all adhesives shrink to some degree as they cure, often causing fabrics to pucker, try to find an adhesive formulated to cure with minimal shrinkage.

Urethane adhesive patches dry clear and are extremely flexible and waterproof. This type of patch is perfect for tent netting, wetsuit tears, holes in fabric or leather footwear, Hypalon boats, snowshoe decking, and just about any other patch area that's smaller than a quarter. This type of patch is not really a trail repair; best results depend on careful prep work, and the adhesive should cure undisturbed.

- Clean and prep both sides of fabric.
- Follow procedure for taped patch, except the tape should be placed on the back side of fabric (adhesive forms the outside patch).
- Turn over and apply urethane adhesive to exterior, covering tear plus ¼ inch.
- Lay flat and allow full cure time.

SEWN PATCHES

A sewn patch can be done with a patient hand in the field but is usually performed at home with a machine. A sewn patch requires more finesse

THE BEAUTY AND PERILS OF DUCT TAPE

As the heart of most repair kits and the silver lining to many a catastrophe, duct tape certainly qualifies as the "eleventh essential." One day we asked everyone who called or dropped by to recall their most recent use for duct tape . . .

- Climbing skin
- Ski pole strap
- Heels ("Duct tape is much better than moleskin and sticks for many days," says outdoor writer-photographer Steve Howe. "The shiny surface doesn't catch on socks and peel off.")
- Therm-a-Rest
- Windpants
- Gaiters
- Boots (along with some wire)
- Kayak crack
- Split canoe paddle
- Mousebitten pack
- Holey gloves
- Sunglasses
- Cracked battery cover on camera

Silver solution

Despite its wonderful versatility, there's nothing a repair specialist hates more than duct tape. In her years as a custom gear designer and "surgeon" at Needle Mountain Designs, Peggy Quinn has had to work around thousands of gummy blobs left by emergency duct tape applications. The silver solution may be terrific in the field, warns Quinn, but you may create a need for more extensive repair if tape is left to bake into the fabric indefinitely. Gray tape's tenacious adhesives are tough to remove even with solvents and abrasive cleaners (which can damage fabrics). Additionally, it's difficult to stitch through any residue—broken needles, gummed-up thread, and vile curses are guaranteed.

Similarly, those who rely on duct tape to patch a kayak hull should be forewarned that the stuff sticks just as determinedly to fiberglass.

Consider any tape a temporary fix.

than most people realize, and it is commonly botched. Master gear-fixer Bob Upton of Rainy Pass Repair has rescued hundreds of failed home repairs and half-baked efforts to fix tents and garments (see photos on page 10). He recommends turning a patch job over to an expert whenever possible. "People think they'll save money doing a repair themselves and end up spending more because we have to *undo* everything they did," says Upton.

Part of the difficulty lies in the fact that a small patch often isn't effective—an entire panel of fabric may need to be replaced to ensure a successful repair, which involves meticulous de- and reconstruction of the damaged item. Knowledge of how a particular fabric stretches and accepts stress is also important. If you don't sew in the first place, save yourself time, money, and a big headache by sending your damaged gear to its original manufacturer or to one of the repair specialists listed in appendix G, Materials Resources. The same goes if the garment or tent is new: send it to the manufacturer or to a qualified repair center to assure a virtually invisible repair that will last at least as long as the manufacturer intended the gear to last in the first place.

Another point to consider when facing a big patch job is whether your repair will be too strong for the surrounding fabric. For instance, our friend Steve asked Annie to fix his tent fly, torn at a stake-out loop. While making the repair, she accidentally punctured another area of fabric a little too easily and realized that the fly had succumbed to ultraviolet (UV) degradation. Further efforts to save it were moot.

SHADES OF GLUE

Throughout this guide you will encounter many references to urethane adhesive patches, whether for a wetsuit, fabric boot, or tent. While there are many urethane products available, those manufactured by McNett Corporation in Bellingham, Washington, are formulated especially for outdoor uses.

McNett offers shades of glue for various applications, and the biggest difference between them is their viscosity, or resistance to flow. For example, you'd need a stiff adhesive to patch a boot toe bumper so the glue won't flow away while hardening; conversely, a thinner mix will penetrate stitching better when seamsealing a rainfly.

The three main choices are (these options hold true for other makers' sealers as well; ask a knowledgeable salesperson for advice):

- *Freesole*—Engineered for high abrasion-resistance, this is the thickest, stickiest goop you'll find. Ideal for patching footwear or filling gouges.
- *Aquaseal*—This medium-weight formula needs the support of a fabric to stay in place while hardening. Best uses: wetsuit repair, general fabric patching.
- *Seam Grip*—McNett's thinnest adhesive is designed for maximum stick and flexibility; like the name says, use it for seamsealing or when you want to penetrate a material, as when patching a self-inflated sleeping pad.

REINFORCEMENT PATCHES

If a snap, grommet, or webbing loop pulls out, it's because the fastener is stronger than the surrounding fabric. Similarly, if a load is greater than the seam strength, the fabric will give way. Simply replacing the fastener does not cure the disease; you must create a reinforcement patch to evenly distribute load stress so the fabric will hold.

Use a heavier fabric than the original for a reinforcement patch. A round patch will evenly distribute stress on the fabric; if that's not possible, at least use rounded edges on the patch. Follow the patching instructions above, then replace the fastener as needed (see pages 15–18).

Bob Upton of Rainy Pass Repair in Seattle enjoys showing the difference between a typical home repair and a professional's approach to stitching outdoor gear.

Typical home patch job.

Pinch patch (bags, insulated garments).

Mock-felled patch (tents, other stressed fabrics).

Unfinished patch with heat-sealed edges (heavy fabric bags and packs, mosquito netting).

Zippers: The Full Disclosure

See also Drysuit Zippers, page 39

Whatever you do
watch out for your lip
don't let it get bloodied
in the doggone zip.
Watch too for beards
scarves and hair
none of these
belong in there.

Karen van Allsburg

Ever stop to count the zippers you're heading into the backcountry with? Your pack, tent, raingear, gaiters, and miscellaneous pouches all feature zipper closures—an average weekender will use about two dozen of the buggers. Despite their ubiquitousness, most people have never examined a zipper's anatomy and thus unnecessarily fall prey to the dreaded *Gaposis* on a cold winter's night.

The modern zipper is essentially similar to Whitcomb Judson's 1891 invention. Today's outdoor gear employs two general types of nylon zip-

PATCHING TIPS FOR THE STRONG-HEARTED

- Stop the tear in its tracks. Run a few stitches perpendicular to the rip to prevent further tearing. In vinyl or plastic, make a small round hole at the end of the tear to help keep it from spreading.

Whether cut from tape or fabric, a round patch offers no snagging edges & will transmit/absorb an even load on stressed fabric.

- The best patch is sewn through existing seams, preserving the overall strength and waterproofness of the garment or shelter by minimizing the number of stitch holes.
- To open up an area larger than the patch, clip seam stitches individually with scissors. Never tempt fate by using a razor knife. You may have to remove a bar-tacked webbing loop—remember to mark its placement.
- Try to use a repair material that matches the original fabric weight as closely as possible. Also try to match the weave when cutting the patch so that patch threads lie along the same angle as the original material.
- Trace the angles onto your patch fabric, allowing extra fabric for turning edges under, if appropriate, and for splicing into a seam.
- Heat-seal patch edges. If you're turning edges under, press with a warm iron (on the uncoated side).
- Don't pin the patch to the fabric being repaired, or you'll risk further tearing of fabric. If you need to stabilize the patch, tack it with a dot of quick-setting adhesive, like Superglue.
- Practice machine-stitching on scraps to determine tension and stitch length (generally 10 to 12 stitches per inch in most light- and midweight nylons). Do this before you start stitching on your favorite pack, and you'll save yourself (and the pack) lots of grief.
- Splice in your patch, removing from the machine at regular intervals to smooth fabric; make sure the patch is lined up and the stitches are even. Before beginning the second line of stitching, remove from machine and review your work.
- For large patches, trim away original damaged fabric to within 1 inch of the patch stitching. Fold the cut edges of the fabric under and incorporate them into the second, inner line of stitching.
- Close up opened seams, replacing webbing with bar tacks if necessary.
- Seal along stitch lines (see pages 20–24).

---

pers: *toothed* and *coil*. Both work with the same basic parts and are easy to troubleshoot once you identify them.

Toothed zippers have metal or molded nylon teeth shaped like interlocking puzzle pieces and generally operate more smoothly than coil types. Toothed zippers can take various forms: a *one-way separating zipper* has a stop at one end and is open at the other (this is the most common type, found on most clothing); a *two-way separating zipper* can be opened at both ends (like on parkas or sleeping bags).

Coil zippers utilize interlocking coils woven into the zipper tape; they're about twice as strong under stress as toothed zippers. The slider or sliders (there can be two or more) either open or close

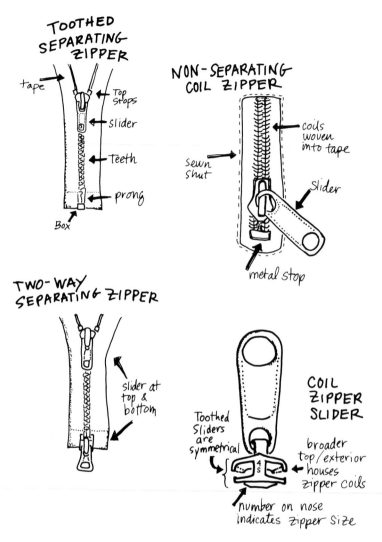

TOOTHED SEPARATING ZIPPER

tape

Top Stops

slider

Teeth

prong

Box

NON-SEPARATING COIL ZIPPER

coils woven into tape

sewn shut

Slider

metal stop

TWO-WAY SEPARATING ZIPPER

slider at top & bottom

COIL ZIPPER SLIDER

Toothed Sliders are symmetrical

broader top/exterior houses zipper coils

number on nose indicates zipper size

ZIPPER PARTS

Sliders have the onerous and underappreciated task of meshing two rows of zipper teeth or coils together into an integrated fastener. Inherently mechanical, a slider is usually the first part of a zipper to malfunction because it operates within very close tolerances.

Insert pins and retaining box are permanent, dovetailed parts of toothed zippers. The box, on one tape of a one-way zipper, receives the insert pin from the other side. On a two-way zipper there are two pins, or prongs; the bottom slider serves as a box.

Stops, made of either metal or plastic, can be removed and replaced (metal stops can be pried off and reused). Stops prevent the slider from coming off either end of the zipper. They are found at the bottom and both top ends of a separating zipper; one stop straddles both rows of a nonseparating zipper at each end point.

Tape is the fabric to which the teeth and pins are molded. Tape on a toothed zipper has a reinforced area at box and pins. On a coil zipper, continuous nylon coil is woven directly into the tape; since coil zippers are cut to length, they have no reinforced areas of tape.

ZIPPER SIZE

Zipper size is usually designated by a number on the slider's nose; the higher the number, the more substantial the zipper (No. 10 is biggest and strongest). Remember that a No. 5 coil zipper is nearly as strong as a No. 10 toothed zipper, but

the teeth on each pass. This is the type of zipper most commonly found on tents and packs because it works so well in curved applications. Most coil zippers are self-healing—a pass with the slider will reunite split sides immediately.

Nonseparating zippers have closure stops at both ends. They can be either toothed or coil. In order to replace a worn slider, you'll have to remove the metal stop or stitching at one end.

the larger zipper should withstand more use, dirt, and strain before it fails. Consideration of their differing capabilities is just as important as the size.

TROUBLESHOOTING
Broken or Missing Element

A missing tooth, box, or pin will allow the slider to come off and disappear into space. While none of these parts is repairable as such, there are a few stopgap measures you can take to maximize your zipper mileage.

If a tooth is missing near the top or bottom of a separating zipper, you can insert a stop in place of the tooth to prevent losing the slider. This can be a regular zipper stop, a few turns of thread, or several drops of epoxy, seam sealer, or Superglue. If a tooth is missing in the middle of the zipper's track, place a stop across both rows or sew the rows shut at that point—you'll be able to zip halfway until you replace the zipper. Keep a spare stop in your kit.

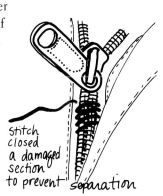

stitch closed a damaged section to prevent separation

Mashed Coils

Nylon coil zippers may be crushed in spots by fancy footwork or hardware abrasion. The slider will not be able to mesh this area properly, and the zipper will split open at the most inopportune moments. It's sometimes possible to realign coil loops with a straight pin: Slide the pin under damaged loops one at a time and tug very gently to pull them back into shape. Next, replace the slider to help straighten the coils. If this doesn't work (or if repair efforts make even more of a mess), simply stitch the damaged section closed. You'll have to decide for yourself if you can live with reduced function, that is, a pullover jacket instead of a zip-front, or tight access to once-roomy pockets.

Broken Slider Pull Tab

Extremely common, with uncommon remedies, is the broken pull tab. Replace it with ribbon, a fishing swivel, a paper clip, a whistle, twine—you are limited only by your imagination. You might find this a most stylish use for leftover single earrings.

Worn Slider,
a.k.a. Zipper Won't Stay Zipped

This is the most common coil zip failure. The tolerances inside a slider are very tight; it doesn't take much wear to loosen it up and, poof—the zipper *appears* to work but keeps popping open. A slider gets worn from plain hard use, but it tires more quickly from grit trapped along the elements. Especially trying for a slider is the typical ape-armed human reaction when fabric gets jammed in the zipper. Rather than yanking on the pull, fetch your pliers and pull the fabric out. Otherwise you'll likely bend the slider or bust the pull tab.

If the zipper stays open after a pass with the slider, you might be able to remedy the situation with a delicate pinching operation. First, open the zipper. This is sometimes difficult, so carefully align the elements and feed them into the slider. (If the slider is truly stuck, pry it off with a screwdriver and replace as described below.)

When the zipper is open (separating zipper) or all the way to its starting position (nonseparating), begin gently, tentatively goosing with pliers. Squeeze just a little on one side, then on the other, with equal pressure. Try the

NON-SEPARATING ZIPPER IN POSITION FOR PINCHING SLIDER

zipper. Repeat the process two or three times until you have properly tightened the slider.

Caution: Heavy-handed squeezing may over-pinch the slider and make it refuse to work, or even worse, it may smash coils. If the slider sticks, pry it off and replace it.

REPLACING THE SLIDER
Separating Zipper

Separate the zipper (you may need to pry off the old slider). Remove the stop on top of the slider (box) side of the zipper and take the slider off. Check the size of the slider before tossing it aside; better yet, take the old part along when you shop for a replacement. Replace the slider, then the stop.

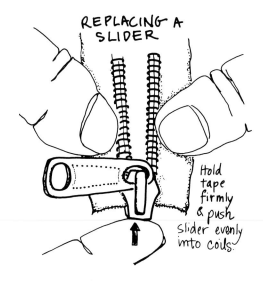

REPLACING A SLIDER

Hold tape firmly & push slider evenly into coils.

Nonseparating Zipper

Remove the stitching surrounding the bottom of the zipper. Be patient and clip the stitches one by one, or you'll end up doing a patch job too. Remove the offending slider to separate the zipper. With the zipper facing you, insert one row of elements evenly into the larger (top) side of the slider; hold this side firmly while you insert the opposite row of elements into the slider an equal distance.

Hold the inserted ends of the zipper tape securely and push the slider to initiate meshing of coils. Whew! This tender operation accomplished, you will need to insert a stop at the open end. Do this with a metal stop across both rows or by restitching the placket shut.

Caution: Before zealously removing stitching on a down jacket or sleeping bag, check to see if the filling will leak out. Work the down away from the zipper area. Staple, pin, or run a line of stitching along the seam before clipping the zipper stitches. Be ready with a plant mister, and spritz water on any escaping plumes. This makes the down clump together rather than flying up your nose.

Remember to quit while you're ahead. You can easily "fix" a zipper to death, which will require replacing the whole shebang.

REPLACING A ZIPPER

The easiest way to remove the old zipper is simply to cut it off, trimming the zipper tape close to the fabric. Stitch in the new zipper behind the old one. This will save you a load of tedious stitch-plucking and is especially useful on down-filled products. Mental health tip: pay someone else to replace your heavily stressed pack zipper (see appendix F, beginning on page 232) or consult a sewing guide.

PREVENTIVE PRACTICES: THE ZEN OF ZIPPING

Practicing mindfulness is a good way to extend the life of any zipper. As you link the two sides (yin and yang), say, "I am joining the zipper teeth gently now," and continue with this awareness as you pull the slider along the path to enlightenment.

Aside from this, the best thing you can do for your zipper is to keep it clean and free of sand or grit. Regularly irrigate your zippers with the pressure jet from a garden hose. Opinions vary regarding zipper lubricants like soap or wax; some folks argue that lubricants simply attract more grime. A little dry graphite lubricant on the joined zipper may be an effective compromise. The best case for wax is as a protectant for zippers regularly exposed to salt water (wetsuit or drysuit) or on a rough patch of a coil zipper. Use solid wax like beeswax (or a candle stub in the field); liquids like TriFlow or spray silicones will spread and may stain fabrics.

Seams inside packs and what-have-you will fray and unravel over time. Loose threads cause untold frustration as they catch and bend a slider. Periodically check for these grabbers; trim, then burn back with a soldering iron, lighter, or candle. Alternatively, run a bead of seam sealer along the frayed fabric edge.

Maybe your zipper seems poorly suited to its task. If you're perpetually overstuffing a pack and the zipper bulges warningly, consider mounting some compression straps to ease the pressure.

(See also pages 222–23 for the Zipper Rescue Kit, a terrific resource for zipper parts, trivia, and advice. In fact, much of the information shared here can be traced to zipper sage Mike McCabe, who developed the kit.)

Fasteners

Fasteners have evolved just as dramatically as the rest of outdoor equipment. When was the last time you actually *buckled* a piece of outdoor gear? Gone are the wretched metal hip belt buckles that rusted and annoyed; they've been replaced by lightweight, molded nylon buckles that crack and annoy. Progress has also eliminated (for the most part) welded D-rings and substituted one-piece, synthetic versions. While notions are lighter, sleeker, and more efficient than earlier generations, outdoor gear closure systems still break. This very general listing of fasteners (there are zillions of superspecialized molded styles available) highlights the basic stuff you need to know. (See

appendix F, beginning on page 232, for sources of notions by mail.)

BUTTONS

Annie's mother wouldn't let her wear any new sweater until she had "properly" resewn each button. Buttons illustrate a case where thread that's much stronger than the fabric will cause the fabric to tear; that is, don't sew cotton with heavy nylon thread, which may cut the softer cotton. Rather than dropping everything to sew on a button, use a wire twist-tie, scant in these Ziploc days, to secure the fastener in the field. For hardworking buttons, add a protective dot of seam sealer over the threads.

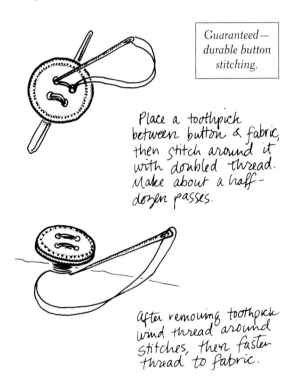

Guaranteed—durable button stitching.

Place a toothpick between button & fabric, then stitch around it with doubled thread. Make about a half-dozen passes.

After removing toothpick wind thread around stitches, then fasten thread to fabric.

BUTTONHOLES

If buttonholes are frayed, stitch around them and create a perpendicular bar tack to ease stress on the fabric (you may need to back with a patch).

VELCRO

Hook-and-loop fastener tape (Velcro is one commercial brand) may be purchased in a fabric shop by the foot or in self-adhesive strips. The strips are useful in a repair kit to back up a failed zipper, but they are difficult to sew through because the adhesive gums up needles and thread. Velcro is so resistant to shearing forces along its length that it often causes the other half to tear away from fabric. Sometimes the tape is sewn too close to an edge and pulls away from stitching. If this happens, add another row of stitches by hand or on a home sewing machine. Be careful and patient—this is thick, tough stuff. Another stopgap repair is to inject a little urethane seam sealer under peeling edges, then clamp Velcro to fabric with a clothespin. Don't close the Velcro until the adhesive has completely cured!

Velcro loses its oomph over time; the loops gradually pull apart, while the hook side becomes clogged by mitten fuzz, dirt, and cookie crumbs. Try combing out the hook side of the tape and gently scrubbing the fuzzy loop side with a toothbrush under water to pill up and extract these freeloaders and fluff up any loops lying down on the job.

inspirational origin of Velcro: the common burdock stuck to dogs' ears & wooly knickers

SNAPS

Snaps are likely to crack and break if made of plastic, like those on some fleece and lightweight raingear. A metal snap will often stay snapped so tenaciously that it tears away surrounding fabric as you try to pop it apart. A reinforcing patch is required before a snap can be replaced—indeed, every snap should be backed by a stout scrap of packcloth or leather. A piece of nylon webbing is ideal.

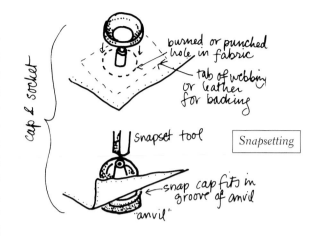

cap & socket

burned or punched hole in fabric

tab of webbing or leather for backing

snapset tool

Snapsetting

snap cap fits in groove of anvil

"anvil"

Snapset kits, which include snaps, setting tool, and positioning anvil, are available at some hardware and fabric stores or leather shops. Tap gently to set the male and snap parts properly. Pounding forcefully will only bend the male part, and your snap will not be secure (though on big snaps you may need to whale pretty hard). Practice on a scrap before you place the real thing.

GROMMETS

Grommets commonly pull away from surrounding fabric. Regular inspection lets you address the problem before a catastrophe strikes. If you note frays, singe fabric with a lighter to forestall doom. Purchase a grommet-setter at a hardware, marine, or sewing shop. Size 0 is the size most often used for backpacks. When replacing a grommet, you'll need to reinforce the fabric, and every grommet requires a piece of backing fabric or leather as well. A scrap of nylon webbing works great for this. Grommets follow the same rules as snaps: Set gently with a wooden mallet; practice first.

BUCKLES

Buckles abound in a variety of shapes, sizes, and functions. The following molded types are available in bulk at most outdoor shops.

Ladderlock buckles give easy length adjust-

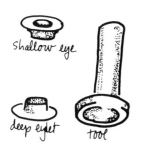

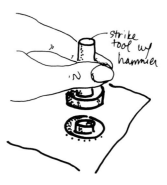

Back snaps and grommets with a swatch of stout nylon webbing or leather.

ment on webbing. They may be metal or nylon and are most common on pack straps. There are a few tricks to threading them for their chosen purpose. Ladderlocks are closed, or sewn, near the webbing's attachment point. One terrific molded innovation: the ladderlock for field repair. This fastener allows you to instantly replace a broken buckle with no stitching required. These may be tough to find, but they are fabulous for backpacking and especially for winter traveling.

Friction-release buckles are nasty little metal units that work by sliding a toothed bar into webbing. These are found primarily on accessory straps. Although they work well to hold, say, a cook kit together, friction-release buckles tend to stiffen and rust. Keep them operating well with a little TriFlow.

Cam-lock nylon buckles use eccentric cams to jam webbing into place. While more efficient in cold weather than friction-release buckles, cam-locks are not entirely trustworthy because slack web can easily become caught and open the buckle. Many people replace cam-locks with side-release buckles.

Threading a ladderlock, then "locking" the webbing

Side-release buckles are everywhere, and for good reason. They're easy to use, to adjust, and even to replace—a given, since they are prone to cracking after prolonged exposure to UV, cold, and general abuse. Nylon side-release buckles are available in several sizes, from ¾- to 2-inch, commensurate with webbing widths. The only problem is that they originate from a bewildering array of manufacturers, and most are not interchangeable. So if one part breaks (usually the female half), you'll likely have to replace both.

Sliders

Sliders, or Tri-Glides, are made of metal or nylon and are used as "keepers" to anchor floppy webbing (like on a pack waistbelt) or to adjust the length of shoulder straps (like on a camera bag). These are available in many widths and shapes.

D-Rings

D-rings are endlessly useful for modifying everything from packs to canoes and are often doubled for use as a friction accessory strap.

CORD LOCKS

Cord locks have virtually replaced knots for fastening drawstrings. Spares are handy additions to any repair kit. Buy them by the handful at your favorite outdoor store.

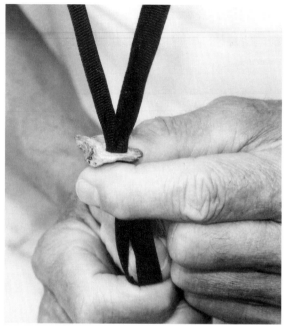

Found objects as repair solutions: a piece of cholla cactus skeleton neatly replaces a lost cord lock on a sunhat retainer strap.

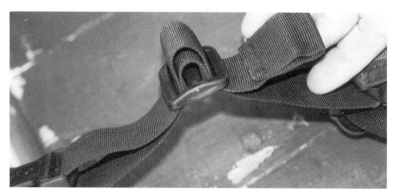

Properly threaded Tri-Glide slider.

Cordage

Matching the right rope or cord to a particular job is literally a knotty problem. Before choosing a rope based on its attractive color scheme or price, realize that suitability really depends on materials and construction. (See also chapter 13, Climbing Gear, and appendix E.)

ROPE CONSTRUCTION

Twisted, or laid, rope—nautical-style rope comprising three smaller strands wound together—is your basic pirate stock. For outdoor use, traditional laid ropes have been largely supplanted by newer braided types. Twisted lines exhibit several faults: they tend to unravel if not carefully whipped or taped at the ends; they're stiff and cranky to coil or handle; and knots tend either to loosen if not pulled tight or to jam mercilessly if heavily loaded. On the plus side, laid ropes can easily be spliced into useful loops at the ends, and dangerously abraded sections are easy to spot.

Braided lines result from weaving a number of smaller cords into a smooth, interlocking whole. Braided lines are the most popular type for general outdoor use. They generally exhibit moderate stretch, hold knots well, and are easy to keep from unraveling by burning the ends.

Breathe fumes at your peril

don't touch the flame to rope or you'll make a sooty mess

Mold soft end with wet finger or by rolling on a hard surface

THE "BUTANE BACKSPLICE"

Kernmantle ropes—cordage with an outer sheath that protects the structural braided core—are favored by rope-conscious climbers. These ropes offer the ultimate in durability, stretch management, friendly handling characteristics . . . and price. The downside is that the exterior sheath can sometimes mask damage along the inner mantle (though tactile examinations can locate bad areas). Kernmantle can be either dynamic (with a certain amount of stretch that will absorb the shock of a fall) or static. Static ropes are used for caving, canyoneering, or fixed lines for ascending because they are not as elastic, nor will they absorb as much water as a dynamic rope.

ROPE MATERIALS

Nylon, that precocious petrochemical, rules the rope roost. Nylon offers the best combination of high strength and low price. Though stretchy to absorb shock and provide amazing strength, it's quite prone to heat damage. Nylon ropes are not suited to applications where loaded ropes may cross one another.

Polypropylene is most commonly found with clothespins and bedsheets hanging from it; though cheap, this type is too stiff and unyielding for most outdoor uses. However, polypropylene is also employed in higher-quality braided lines for marine purposes and river-rescue ropes, for which its high buoyancy is a decided advantage.

Spectra rope sounds vaguely sinister, like all high-tech aramid fibers. And it is high-tech, high-strength, and extremely lightweight. Most often used in climbing applications, Spectra cord's disadvantages are its stratospheric price and its high susceptibility to heat-induced failure. It's pretty much impossible to cut or sew yourself.

BREAKING STRENGTH

When you purchase a rope by the skein, spool, or foot, it comes with the manufacturer's stated strength—which means that a given rope will bear so much load before breaking. Except in the case of climbing ropes, take these numbers as a guide, not gospel, since testing methods vary. The most reliable breaking-strength figures come from those manufacturers who must adhere to strict industry standards.

You'll want to match the characteristics of a rope to its intended job. Obviously, climbing rope should be (and is) the strongest. Roof-rack tie-downs should balance strength and stretch to cinch down boats against 65-mph highway blasts. Remember, stronger is not always better: it's actually better to lash canoe float bags with small cord since it *will* break if the boat hangs up on an obstruction.

CORDAGE DU JOUR

Cord Type	Diameter	Best Use
Nylon accessory cord (a.k.a. paracord)		tent/tarp guylines, bear-bagging, lashing gear or flotation into canoes, utility lashing
Braided nylon	⅜ in.	general purpose use, canoe/kayak painter, roof-rack tie-downs, tarp ridge lines
Braided polypro	⅜ in.	whitewater rescue ropes, throw bags
Braided polypro	½ in.	raft safety lines, boat extrication
Kernmantle	3 mm	tent guylines, bear-bagging, utility lashing
Kernmantle	4 mm	kayak deck rigging, general lashing
Kernmantle	5 mm	roof-rack tie-downs
Kernmantle	6 mm	canoe bow and stern lines, climbers' cordelette
Kernmantle	7–8 mm	fixed lines for mountaineering, haul bag lines
Kernmantle	9–11 mm	climbing ropes

WEBBING

Flat nylon webbing is available by the foot in various widths at better outdoor shops with climbing or paddling departments. Flat webbing is easier to sew than tubular webbing and is commonly used for pack straps, compression straps, bag handles, reinforcing patches, dog leashes, and any number of other vital applications. Flat webbing works great in ladderlock or side-release buckles.

Tubular nylon webbing is available in ¾- and 1-inch widths by the foot. Although it has a silky smooth hand and is the strongest available, tubular webbing is difficult to sew and hard to thread through nylon buckles. It's popular for knotting up climbing runners, but do not attempt to sew your own—noncommercial tacks are unreliable at best. Leave this to a climbing-gear shop or manufacturer.

cut webbing at an angle with a hot knife for easier threading

Seams and Seamsealing

See also sidebar, page 9; and appendix A, Adhesives

Seams are the Achilles' heel of tents, boots, rainwear, packs, and any exposed fabric. A seam is deliberately weaker than the material itself; if it's stronger, stressed fabric may pull away and tear along the stitching. But seams are a necessary evil, adding structure and shape and performance. Without

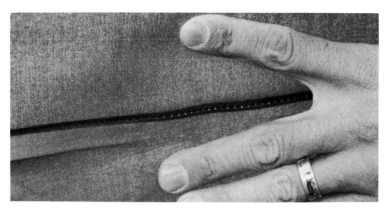

Hundreds of tiny punctures along every stitched seam must be sealed or taped if you expect to stay dry.

coated packcloth or "ballistic" fabric. Nylon tape is folded and stitched over the seam to protect fabric edges—a sign of quality manufacturing. It's not a bad idea to seal the exterior line of stitching on bound seams, but this is overkill if the fabric has not been coated to repel water as well.

Taped

Factory taping is a process by which a waterproof or waterproof/breathable strip of fabric is heat-welded or laminated to the inner side of unfinished seams. You'll find taped seams on almost all raingear (if the garment is lined, you can still spot it through the outer shell), on all Gore-Tex raingear and tents (sealer won't stick to the breathable laminate), and on tents. Seams are taped and repaired by the manufacturer or a reputable repair center (see appendix F, beginning page 232).

them we'd all be loping along in kilts and ponchos.

No matter what a fabric is made of, thousands of tiny stitches along seams amount to so many punctures—which become miniature gushers in foul weather. Most outdoor fabrics sport about 10 to 12 stitches per inch along each seam. Seam-sealing maximizes weatherproofing and also protects stitching in vulnerable locations, as on boots or gloves.

UNFINISHED SEAMS

Unfinished edges (see page 22, top) mean fraying fabric, which eventually allows the seams to pull apart. Dangling threads get caught in zippers (causing damage to the slider) and generally make a mess.

- Trim away any dangling strands of fabric.
- Place a soldering iron or wood-burning pencil in a vise.
- Skim the raw fabric edge along a heated rod to heat-seal the fabric.

If you can't access a fabric edge (such as a corner pocket on a tent) to heat finish, you can seal a raw edge with seam sealer in a syringe.

FINISHED SEAMS
Bound

Bound seams are found inside better-quality packs and luggage, gear made with rugged,

WHAT SHOULD I SEAMSEAL?

- Hiking boots: external seams.
- Telemark boots: welt and toe seams, plus a layer over toe welt (see pages 86–87).
- Mitts and gloves: internal seams of shell layer on system gloves and mitts, perhaps an exterior coat to add texture to slick synthetic palms.
- Raingear: any untaped, internal seam, or seams where the factory tape has peeled.
- Tents: internal floor seams and hardware, all rainfly seams, external side of exposed taped seams. (Optional: all seams.)
- Packs and luggage. (Optional: unbound internal seams, exposed external seams when fabric is coated to repel water.)

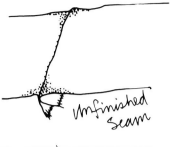

Unfinished Seam

Lap-felled seam

Bound Seam

Taped seam

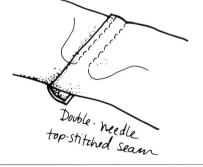

Double-needle top-stitched seam

SEAM SEALERS DIFFERENTIATED

Seam sealers are essentially adhesives, formulated by suspending plastic or urethane material in a water or solvent base. Once applied to a seam (or exposed to air or moisture), the solvent base evaporates or reacts, leaving a film coating of cured, solid material stuck to the fabric. The favored coating, whether water- or solvent-based, is urethane, valued for its flexibility, resiliency, and abrasion-resistant properties.

Water-Based Sealers

If you are a fairweather camper and don't head out frequently in extreme conditions or frigid temperatures, you are an excellent candidate for water-based seam sealer. Water-based products are made under more environmentally friendly circumstances and are somewhat less toxic to manufacture, use, and dispose of than solvent-based sealers. Water-based sealers come in liquid form in sponge-tipped bottles and are easily applied to uncoated fabric.

The big drawback to water-based sealers is that they tend to have low abrasion resistance, become flaky, and must be reapplied every few seasons (or more often). Water-based adhesives simply float on the surface of any previous coating, making it paramount that you remove old coatings before applying

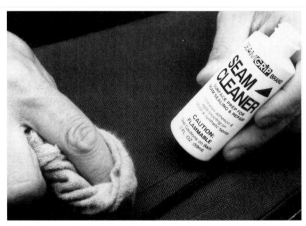

Before sealing, clean all seams with solvent.

seam sealer. Therefore, you must first use a solvent-based precleaner or alcohol to prepare seams.

Solvent-Based Sealers

Solvent-based sealants remain stretchy and flexible through temperature extremes and resist flaking and peeling, even in subzero weather. More viscous and less likely to spill than other liquid sealers, they are usually applied using a small artist's paintbrush or an irrigating syringe, which allows you to coat individual stitches.

Toluene is a solvent base for the most frequently recommended sealers on the market. Experts, manufacturers, and repair services tend to overlook toluene's less-redeeming qualities—it's banned for sale in some regions for its mind-altering capabilities—because the products work better than any others available. The solvent penetrates previously applied coatings and chemically bonds solid sealant to fabric, resulting in a permanent, one-time-only operation.

Sealer manufacturer McNett Corporation offers its views on toluene-based sealers: "As with any solvent product—from gasoline to MEK [methyl ethyl ketone] to kero—users should follow basic, commonsense safety precautions (work in a well-ventilated area, and avoid inhaling the fumes). The permanent nature of a single application of solvent-based sealer means there's less repetition and less packaging waste than with a water-based product."

Environmental regulations become more rigorous daily. While the development of effective, less-toxic alternatives to solvent-based adhesives is certainly imminent, the products and uses recommended here are state-of-the-industry.

SEAMSEALING TIPS
- Work in a ventilated area, even if using water-based sealant.
- Keep kids and pets away from work area.
- Have a rag handy to wipe off drips or smears

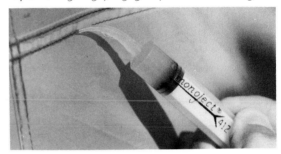

A plastic irrigating syringe gives you that clinical edge.

immediately. Paper towels tend to catch and make more of a mess. The best rag is a square cut from a PakTowl moistened with a bit of alcohol.
- Seams should be clean, dry, warm, and taut; erect the tent when preparing to seal it. Whenever possible, seamseal a new tent or garment before using.
- Prepare the surface to be sealed by buffing gently with a brush, then sponging a commercial precleaner or alcohol along the stitching. This removes any factory water-repellent finish that might interfere with a good sealer bond. (See chapter 2, Fabrics and Insulations.)
- Sealers bond best to the uncoated side of the fabric and to the exterior shell of a waterproof/breathable laminate. Also seal the inside roll of a lap-felled or overlapping seam.
- Use a syringe to inject sealer along the folded edge of seams.

- Run a thin film of sealer along stitch lines, spreading any runny spots with a fine brush.
- Several thin coats of liquid sealant are better than one goopy coat; each successive coat is applied while the previous coat is still tacky. (Seam Grip brand sealant requires only one layer.)
- Pay extra attention to exposed snaps or bar tacks on webbing loops. Use a syringe to drop a bead of sealer into the center of the snap itself.
- Allow full cure time and then some before storing any freshly sealed gear. Otherwise, your new jacket or tent may securely stick itself together. Some manufacturers suggest dusting newly sealed items with a very light layer of talcum, but if the adhesive has fully cured this is unnecessary.

Note: For ultimate protection, Bibler Tents recommends sealing exterior taped seams to prevent water from entering and channeling along the tape.

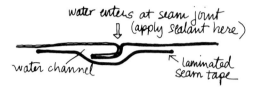

Ultimate weatherproofing theory and practice by Bibler Tents.

CHAPTER 2

Fabrics and Insulations

Wool is by no stretch of the imagination an ideal invention, except perhaps for the sheep.

Davidson and Rugge,
Complete Wilderness Paddler

residue is a desiccant and attracts water, which invites mildew. Chemicals like battery acid and some insect repellents, and even harsh detergents, also damage fibers of any origin.

Unraveling Fabric Mysteries

Outerwear is anything one might wear outside, though the fact that Annie's mom wears a flannel granny gown and sawed-off hip waders when she takes the dog out each morning does blur distinctions somewhat. For outdoor enthusiasts, outerwear generally implies layers of garments that protect against the elements: next-to-skin, insulation, and outer shell. While these layers vary considerably, they are all made of fiber; identifying their composition will tell you how to care for them.

NATURAL VERSUS SYNTHETIC

Fibers fall into two basic categories: natural (like cotton, wool, flax, hemp, or silk) and synthetic. Natural fibers are inherently breathable. Synthetic fabrics may allow air transfer, but the fibers themselves do not. Natural fibers are absorbent and will shrink, whereas both factors are minimal in synthetics. Besides obvious rips and scuffs, any fiber's worst enemy is the sun, with mildew running a close second. No fiber or fabric will endure prolonged contact with salt water. Dried salt

Cotton

Cotton has not been completely forgotten as a useful outdoor fabric. Nothing beats its breatha-

bility and comfort, but when it comes to water, cotton does exhibit some drawbacks (not to mention that cotton production accounts for one-tenth of all pesticide use worldwide). Once wet, cotton fabric swells, tightening the weave against drops of water. However, wet cotton does not withstand water pressure, and leaks. (Remember your dad's warning not to touch the tent wall?) This absorbent quality also means that cotton offers zero insulation once saturated. One solution is to coat cotton fabric with tent wax, available at well-stocked outdoor shops. Another is to wash the fabric in a water-repellent treatment like Nikwax Cottonproof, which works pretty well on cotton and cotton blends, like your old favorite 60-40 parka.

Waxing Poetic

Rewaxing a waxed cotton anorak or tent is a lot like treating boots. Always apply wax to clean fabric. Look for "nontack" wax, which provides a smooth, flexible surface without attracting dirt and grit. Figure about 3 ounces of wax per garment.

- Place clean, dry garments in a dryer (at "low" setting) or near a heat source to warm them before treating the outside of the fabric.
- Lay the garment flat on a clean, protected surface (butcher paper is ideal).
- Use a warmed rag to apply wax generously to seams, joints, and elbows (the areas most likely to leak). Next, systematically coat the entire article. Some waxes are now available in pump sprays.
- Place the garment on a hanger. Inspect for even coating and wipe away any excess wax. Hang to dry overnight in a warm, ventilated spot away from a direct heat source.

Treatment of cotton canvas tents follows the same procedure, with these variations:

Wait for a clear, dry weather forecast. Set up tent in full sun, then follow the rays as they warm wall surfaces, applying wax as recommended above. Heavy canvas tents are especially prone to mildew either because they are not fully dry when stored or because their storage location is a cool, damp cellar. Periodically air your cotton-wall tent, especially if you never use it. Review appendix B, beginning on page 216, for preventive-care tips, or try Rainy Pass Repair's Mildew Removal Recipe, offered below.

The procedure for treating cotton garments with wash-in water repellent goes as follows: Prewash garment thoroughly, using nondetergent soap (this removes detergent residues that might inhibit the waterproofing polymers from adhering to the fabric). Follow instructions covered in DWR Wash-In Tips (sidebar, page 33).

Another treatment for waterproofing cotton involves silicone or Scotchguard spray products. This is a favorite solution for making our beloved wide-brimmed poly-cotton "boonie" hats serve as well in the wet as they do in the blazing sun. Spritz the hat with several coats of spray, letting it dry thoroughly between coats. We've found that this treatment will last most of a summer, though maybe the vast amounts of soaked-in bug repellent present in these hats has something to do with it. And no, the irony of using propellant-heavy commercial sprays to treat natural fibers does not escape us.

RAINY PASS MILDEW REMOVER

Phase I: Mix ½ cup Lysol in 1 gallon of hot water.
- Wash mixture into setup tent with sponge and allow to dry completely.

Phase II: Mix 1 cup salt and 1 cup lemon juice in 1 gallon of hot water.
- Wash tent with this mixture and allow to dry.
- Rinse tent with fresh water and allow to dry before storing.

Silk

Silk is popular for use in socks and long underwear because of its fine wicking ability, soft hand, and elegant drape. It requires little care other than hand-washing with gentle soap and hanging to dry.

Wool

Wool takes on many tasks with equanimity. It is durable and water-resistant as an outer layer, puffy and resilient as an insulating layer, stretchy and breathable (and in the cushy New Zealander knits, remarkably comfy) next to skin. Each wool fiber bears its own protective lanolin coating, which will shed dirt and water for years.

To care for any wool garment is to protect its wonderful natural qualities. Regular shakes, brushings, and spot-cleaning are better for the life of a wool garment than countless dry cleanings. Handwash with mild, nondetergent soap and block dry. Try a small vegetable brush (the wooden-back, yellow bristle type), Sweater Stone, or piece of pumice to remove pills. Don't shave with a razor, or you'll risk slicing the knit.

One oft-undervalued quality of wool is that it shrinks, something appreciated by herding cultures for centuries. Wet, agitated wool fibers cling to one another to form thick, lofty felt. If you've ever accidentally shrunk your favorite cardigan, you remember how tight the knit became. Boiled-wool sweaters offer fabulous insulation that's both breathable and somewhat water-repellent. Make your own boiled-wool layer by purchasing an oversized wool sweater at the Goodwill store, then callously washing and drying it until it shrinks to fit you.

Hemp

Hemp has made an impressive comeback in the outdoor industry for many reasons. Requiring no pesticides for cultivation (a real problem with cotton), hemp is durable, naturally water-resistant, and nonpolluting. Depending on the extent of refinement, hemp fibers are suitable for making

SO YOU DON'T WANT TO WEAR FUR

Creatures compressed in early Cretaceous
extracted, pumped and canned
by supertankers then poured
into refineries

Extruded as polymers
measured by diameter
per 9,000 meters of monofilament

Spun into yarn and
knitted into gray cloth

by a small gray town then
Agitated, stamped, rolled
dyed and clipped
teased, bonded, cooked then shipped

To Asia, or Mexico
for cutting and assembly
into garments specified by
earnest lifestylers and

Marketed bi-annually
in four-color catalogs with
environmental messages
mailed directly then

Closed-out by containers
last year's styles
half-price dinosaurs

A.G.

coarse backpack fabric or fine clothing; its dirt-shedding luster is eminently hand-washable; and tighter weaves suffer little shrinkage. Hemp clothing has proved popular primarily with countercultural types like snowboarders and mountain bikers.

Wearing Dinosaurs

Synthetic fabrics roared into life during the 1920s as something for postwar petrochemical plants to manufacture. Many early man-made fabric names (like nylon) began as trade names of the same players who now bring us ripstop, fleece, and Gore-Tex. Petroleum-based fabrics have entered all aspects of twentieth-century life, including your grandfather's hip joint.

Sadly, these miraculous fabrics are based entirely on a limited, extracted resource, and though they are affordable, we have yet to bear their price. While not quite ready to give up our wetsuits or cagoules or Lycra ski bibs, we are very conscious of "wearing dinosaurs."

High-tech synthetics beat natural fibers cold when it comes to their lightweight, quick-drying, elastic, and nonallergenic qualities. Synthetics are a fabric engineer's best friend—they bond easily in blends or layers to outperform natural fibers, as in waterproof-breathable laminates and the latest microbally treated, electrostatically charged underwear knits.

Requiring the same gentle care as natural fabrics, tired plastic fabrics can be periodically revitalized with a wide assortment of treatments and conditioners. One caution: most synthetics are especially vulnerable to DEET (N,N-diethyl-meta-toluamide), a common insect repellent that also happens to be a fine plastics solvent.

Polypro, Etc.

Synthetic underlayers quickly became de rigueur for mountaineers and other outdoor enthusiasts for their fabulous warmth-to-weight ratio and unsurpassed hydrophobia. Ever-popular polypropylene (or polyolefin) represented the first generation of these keep-you-dry fabrics. The main care consideration with polypropylene is its low melting point (*do not* put in dryer!) and odor-absorbing tendencies. Polyester underlayers (Thermax, Capilene, etc.) generally have a softer feel, less odor retention, and can be machine-dried.

New to the outdoor undie world is a whole raft of wondrous blends that have been microbally treated to minimize the poly-pew factor. Some of these fabric treatments include pesticides (!), though there are currently no reports of irritation from wearing these garments.

The latest wrinkle involves fabrics treated with zeolites, which incorporate aluminum silicate—the active ingredient in common underarm deodorant. Other hyper-tech blends resort to electrostatically charging the fibers' molecular structure to repel moisture. Whether this means you can't work at your computer while garbed in backcountry lingerie remains to be seen.

Hang-drying is recommended for all underlayers, natural or synthetic. If you must dry by machine, choose a low or delicate setting and don't use fabric softeners or dryer sheets, which can hamper the insulating and wicking power of many knits. Indeed, dryer sheets have been known to make a sort of greasy stain on these garments if stuck to the fabric for any length of time.

Fleece

Thanks largely to the progressive, trendsetting folks at Malden Mills, outdoorspeople today are an infinitely more colorful crowd than their parents were. Malden began developing synthetic alternative fabrics back in the 1970s, and the rest is history. Polartec and most all fleece can trace its origin to lowly acrylic or polyester griege (gray) goods that resemble jersey knit. After much dying, fuzzing, trimming, and other proprietary manipulations, fleece emerges as a lightweight, nonabsorbent, itch-free wool substitute.

Any parent will tell you that fleece is the best thing that's happened to kids' clothing since the snap. It follows, then, that fleece is virtually care-free. Cold-water machine wash, lift the lid, and remove a nearly spun-dry garment. If pilling is a problem, wash garments inside out, or try scraping the fabric with a vegetable brush, Sweater Stone, or piece of pumice while still damp. *Never* wash your pile gear with bath towels, unless you actually prefer looking like a giant lint magnet.

When choosing from among the now 150-plus variations of synthetic fleece fabrics, there are a few more considerations than style. For instance, an aerodynamic, superstretchy pair of tights relies on added Lycra content for shape retention. While this is great for sleek layering, the trade-off is that Lycra *absorbs* water, so the garment will take longer to dry and will feel cold and clammy on wet-weather trips.

Syntho-Green

A few years back, many garment manufacturers made a highly publicized switch to PCR (postconsumer recycled) fleece reclaimed from plastic bottles. When the media hype died down, so did most companies' commitment to using less of the crude, and they reverted to "virgin" fleece. Other recycled woven synthetics are being developed, like climbing webbing and packcloth; we hope that packs and outerwear will follow suit.

Believe it or not, recycled fibers are old news. Wellman, Inc., the largest supplier, has been turning out recycled polyester fiber (used primarily as insulative batting in textiles and furniture) since 1964. But while recycled synthetics technology has existed for a generation, consumer demand has not. Once consumers begin seeking out recycled products, it becomes a matter of adapting technology—and marketing hype—to fit the need.

Remember, though, that buying such "green" gear is still consumerism, and runaway consumption forms the core of our environmental rotten

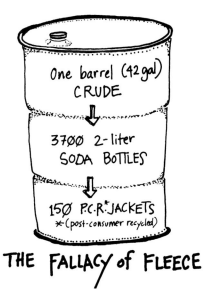

One barrel (42 gal) CRUDE
⇩
3700 2-liter SODA BOTTLES
⇩
150 P.C.R.* JACKETS
*(post-consumer recycled)

THE FALLACY of FLEECE

apple. Purchasing a new fleece sweater may keep 10 or 20 soda bottles out of a landfill, but this does little good if you continue to purchase beverages and foods in plastic containers, which according to U.S. Food and Drug Administration mandate must be made from virgin plastic and which often are not recyclable at the local level.

Stinky Synthetics

Mark Jenkins, minimalist traveler extraordinaire, once told us how, upon climbing Mount Everest, he wore the same polypro shirt for two weeks, then stuffed it away and donned a fresh polypro shirt. After another two weeks, he exchanged the second for the first, which by then smelled "fresh."

Most outdoorspeople have experienced the horrific odor-holding power of polypropylene. A few years back, while filming in the Bugaboos, Annie was horrified when Scottie, her favorite soundman, asked her *p-l-e-a-s-e* to retire her favorite zip turtleneck. Fortunately, as mentioned above, most manufacturers of outdoor clothing are busily addressing this social malady with odor-fighting antimicrobial finishes. Unfortunately, due to the legendary longevity of polypro, the stink problem lives on. Want to salvage a smelly synthetic? Try soaking it in a tub with a few splashes of liquid soap and white vinegar or highly diluted citrus cleaner, then wash as normal. (See appendix B, beginning on page 216.)

WATERPROOF FABRICS

A stroll through your local outfitter's store will introduce you to the thoroughly confusing world of waterproof, waterproof-breathable, and water-repellent fabrics. Manufacturers' hangtags extol the singular virtues of their proprietary innovations, yet there are just three basic ways to add water-repellency to nylon or polyester fabric.

Coated, nonbreathable fabrics bear a urethane-based water barrier on the inside of the garment. These fabrics are used primarily for foul-weather gear and are inherently waterproof, but

they do trap perspiration. If the manufacturer has not sealed the seams with tape, you'll need to add seam sealer or periodically touch up the seams (see pages 20–24 and 36).

The waterproof coating of nonbreathable fabrics tends to peel off when repeatedly subjected to mineral salts—a particular problem for many paddle jackets, which are bombarded by sweaty salt within and sun-dried sea salt without. To extend their service life, turn them inside out to dry, and rinse regularly with ample douches of fresh water.

Coated, breathable fabrics often carry trade names like Ultrex, Helly-Tech, etc., but most employ a polyurethane coating that blocks liquid water entry but still offers some permeability to water vapor, a.k.a. *breathability*. Garments made with these fabrics may also benefit from some owner-applied seamsealing, but they are usually lined, denying access to the seams. In fairness, most coated breathables sport factory seam tape.

Coated fabrics of either type (sometimes

SOLUTION-COATED FABRIC — outer shell fabric w/ DWR — microporous coating

WATERPROOF-BREATHABLE LAMINATE — outer shell fabric w/ DWR — liner fabric — microporous membrane (Gore-Tex)

referred to as *solution-coated*) can be revitalized by a spray-on or launder-in water-repellent treatment, described below. Do not machine-dry unless the manufacturer suggests it. A peeling coating means that your garment has seen better days, and there's little you can do to stop the flaking (see page 36). You can delay the onset of flakes and peels by periodically rinsing both inside and out with clean water—especially if you sweat a lot—and letting the garment dry thoroughly before storing. If the garment is new and the coating peels, return it to the manufacturer.

Waterproof-Breathable Laminate

Waterproof-breathable laminate (typically Gore-Tex) implies a microporous Teflon membrane (otherwise known by the tongue-twisting moniker *polytetrafluoroethylene*) bonded to a tough outer fabric. Three-layer Gore-Tex is a sandwich of shell, membrane, and tricot liner, while two-layer Gore-Tex has a separate, free-hanging liner. Gore's new PacLite fabric saves weight by dispensing with inner linings, protecting the Teflon layer with raised rubbery dots.

Whatever its form, Gore's layered membrane allows water vapor (sweat) to pass through, but not water droplets (rain). Highly stable, the membrane itself is damaged only by punctures or abrasion; myriad outer shell fabrics are employed to protect the whole shebang from committed bushwhackers and shameless granite-grovelers.

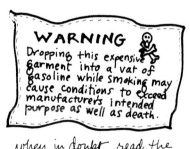

WARNING
Dropping this expensive garment into a vat of gasoline while smoking may cause conditions to exceed manufacturer's intended purpose as well as death.

when in doubt, read the label, stupid

Gore-Tex does have different care requirements from other fabrics, and its performance greatly benefits from periodic maintenance of the stuff's exterior water-repellent finish. Machine-wash using nondetergent soap, and follow this with a spray-on or launder-in water-repellent treatment (see page 35). Careful machine-drying restores water repellency to the shell fabric, as does a thoughtful ironing of the outer fabric with a medium-temperature setting (amazing but true). All Gore-Tex seams are factory-sealed with Gore-Tex tape; peeling seams should be returned to the manufacturer or an authorized service center for warranted repair.

Restoring Water Repellency

Any waterproof garment is only as effective as its DWR—that's durable water repellency or repellent—an outer fabric's water-phobic quality. Instead of cursing your expensive rainsuit after an unexpected soaking, revitalize it. Most DWRs are fluoropolymer coatings to the shell fibers, which make water bead up and run off the surface instead of spreading out and soaking in. Time, dirt, wood smoke, abrasion, bug juice, general trail mileage, and laundering will hinder the DWR's function, allowing water to saturate the outer fabric and make you feel clammy even though the garment isn't really leaking.

The easiest way to restore factory DWR is to machine-dry the garment at medium heat (unless otherwise forewarned by the manufacturer). Before drying, always fasten wrist and ankle closures on one side to those on the other; this keeps garments from turning inside out in the dryer cycle. Don't dry the garments along with fabric-softener sheets, which will counteract the repellent's effects. Next, ironing, as mentioned above, will reactivate DWR (again, read the label instructions—ironing is not good for many coated fabrics). Before ironing, wipe the cool iron sole plate with denatured alcohol to make sure it's clean. As your garment ages and seems less responsive to these steps, consider a conditioning treatment.

Water-Repellent Treatments

DWR treatments are available in two forms: spray and liquid wash. Look for fluoropolymer spray treatments like 3M Scotchguard, DuPont Teflon Fabric Protector, or Nikwax TX Direct Spray-On.

Silicone sprays do shed water, but can inhibit seamsealer adhesion. Wash-in DWR enhancers assure you of even coating and come in recyclable plastic containers. Look for Nikwax TX Direct Wash-In, which is a liquid version of the original

TEN TRAIL-TESTED TIPS: FINDING BETTER RAINGEAR

These tips assume that you're searching for general-purpose, active outdoor raingear that's suitable for hiking, backpacking, light winter use, canoeing, etc. We also assume that you don't have the budget to dedicate a perfectly specialized suit to your every outdoor endeavor.

- **Choose a waterproof-breathable fabric with factory-taped sealed seams.** Pick a nonbreathable coated fabric only if low cost is your overriding concern.
- **Choose a hip-length jacket generously cut to accommodate layers underneath.** But don't go oversize, or you'll look (and feel) like a little kid wearing your big brother's raingear. Most rainwear is cut loosely to allow freedom of movement and room for insulating layers.
- **Look for articulated sleeves and knees for full freedom of movement.** Better raingear has carefully shaped panels at the joints, so it offers minimal constriction to high-stepping hikers or face-planting skiers.
- **Look for reinforced panels at high-wear areas.** Heavier fabric patches at elbows, shoulders, knees, and seat fend off the hard knocks of trail life while allowing the rest of the garment to be of relatively lighter fabric to save weight.
- **In general, fewer seams mean better waterproofing.** Even factory-sealed seams can (and will) leak eventually. Fewer seams mean fewer potential leakage points.
- **Insist on a full-coverage hood with integral brim.** Good hoods snug down around your head and neck, protect the chin area, and swivel with your head. The integral brim sheds water much better than a baseball cap brim, which will just funnel water down your neck. Reject detachable or zip-in hoods: Murphy's Law ensures that they will, indeed, be missing just when a big thunderstorm hits.
- **Vents are your friend.** No matter how breathable a shell fabric might be, you'll be glad to open up underarm zips or venting pockets when you're halfway up Mount Massive, laboring underneath a 40-pound pack.
- **Check pocket placement.** The way pockets are located on a garment tells you a lot about their designer's connection to the activities you have in mind. Can you easily reach into the lower jacket pockets while wearing a backpack waistbelt? Are there adequate storm flaps over the zippers to curb leakage? Are pocket linings set in so that loose items are less likely to fall out when you've hiked three days into the boonies?
- **Love those one-handed drawcord locks.** A simple loop of fabric holds drawstring cordlocks so you can tighten or loosen them with one hand. Sounds elementary, but it's a big deal when your hands are freezing or you're clinging to a mountainside.
- **Choose muted colors if possible.** Granted, bright is right in hunting season or to keep powerboats from bearing down on your kayak. Otherwise, choose muted shades that are easier on the eye and on the environment. Brown and beige dyes contain the least toxic compounds.

DWR WASH-IN TIPS

- Prewash your garment so the DWR will bond to the fabric's fibers and not to dirt on the fabric.
- If you want the outside of a garment to receive the most treatment, wash right side out, and vice versa.
- If using a washing machine, let water fill the drum completely before adding the DWR emulsion. Let the machine disperse liquid for about 5 minutes, then stop the process to allow the garments to soak before completing the wash cycle.

DWR used by many manufacturers. The only time when a liquid is not the better choice is when the garment includes a free-hanging wicking liner, whose performance would be hampered by a launder-in DWR treatment. Follow any DWR retreatment with a trip through the dryer to enhance the bond between waterproofing polymers and fabric. Then keep garments clean — dirt attracts water and masks the hydrophobic action of water-repellent treatments. Sluice the crud off with clean creek water if nothing else.

CARDINAL RULE

Do not store any fabric wet!

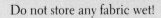

Insulations

See also Sleeping Bags, beginning on page 54

Lacking fur or feathers, humans have trapped and skinned and plucked and emulated these organic insulators for centuries. Regardless of origin, insulation works by acting as a barrier against heat loss; generally, more volume means more insulation. Machine-laundering is known to be hard on all insulated garments, but most people simply don't take the time to hand-wash (see pages 34–35).

DOWN

Down's legendary compressibility gives it the greatest warmth-to-weight ratio of any insulation, the latest synthetics included. Down compresses to a very low volume, then springs back to fill as much space as allowed. Down is not feathers, but the soft underplumage of waterfowl, yet "leaking feathers" is a common complaint with down garments. Read the label carefully when purchasing, and make sure you're looking at a down garment and not "down blend"—feathers have little insulating value and are nothing more than cheap filler.

The main drawback to down is its lack of insulating power when wet. There are some wash-in down conditioners available (Kenyon, Nikwax) that add a DWR coating to individual down plumes, enhancing the down's natural resiliency with a bit of water-repellent boost.

Down-filled garments or bags should not be stored tightly stuffed in their sacks, but should be hung or kept in a large, breathable cotton sack. When stitching a tear or zipper on a down garment, use the smallest needle possible to keep holes (a.k.a. down escape vents) to a minimum. If you're replacing a zipper, make sure the down is contained by a line of stitching before opening zipper stitches. Otherwise you'll be gasping for air in a room full of plumes. One trick recommended by Bob Upton at Rainy Pass Repair is to wet the down before attempting to work around it.

SYNTHETIC FILL

Synthetic fill is every bit as delicate as down, despite what you read in the magazine ads. Recent years have witnessed notorious "fill wars," with major petrochemical concerns pitting their engineers' latest efforts to counterfeit goose down against those of other concerns in advertising-heavy battles. They're making progress toward truly durable syn-fills that mimic the compressibility and weight-efficiency of down, but Mother Goose has a 20,000-year head start.

Most synthetic fills use polyester fibers held together in thin bats by a resinous bond. This binder can be especially susceptible to heat damage—in car trunks, hot water, and clothes dryers. Hand-washing is recommended by manufacturers. Synthetic-filled items should be stored like their down counterparts—by hanging or in breathable cotton bags. Storing fiberfill garments fully compressed will merely ensure a chilling experience later.

NEOPRENE

See also Wetsuits and Neoprene Care, beginning on page 37

Cleaning Methods
DRY CLEANING—NOT!

Dry-cleaning processes employ ethylene-based solvents that are harmful to down and synthetics. Even Stoddard Process, often touted as better for down products, uses distilled kerosene. Most down garments and bags sport a "Dry Clean Only" label largely to prevent careless machine-washing, even though the solvents are harmful to both down and synthetic fills (as well as to shell fibers). Spare your gear and the planet—limit your dry cleaning.

KINDER, GENTLER HAND-WASHING

Although you shouldn't wash outerwear any more than absolutely necessary, hand-washing is recommended, especially for insulated products. About as much fun as bathing a dog, and more

time-consuming, this process is definitely worth the effort. Remember to clean your pockets! Turn them inside out and brush away lint, cookie crumbs, or anything likely to stain.

Use nondetergent, powdered soaps that do not employ surfactants (surfacing agents that will leave film or residue on fibers and reduce water repellency). Ivory Flakes and Dreft are recommended for hand- or machine-washing of outdoor gear. Dr. Bronner's Liquid Castile soap is also suitable for many applications. (See appendix B, Low-Tox Cleaning Solutions, beginning on page 216.)

- Spot-clean any stains by scrubbing with a little cleaner and warm water (a tooth-brush works great).

"OUT, OUT DAMNED SPOT!"

Make a paste with your favorite powdered soap or stain rem & scrub with toothbrush

- Fill bathtub with lukewarm (not hot) water, then dissolve a small amount of cleaner in the water.
- Immerse items to be cleaned, then knead gently until thoroughly wet. Do not twist or wring the garment at any point.
- Allow to soak for about 30 minutes.
- Drain soapy water, then press water out of the garment by hand.
- Refill the tub with warm water, let garment soak for 15 minutes or so, then knead to remove soap. Drain the tub and compress water out of the garment.
- Repeat the rinsing process at least once more; several times is ideal.
- Lift the garment gently, then block dry on a towel or screen.
- Allow to air-dry for a time before machine-drying. Wool, silk, and synthetics should air-dry; down products require the air and rotation of a machine dryer to redistribute and loft the filling.
- Machine-drying down: use low or delicate set-

ting. Add a few clean, dry towels to absorb water. Skip the tennis ball or shoe. Check the dryer often and replace the towels when saturated.

KINDER, GENTLER MACHINE-WASHING

Okay, so it's unrealistic to hand-wash your gear. If you're going to machine-wash, try to use a front-loading commercial washer rather than your home, top-loading spindle type, which twists, agitates, and damages insulating fibers and baffles, not to mention what it does to drawcords. A big commercial machine's tumbling action is also good if you're using a launder-in DWR treatment or down conditioner, because the fabric is less likely to crease and more likely to be evenly coated. Remember to use a nondetergent cleaner only.

Caution: Open zippers and Velcro tabs can wreak havoc in the wash cycle! Velcro is extremely abrasive to linings and coated fabric surfaces. Batten down your jacket thoroughly before washing. Securing opposite cuffs with Velcro or snaps is a good way to prevent the sleeves from turning inside out or becoming hopelessly twisted.

STICKY STUFF

Pitch, chewing gum, wax, and weird gooey stuff lodged in a sweater or the seat of your pants is unpleasant, but easily removed. On the trail, try slathering the spot with peanut butter or cooking oil, which penetrates and loosens unwelcome bonds. At home, place the garment in the freezer. Once hard, at least some of the substance should crack off. Other solutions (after removing as much of the substance as possible): Rub the spot with egg white, then soak in vinegar before laundering, or apply citrus cleaner directly to the mess. Don't go overboard chemically trying to remove the substance, or you may damage the fabric! Test a non-visible area of fabric for color-fastness before trying

denatured alcohol or (as a last resort) nail polish remover on the sticky stain. (See appendix B, Low-Tox Cleaning Solutions, beginning on page 216.)

STAIN REMOVAL

The best way to deal with stains is to prevent them with Scotchguard or other surface treatment that repels liquid. The sooner you attend to a spot, the easier it will be to remove. Commercial "stain sticks" are effective cleaners. Try making a paste with regular powdered soap and water and then working it into the offending mark with a toothbrush. We stick to varying mixtures of borax, baking soda, lemon juice, egg white, or vinegar and hope for the best.

"I SEE YOU HAVE A PET"

More than one person has remarked upon the hairy state of our fleece garments. If you live with animals, the best way to remove their omnipresent hair is with a Sweater Stone,

Animal lovers should consider pet hair color when purchasing fuzzy garments.

pumice, or stout clothes brush while the garment is still damp.

Patching

Duct tape is the most popular material for patching synthetic raingear, down vests, and just about everything else in the field. Kenyon K-Tape self-adhesive nylon repair tape is easy enough to carry in your field repair kit, though. Tenaciously sticky and available in both taffeta and ripstop, K-Tape is washable and comes in about two dozen colors.

The trick for taping any tear is to clean and dry

the fabric, then singe any frayed bits with a butane lighter. A swipe with an alcohol swab from your repair kit will hasten drying and ensure a good bond for adhesive patches. Rounded corners on the tape patch are also important. Another popular field and home repair is a urethane adhesive patch (see pages 7–10; and sidebar, page 8). Remember that tape should be considered a temporary patch.

Seamsealing

Outerwear construction is so detailed these days that it's rare to find an untaped seam on any type of coated raingear. You can spot the outline of a taped seam through the outside of the garment. (See pages 20–24.)

Coating or Recoating Synthetics

If the waterproof coating on your favorite jacket is beginning to flake, you have a couple of options to buy a few more outings before the inevitable honorable retirement. Look for a liquid, water-based polymer recoating agent like Aquaseal Poly Coat or Kenyon Recoat 3.

One pleasingly economical stopgap is Thompson's Water Seal (an all-purpose deck sealer from the hardware store). Three ounces should cover about 10 square feet. Always apply to the uncoated side of the fabric (if you apply it to a flaky original coating, the new layer will just peel along with it, and probably exacerbate the problem).

- Thoroughly clean the surface to be coated. Hang the garment in an open, ventilated area or lay flat on a clean surface.
- Use a bristle brush or a small pump sprayer for consistent application.
- Thoroughly spread out any puddles or excess coating, which might blister and peel once dry.
- The fabric should be saturated.
- If applying a second coat, do so while the first coat is still tacky (within 30 minutes) to achieve a secure bond.
- Allow to air-dry for about three days before storing. When storing

handheld sprayer for sealants, gelcoat

for the first time after recoating, sprinkle a little talcum powder on the coated areas to keep the fabric from sticking to itself.

CHAPTER 3

Specialty Garments

Wetsuits and Neoprene Care

See also chapter 1, Essential Techniques; chapter 2, Fabrics and Insulations; Sprayskirts, beginning on page 200; and appendix A, Adhesives

Neoprene is the best wet insulator, barring seal blubber and sea-otter fur. Like other synthetics, neoprene has evolved from its first generation of sticky, bulky black rubber to the sleek, laminated forms we see today. Neoprene of varying thickness is now sandwiched between soft nylon fabric skins for comfort and ease of wear. Neoprene garments take many forms, from Farmer John wetsuits to socks, paddling gloves to ski pants, beanies to sprayskirts. The new generation of chest-high neoprene waders are just the ticket for paddling sit-on-top kayaks in chilly waters and may just be the warmest, nicest foul-weather bibs ever invented.

The finer points of wetsuit care have come from our neighbor (who prefers the moniker Neoprene Queen), an avid scuba diver and sea-kayak guide. Neon costumes festoon our street during the summer months, because after each outing she carefully rinses and line-dries her wetsuit, whether she's been floating in the salt sea, the local YMCA pool, or a nearby lake.

"Few people realize," says the Neoprene Queen, "that fresh water is just as hard on synthetics as salt or chlorine—thanks to organic matter and pollutants. These contaminants are harbored in open cells of the neoprene." Sweat (body salt) also fatigues the fabric. Neoprene begins to deteriorate from the very day of manufacture simply because of chemistry. Even if you treat your wetsuit with gentle reverence, its insulative value gradually decreases with time.

Maximize the life of your neoprene gear with a thorough rinse using a powerful water jet (hose or shower) both inside and out, paying special attention to zippers. Do this every time you wear the garment. Occasional conditioning by soaking in a tub with Aquaseal Wet Suit Shampoo (available at paddle or dive shops) is a good idea. Hang dry wetsuits inside out on a stiff, shaped hanger to avoid creases, which will crack with age.

SUN DAMAGE: ULTRAVIOLENT RAYS

Nothing hurts neoprene gear more than solar exposure. The nylon-face fabrics have proven particularly susceptible to UV degradation—

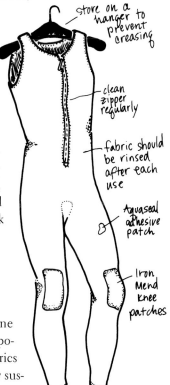

store on a hanger to prevent creasing

clean zipper regularly

fabric should be rinsed after each use

Aquaseal adhesive patch

Iron Mend knee patches

witness the tattered hatch covers on our much-used 21-foot double kayak. The neoprene foot straps on Dave's favorite sailboard are so sun-rotted that they've faded from bright pink to a ghastly bruised rose, and the outer skin is falling off in scabrous chunks.

To extend the service life of neoprene items, minimize solar exposure fanatically. Hang-dry neoprene gear out of the sun, and take it off the line as soon as it's dry. It should be stored hanging in a dark closet or loosely rolled up (not folded) in an opaque storage box. Keep kayak hatch covers stashed safely away inside the boat, not stretched over the hatch, where they'll lose resilience and bake in the sun.

Preventive maintenance includes regular spritzing with a UV inhibitor like Formula 303 Protectant, a treatment that also helps extend the life of original colors.

PUNCTURES AND TEARS

Sun-seared or much-used neoprene suffers additionally from abrasion and punctures. Small tears (usually in the outer skin) should be patched with Aquaseal, Goo, or other polyurethane adhesive. One glance at a Maine coast urchin-diver's gloves will tell you that Aquaseal is the goop favored by professionals.

Your neoprene waders will last longer if you are extra careful about keeping grit and pebbles out of the footgear you wear over their integral booties. Snug-fitting high-top wading shoes resist picking up sand and gravel better than floppy old sneakers or open-toed river sandals. One fly-fishing friend swears by army-surplus jungle boots. He hot-rodded the army boots for river duty with add-on felt soles, which offer decent traction on moss-slicked rock.

Ruthless tugging of friction-prone suits or booties while putting them on or taking them off will inevitably cause tears at seams. Neoprene is difficult to stitch on a home machine. It's better to hand-sew neoprene with nylon thread, but close inspection may reveal that you've torn through both the nylon outer skin and the neoprene itself, indicating that a structural patch is the only answer.

NEOPRENE PATCH

Patching neoprene requires a bridge to join intact areas of the nylon fabric. The simplest and most effective patching material is McNett's Iron Mend, a heat-activated nylon adhesive tape. Iron Mend comes in a precut kneepad size (10 by 6 inches) in many colors—you can cut smaller patches from the sheet. Worn or abraded areas like knees and elbows or stressed areas at crotch, zipper, or where a sprayskirt stretches over coaming will benefit from an iron-on preventive patch. For just a preventive patch, skip the preliminary Aquaseal patching steps outlined below.

- Review patching techniques (see pages 7–10).
- Make sure the neoprene article is clean and dry. A little swab of alcohol on the area to be repaired will remove any lingering oils and improve patch adhesion. Allow to dry.
- If the hole is larger than your fingerprint, plug it with a piece of neoprene material or thick PU repair adhesive like Goo or Freesole.
- Join torn areas (and plug materials) together and apply a masking-tape backing.
- Create an adhesive patch using Aquaseal or another midweight urethane repair material and allow to cure.
- Remove masking-tape backing and clean area with alcohol. Allow to dry.
- Wipe off sole plate of a cool iron with a little denatured alcohol to remove any contaminants.
- Preheat iron to *acrylic*, *low*, or *delicate* setting, with no steam.
- Cut Iron Mend to cover damaged area plus about 1 inch, remembering to round edges of patch.
- Place article on flat surface (ironing board, bench, counter).

- Position Iron Mend over damaged area, coated side down. Place silicone release paper (supplied with tape) over the area to be ironed.
- Hold iron on the patch with firm, steady pressure for about 10 seconds; make sure you heat the entire patch.
- Allow the repair to cool before testing edges for security. You may need to apply more heat and pressure. If after the second application of heat the patch does not stick, start over with fresh tape.

Drysuits

The reason for owning and wearing a drysuit is to guarantee (as much as possible) against getting wet in very cold and exposed environments like windy, open seas or gnarly whitewater. Failure by way of leaking fabric or worn gaskets can be more than uncomfortable—the hazards of hypothermia become very real.

The two big reasons for taking good care of your drysuit: first, it's a *very* expensive, specialized toy; and second, this toy can literally save your life.

FABRIC CARE

Drysuits are usually made of coated nylon fabric with welded seams, while top-end suits employ Gore-Tex or other laminates (see chapter 2, Fabrics and Insulations, for specific care recommendations and tips on how to revitalize water-repellent fabric finishes).

Drysuits usually work so well that you'll crank out enough sweat to make you wet from the inside. The best way to keep your drysuit dry is to wear a thin next-to-skin layer of moisture-managing synthetic (polypro, polyester, etc.), which keeps the dankness away from your skin and prevents condensed perspiration or slight leakage from pooling.

Pollutants and dirt should be washed off the outside of the drysuit after each wearing. Salty condensation from your own body can cause mildew inside the suit. Turn the suit inside out and rinse with fresh water and allow to completely dry before rolling and storing in a cool, dry place. Placing the suit in a loose-weave cotton bag (as you would a sleeping bag) is also a good habit.

Finding an elusive leak in a drysuit may drive you to distraction. You might try hanging the suit in a darkened room, shining a flashlight inside it and looking for pinpoints of light. When you find such a spot, mark it, then patch it with a dab of urethane adhesive. Larger rips will require a fabric patch. Drysuit patches should be applied to the interior (coated side) of coated fabrics with urethane adhesive and allowed to fully cure before folding or wearing. Gore-Tex suits typically must be patched on the outside. Stitched patches are not recommended, for obvious reasons.

DRYSUIT ZIPPERS

When buying a drysuit, a lot of what you pay for is the watertight zipper, which is heat-seated or welded into position. Unlike your average coil or toothed zipper, these watertight versions are not repairable by normal humans, and damaged suits must be returned to the factory for an expensive replacement.

When opening or closing a drysuit zipper, pull the zipper string at an angle (about 30 degrees) to minimize friction. Pulling directly at the slider will cause it to dig into the zipper teeth or coils. Get a friend to close or open the zipper for you. By doing it solo, you place pressure on the teeth in the wrong direction.

Always irrigate the zipper with clean, fresh water after wearing. Some people use wax to lubricate a metal zipper. Others insist that the zipper must be stored fully closed or fully opened—never partway—or the delicate coils may kink. If you make a habit of zipping only to take the garment on or off, you'll conserve the zipper. Make sure that nothing heavy is placed on top of the zipper during storage, or it may become deformed.

GASKETS

Natural gum latex gaskets provide the ultimate moisture seal and are the most sensitive part of the drysuit. Gaskets may last anywhere from a few months to five years, but the average life span is about three years. Gasket replacement is such a pain and so expensive (about $75 just for the parts) that after you're forced to do it, you'll definitely take better care of the next set.

The first line of defense is always to ease into your suit mindfully, working the seals carefully over head, wrists, and feet. Resist the urge to just yank it on, or you'll almost certainly tear the seals, especially if they are aging and weak.

Gaskets are especially vulnerable to damage by heat and petrochemicals, including most forms of water pollution and suntan lotions. DEET is absolutely lethal. The secret to gasket longevity is simple: Keep the rubber clean and cool.

As rubber stretches, its pores open to chemical contamination; when the gasket becomes slack, pores close around the entrapped dirt, salt, or pollutants, which go right to work breaking down the rubber. Wash with gentle soap and water after each wear. After cleaning, apply a food-grade silicone or 303 Protectant to provide lubrication as well as a barrier against chemicals. Don't apply the lubricant without cleaning the gaskets first, though, since this will seal in any dirt. Storing your suit in a cotton bag will minimize airflow around the seals.

Protect the drysuit from heat. Even more damaging than UV, the heat inside a car trunk is enough to dry out rubber, or worse, turn it to tarlike goo. Keeping the gasket rubber cool is extremely important.

When you first purchase a drysuit, the gaskets may be uncomfortably tight. Don't be tempted to pare them down without first giving them time to stretch. You can assist the breaking-in by pre-stretching the gaskets around neck-, wrist- or ankle-sized forms: coffee cans, juice cans, salad bowls, cook pots, or the subversive's solution, a traffic cone. Here's an actual use for your Lava Lamp.

If your neck gasket proves truly unbearable, you can trim it with very sharp scissors, but only ⅛ inch at a time. Make sure to trim evenly; leave no nicks, which will inevitably split on the first day of your next big trip. It's important to be patient because the seals do stretch, often to a fault.

Many drysuits are now equipped with overcuffs designed to protect the seals from UV, dirt, and what-have-you. While they may be effective in prolonging gasket life, overcuffs can be somewhat in the way when it comes time to replace the seals—and you will have to replace them. Do everything you can to delay that sorry day.

Patching Gaskets

Although rare, a punctured seal may be repaired with a bicycle tube patch kit.

Prevent the Black Plague

Nothing's more disappointing than pulling a drysuit out of storage to find that the seals have disintegrated into a pulpy goo smeared all over the body. The only way to get the stuff off the fabric is to scrape it away, then clean carefully with acetone—but don't scrub too hard, or you risk damaging the fabric coating with the solvent. This ruinous black blight is a nightmare to remove, but it could have been avoided.

As you inspect the gaskets, if you notice that the latex is losing its resiliency and starting to feel a little tacky, remove and replace them immediately, before goo sets in. Once the seals have lost their integrity, removal is very unpleasant and dependent upon the use of a solvent. Even if you don't plan to seat new gaskets until next season, remove the old ones now, while the job's easier, then clean and store the suit.

Replacing Neck Gaskets: Two Methods

Replacement neck gaskets are available at paddling, dive, or sail shops or from the manufacturer.

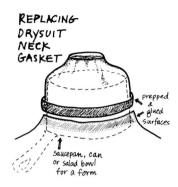

REPLACING DRYSUIT NECK GASKET

prepped & glued surfaces

Saucepan, can or salad bowl for a form

Gasket replacement is one of those potentially messy jobs you may wish to assign to someone else. Consider shipping your suit to its manufacturer, who will replace seals for a nominal fee (and you're guaranteed a professional-looking finish).

Either method requires

- A gasket mandrel or form to hold the end of the drysuit open and provide a place to position the replacement gasket. A 2-liter beverage bottle works well for most wrists; a 3-liter bottle for most ankles; and a medium-sized kitchen pot for necks. Get creative; try a salad bowl, traffic cone, coffee can, or waxed-paper container. The mandrel is best wrapped with waxed paper to prevent adhesive mishaps.
- Prepare the gluing surface of the new gasket (the bottom 1 inch) by gently sanding with fine-grit (220) sandpaper, then cleaning with denatured alcohol. Some manufacturers provide prepared replacement seals that require only a quick wipe with solvent before adhesion.
- Place the form inside the suit opening and stretch a new (prepped) gasket into position as shown, peeling up the last inch for gluing.

Method 1: Breakable Bond

Use a urethane adhesive such as Sta-Bond, popular for vinyl raft repair, or the proprietary adhesive recommended by your drysuit manufacturer (see appendix G, Materials Resources, beginning on page 236). This method is very clean, neat, and professional-looking.

- Remove old gaskets by heating the bond with a hair dryer or heat lamp, which warms the glue enough that you can peel the rubber away easily. DO NOT use an open flame.
- If heat removal is not an option, resort to MEK (methy ethyl ketone), applied with an acid brush, to soften the glue. Keep the MEK away from any heat source. (MEK is available in the paint department of auto parts stores. This nasty stuff requires skin and eye protection.)
- Leave residue on the fabric—this provides a good adhesive base that requires no preparation. Remove any lumps of old adhesive, though.
- Attach parts to form as illustrated.
- Apply a thin coat of adhesive to each piece and allow to dry so it is not tacky. Apply a second coat of adhesive to the neck gasket and allow to dry. This method allows adjustment during positioning.
- Roll gasket into position.
- Use a hair dryer to heat the glued surface (the heat will activate the glue). Carefully burnish with your finger or corrugator to dispel any air bubbles.
- Allow to stand overnight to cure.

Method 2: Unbreakable Bond

Some adhesives chemically bond so completely that you must cut off the old gasket at the edge of the fabric. To replace, you must glue to the old gasket—a rubber-to-rubber surface. A relatively thin urethane adhesive like Aquaseal is normally recommended for this purpose.

- Prepare the gluing surface of the old gasket by sanding and cleaning with denatured alcohol.
- Use masking tape to protect the fabric, since Aquaseal is pretty goopy and stays wet for a long time.
- Attach both parts to form as illustrated.
- Apply a thin, even coat of Aquaseal to both surfaces.
- Gently roll the gasket into position.

- Use your fingers to carefully burnish the bond, working out any air bubbles or lumpy spots.
- Wrap the glued joint with a band of waxed paper, held tightly in place with a wrap of masking tape.
- Allow to set overnight in a warm — not cool — spot. Place a "Do Not Disturb" sign nearby.

Shelled Gloves

Gauntlet-style overmitts and gloves should be maintained and periodically treated like the rest of your outerwear. Ice climbing, sweat, and a season of skiing take their toll faster on gloves than on any other garment. Give your gloves a preseason tune-up.

- Wash gloves with nondetergent cleaner and dry thoroughly.
- Turn inside out and seal all seams, preferably with Seam Grip, which is the most waterproof sealer. Allow to dry.
- Turn right side out and apply a spray-on DWR treatment.

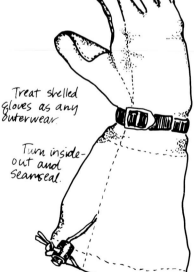

Treat shelled gloves as any outerwear.

Turn inside-out and seamseal.

- Increase the gripping potential of glove palms by putting them on and dotting Aquaseal on the palm area. Spread fingers wide and allow to air-dry for at least 24 hours.

Gaiters

No serious hiker should be without gaiters. From a global standpoint, these stout leggings help prevent the dreaded proliferation of "trail spread" — that erosive condition that results from gaiterless walkers who go *around* puddles and mudholes in the trail. From a personal perspective, you can think of gaiters as tents for your boots, which will make your footwear investment last much longer. The fabric and seams may be weatherproofed and cleaned, and fasteners maintained as needed.

Other tips:

Think of gaiters as little tents for your boots

- Patch crampon lacerations immediately with duct tape or nylon tape. Once home, these are a great application for little urethane patches (Annie's gaiters look like a crazy quilt, Dave's just have lots of unfixed holes).
- Puttee or Outdoor Research Crocodile owners will find that the underfoot Hypalon straps eventually fray, tatter, or become unstitched. Melt back frays with a flame. Inspect for abrasion and weakening around buckle holes. Protect and enhance stitch rows with a coating

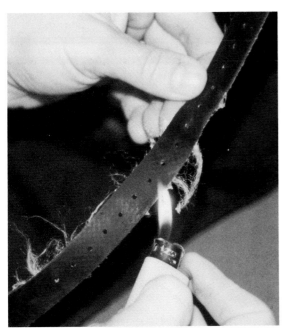

Melt back fraying strands on Hypalon straps.

of urethane seam sealer. (See appendix G, Materials Resources, beginning on page 236, for sources of replacement straps.)

- A lost strap or lace hook is quickly remedied in the field with baling wire, which doesn't ball up with snow.
- Give strap buckles, zippers, and snaps a preseason rubdown with a silicone-saturated cloth. Prevent frozen-finger fumbling and frustration!
- Clean mitten lint and other accumulated schmoo out of Velcro closures. Accumulated wool fibers will mat together like felt, making closure difficult.

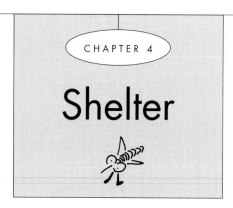

CHAPTER 4

Shelter

Tents

Staying overnight in the wilderness wouldn't be nearly as much fun without a tent in which to hide from the elements. Your tent probably bears more exposure than any other piece of gear, so it should come as no surprise when your three-year-old shelter begins to look a little worse for wear. Dirt, sand, leaves, sticks, salt, and stones grind away at the floor, zippers, and door panels. Meanwhile, the sun, acid rain, pollen, pitch, and powerful gusts pummel the fly and canopy.

UV radiation hastens the demise of most tents; direct sun can weaken both the rainfly and the tent body so dramatically that after just one season coatings peel, hardware pulls out, and the smallest scrape produces a nasty tear. Pitch your tent in the shade whenever possible; glacier and high-altitude campers might wish to pitch a sacrificial tarp over a valued tent. Manufacturers all advise against leaving any nylon tent pitched for a long period. The worst possible fate for a tent is to be left standing in your backyard all summer.

Protect your guesthouse by pitching it under an "Alaskan rainfly," a.k.a. a tarp. One feasible way

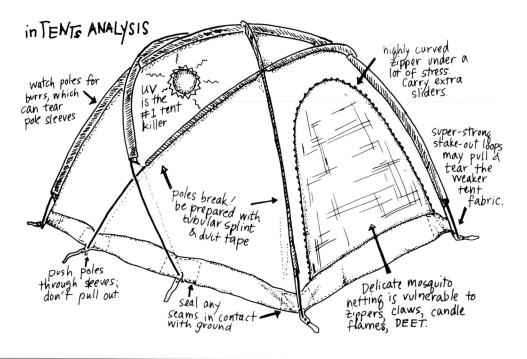

in TENTs ANALYSIS

watch poles for burrs, which can tear pole sleeves

UV is the #1 tent killer

highly curved zipper under a lot of stress. Carry extra sliders.

super-strong stake-out loops may pull & tear the weaker tent fabric.

poles break! be prepared with tubular splint & duct tape

push poles through sleeves; don't pull out.

seal any seams in contact with ground

Delicate mosquito netting is vulnerable to zippers, claws, candle flames, DEET.

TIME-TESTED TIPS FOR FINDING THE RIGHT TENT

- **Know your needs.** The clearer you are about the intended uses for your new tent, the easier it will be for you to resist the blandishments of pushy "sales associates" who think *they* know what *you* need. If you travel solo or by bike, a simple bivy shelter and tarp may suffice. Fair-weather trekkers won't like lugging a heavy mountaineer's tent, and vice versa. "Convertible" tents are stout enough for most winter duty, yet they have zip-out panels to catch those cooling summer breezes.

- **Be a spatial skeptic.** Don't believe manufacturers' capacity guidelines until you've crawled inside with partners and gear. Be frank about your own tendencies: are you a committed minimalist or more of a sybarite? Claustrophobes generally prefer one size larger than tentmakers' estimates.

- **Pooh-pooh the price.** Good value is a distinctly subjective concept. Even the priciest shelter costs less than a month's rent. Light-duty users can afford to let price dictate decisions; otherwise, function and workmanship rule your choices.

- **Stand up to the weather.** Better tents are completely freestanding—that is, no guylines required. Realize, however, that even "free-standing" tents must be staked down, and you'd better be ready to add guylines when stormy weather threatens.

- **Look for factory-sealed seams.** More and more tents now come with factory-taped sealed seams. This saves you the pleasure of inhaling noxious fumes while slathering seams with sealer yourself.

- **A vestibule is best.** Every outdoor abode needs a mud room, a place to shed wet gear before tracking into the inner sanctum. A built-in vestibule only adds a pound or so to the overall weight; avoid floppy, tacked-on optional ones. We prefer vestibules front and rear; one for gear storage, plus a "beastibule" where soggy dogs are banished.

- **Color counts.** Minimize the tent's visual impact by blending it with its surroundings. Light-colored tents stay cooler in hot, sunny climes. Conversely, a darker-hued tent warms right up on a bright winter day—enough to function as a serviceable solar dryer for sodden clothes and sleeping bags.

- **Fight your weight fixation.** Unless you're prepped to accept privation, accept the fact that shelter is heavy. Typical three-season tents weigh about 3 pounds per person. Convertible designs run about 4 pounds per person, while true bombproof mountain tents often run 5 or more.

- **Vent your tent.** Make sure there are plenty of ventilation options available; you'll sleep cooler on a steamy summer eve, dryer in a dank fall rain. Look for vents (zippable doors or windows) that let cool air enter low and hot air exit high.

- **Buy better stakes.** The skimpy aluminum skewers that are standard issue with most tents are great for restraining pet squirrels but not for holding fast against a storm. Improve your stake selection with a half-dozen 6-inch nylon skewers (I-beam cross-sections are best), and carry two or three 10-inch nylon I-stakes to anchor key stake-out loops at tent ends and vestibule.

to minimize UV damage is to coat your exterior tent fly with 303 Protectant. Normally recommended for boat hulls, this water-based "sunscreen" for petroleum-based materials works fine on fabrics too.

FIELD TIPS

Here are a few simple procedures for tent care in the field:

- Establish (and enforce) "house rules," such as no footwear to be worn inside the tent, and always roll up and secure door flaps so they don't languish underfoot in the mud. Meticulous campers might carry a scrap carpet "doormat" to curb tracking.

- Before packing up each morning, remove the fly and drape it upside down to dry the inside. Make sure the tent body is also dry. Pull up the stakes and lay the tent on its side while still erect to let the floor air. Before removing the poles, open the doors completely and shake out any debris.

- *Never* store a wet tent. If it is soaked when stuffed in your pack, remove as soon as possible and set it up to dry. We've ruined more than one tent by neglecting to thoroughly dry the thing after a soggy trip. Even a little morning dew can cause mildew in a few days. Once mildew establishes itself in dark, star-patterned splotches, coatings begin to delaminate.

- It's possible to "overpitch" a tent. Most tents have a series of grommets on the stakeout loops into which you plug pole tips. While the fabric should be taut, maxing the poles into the tightest grommet may unnecessarily stress the fabric. Save those last holes for damp weather (when fabric sags) and to tauten older, stretched-out tents.

- You can also "underpitch" a tent, which is a more certain formula for disaster. Indeed, many tent sagas are due to feeble pitch jobs. A floppy tent, poorly placed and staked, is a wind victim ripe for a proper flattening. A wall of snow blocks or stone to windward isn't a bad idea in exposed, windswept terrain. Seek shelter behind a handy bush, a tree, or boulder—anything to break the blast of wind on your nylon *dome*-icile.

- A visually superb site is not so great if you can't get solid stakes in the ground. Imagine Annie's chagrin after a day at the crags to find our tent tossed like tumbleweed into a barbed wire fence.

- Pay attention to signs of prevailing wind (leaning trees or snowdrifts) when you're setting up camp. Pitch the low end of the tent into the wind so the entrance will be comfortably downwind.

- When pitching in a stiff breeze, stake the upwind end first before inserting all the poles and trying to erect the tent.

- In rough terrain or during extended trips, consider using a groundcloth to minimize abrasion to the tent floor. The cloth should never protrude from the perimeter of the tent, or water will puddle under the floor. On reasonably soft sites Dave prefers to place the groundcloth inside the tent floor to minimize abrasion to the fabric coating and block seepage of ground moisture. Sleeping out on just the groundcloth is also a nice option for clear nights under the stars, when a tent isn't really necessary.

To Roll or To Stuff? That Is the Question

After measured consideration and much spousal, ah, negotiation, here's our advice on this highly controversial backwoods topic: one *rolls* a clean, dry tent around poles (always varying folds to avoid creasing fabric); one *stuffs* a soaking wet tent.

CLEANING

You say you stuffed soggy gear into the trunk, drove home, got caught up with work, and didn't unpack until a week later? The easiest way to clean and dry a tent is to set it up. Once it's dry, you can shake out cooties, brush seams, and inspect stitching and seams for leaks. Check for any worn areas and whether zipper sliders need attention. Like an aging pet, your tent should be treated gently.

Clean grubby tents with nondetergent soap (diluted Ivory Flakes or Dr. Bronner's) and a soft brush. If mildew has set in or there are sticky sap spots, scrub gently with a little borax or baking soda dissolved in water. Better to live with a stain than to damage the fabric trying to eradicate it. (See sidebar, page 26; and appendix B, Low-Tox Cleaning Solutions, beginning on page 216.)

The powerful jet from a garden hose is ideal for blasting out corners, irrigating zippers, and rinsing off pollen or sea salt.

Don't be tempted to wash your tent in a home washing machine, which can twist and wring the fabric to death, cause delamination, and devastate netting panels. If your inner neatnik simply insists upon a machine wash, at least do it in a commercial front-loading drum-type washer. Use the gentle cycle and warm water. Hang-dry at home; do not machine-dry unless you *want* the fabric coatings to start flaking off.

TENT SEALING

See also Seams and Seamsealing, beginning on page 20

Surprisingly, even those enlightened enough to seamseal don't necessarily coat the right seams, or even the right side, of the tent. Seam sealer should be applied to the coated, inside seams of the tent floor and the "bathtub ring" (where the floor is attached to the canopy). Pay special attention to corners and areas of tension, like sewn webbing loops—zillions of stitch holes wait there to become a showerhead. All rainfly seams should be sealed, as should any exposed fasteners, such as snaps.

Bibler Tents also recommends sealing exterior seams, even if they've been factory taped. In wet conditions moisture may enter stitching and track along the channel behind the seam tape. Seal exterior seams to prevent tracking and to get maximum waterproofness and durability. Some skeptics who've learned from hard use insist that all tent seams, inside and out, top and bottom, should be sealed.

The best time to seal is when the tent is new, before any dirt contaminates seams. Always work in a ventilated but not breezy area (a sheltered deck or barn). You don't want airborne detritus stuck to your tent.

Especially when your tent is new, it's crucial to prepare the seams by buffing with alcohol or seam precleaner, which will remove any surfactants or

"MY TENT LEAKS"

Maybe. Water in your tent could be caused by

Condensation. You crank out a lot of heat and moisture while you sleep. This moisture passes through the breathable, inner tent walls and condenses on the underside of the rainfly. Vent the doors and keep the rainfly tightly guyed away from the tent body. If the rainfly sags and tent walls become saturated, you get evaporative cooling, which makes condensation worse. Try to vent an air intake down low and an air outlet up high.

Groundcloth seepage. If you use a groundcloth to protect your tent floor from abrasion, make sure it doesn't extend beyond the perimeter of the tent. Otherwise, the cloth will channel water into a pool directly beneath your sleeping bag.

Poor site selection. Are you camped in a drainage swale? Is the smallest area of tent upwind?

Seam leakage. If you're an all-season camper, seamsealing is a must—even the teensiest corner leak can soak a sleeping bag.

water-repellent finishes, so the sealer will stick. Otherwise, thoroughly clean the tent as recommended above, using a stiff brush on the seams. Then use a precleaner or alcohol.

Erect your tent and let it warm up in the sun. Don't apply sealer in direct sun, though, or you may catch a nasty buzz. Consider using a syringe for deep corners. Put the rainfly on upside down and seal every seam.

Seal tent seams that are in contact with the ground.

NETTING

Note: If you rely on no-see-um netting in the bush, you may also depend at times upon insect repellents. DEET, the active ingredient in many repellents, is extraordinarily hard on synthetics and fabric coatings. (If it melts nylon, how 'bout your skin?) Use caution storing and applying any repellent, and try not to handle the tent just after juicing up. Consider an herb-based "alternative" repellent or one with a reduced concentration of DEET.

Delicate mosquito-netting doors and panels should be treated with respect—especially if you live in blackfly country. Netting is the most likely part of your wigwam to rip; unfortunately, it is located in vulnerable, high-traffic spots like doors. Practice zipper mindfulnes's when opening or venting your tent. Zippers, along with the claws of inquisitive animals, are archenemies of mesh. Never store food in your tent, and teach Rover not to scratch at the door.

Patching Mosquito Netting

For smaller than dime-sized claw marks and snags, back the net with masking tape, then patch with Freesole or Seam Grip urethane adhesive (see pages 7–10). Allow full cure time (up to 48 hours) before carefully removing tape and storing tent.

Larger tears are easily patched by hand- or machine-sewing. Since netting doesn't fray, there's no need to turn ends under. Simply double-needle stitch the patch with regular cotton-poly thread (nylon thread will tear netting), then carefully cut away damaged netting.

FABRIC TEARS

Tiny rips in a nonstress location are easily repaired: Apply adhesive-backed nylon repair tape to the uncoated side, with urethane adhesive on the opposite side. If the tear is too large to be effectively repaired with standard 3-inch tape, figure it's a sewing job.

Repair tape is also very useful in reinforcing abraded areas, as on a well-used tent floor or pole sleeve. Our local outdoor store puts its Moss demo tents through considerable torture during the course of a summer. Entire busloads of Vibram-clad, ice-cream-cone-eating tourists tromp through these shelters. Thanks to big sheets of nylon adhesive from a local sailmaker (used for numbers and graphics on big sails), the store can eke several seasons out of a tent before the floor disintegrates.

Pole sleeves can tear when a burred or cracked pole is pushed through the fabric channel. Avoid this type of tear by inspecting your poles for snags; always assemble the sections and thread poles gently and deliberately. In the field, use duct tape or nylon tape to patch a torn sleeve. Permanent repair means replacing the entire sleeve, which is best left to the manufacturer.

A tent may tear of its own volition at any point stronger than the fabric or where stress is concentrated: a bartacked seam, webbing loop, or around a grommet. This is especially true of older, sun-weakened shelters. When this happens, tape doesn't cut it—reinforcement is in order.

Structural Reinforcement Patch

Remove stitching at seams and bartacks. If seams are coated with sealer, use embroidery or nail scissors to clip each stitch, then pull threads through the uncoated side. Don't be tempted to take out stitches with an X-Acto knife—one slip and you'll be looking at yet another repair. To work-in new fabric, you'll need to open an area at least three-times larger than the actual damage.

- Pay attention to the construction order as you unfurl seams, joints, webbing, etc., so you'll remember how it all goes back together. Make a sketch if necessary.
- Skim the uncoated side of the area destined for repair with a warm iron to flatten out the fabric—never hold the iron in one place long

This webbing loop proved stronger than the tent fabric; a full-strength repair meant reinforcing the fabric panel before reattaching the webbing—a time-consuming task of de- and reconstruction.

FLAKY COATING

Flakes and peeling are signs of fabric-coating delamination and usually occur as a result of mildew, chemicals (often DEET or stove fuel), UV damage, and general old age. If your tent is new and begins to flake spontaneously, take it up with the manufacturer. Flaking is a sign that the fabric has deteriorated beyond its ability to perform in all conditions.

It's possible to prolong the useful life of your tent with a liquid polymer coating. This process merely delays the inevitable, and since recoat treatments are usually applied to the opposite (noncoated) side, you're still faced with the original coating's dandruff problem.

Recoating solutions can be found at most outfitters and mail-order outlets.

You might also try applying a water-repellent finish spray (not silicone), to the exterior fabric walls of the rainfly. One promising new treatment from Nikwax is designed specifically for nonbreathable tents, raingear, packs, etc. It's called Tent and Gear Proof, a spray-on water-based treatment that contains no petroleum, no CFCs (chlorofluorocarbons), and no chlorinated solvents. We've also enjoyed good results with plain old Thompson's Water Seal applied with a handheld sprayer—certainly the most economical option.

enough for the fabric to get hot, or the coating will delaminate.

- Cut a patch, carefully copying the shape and weave of the original fabric. Remember, patch edges must fold over at least ¼ inch. Turn edges under and iron as above.
- Before positioning the patch on the inside, use nylon repair tape to hold the original fabric together. This is the cosmetic part.
- Position the patch, coated side up. Use a little masking tape or a dot of Superglue to secure—*not* pins.
- Sew or splice in the patch following the original stitching and construction order.
- Seal the outside stitch holes, as well as the torn area, with urethane sealer.

Sewn Patches

Patching your tent is a simple but tactical operation. If the reinforcement is not oriented properly, it will do little to alleviate stress on the weakened area. When cutting a patch, try to mirror the warp/weft orientation of the damaged panel, or try a circular patch, which can even out the load on the fabric (see pages 7–10).

Applying Liquid Polymer Coating

Make sure the tent is clean. Rinse several times to remove any residue and dry completely. As with cleaning and sealing, coating is easily applied to an erect tent. Always apply new coating to the uncoated side of fabric—otherwise the new coating will bond to the old, flaky stuff and simply fall away. Make sure to spread any pooled areas of coating, which will harden, blister, and peel away later.

Since a tent floor is the most likely place to peel, and since you're going to the trouble of recoating, do two layers. Apply the second coat while the first is still tacky. Let the coating dry completely according to the manufacturer's instructions.

Waxing Cotton Wall Tents

See pages 25–26 for the recommended procedure.

Poles

Most difficulties with tent poles start on the ground—when you step on them. Treat poles as precision instruments and they'll last longer.

Shock-loaded, aluminum alloy poles are standard issue with most of today's tents. Pole sections are usually straight when new; they take a bend over time as they are forced into the form of your tent. This is generally nothing to worry about, but a kink at or near a tubing joint should be protected with a repair splint until you can have the section replaced. A recent design trend has introduced prebent pole sections for cases where tight-radius curves would prove too taxing for straight tubing. Prebends really cut down on pole failures.

The skeleton of your tent, like your own bones, suffers from stress concentrated at the joints—the most common point of injury. Always make sure you've completely fitted each section snugly together, or a crack will form at the joint, followed

soon by a break—almost always in a howling rainstorm at midnight. If you spot a crack developing, use the repair splint in your kit to prevent a more serious fracture.

Although it's fun to throw tent poles in the air and let them snap together like a spontaneously generated arachnid, this is really hard on the section ends, inflicting burrs and cracks. Instead, join the middle sections first to allow maximum elasticity of the shock cord, then gently fit sections together. This way you can inspect poles at the same time. Watch for too-tight joints, sand or salt inside the poles, worn shock cord, or cracks along

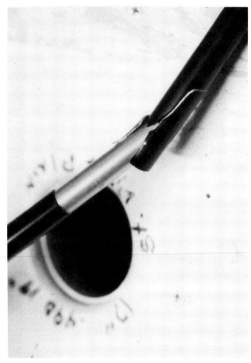

Tent poles usually break at section joints. Once cracked or sheared, tent pole sleeves are next to suffer.

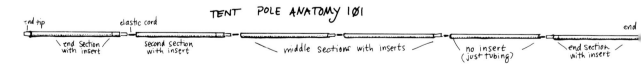

TENT POLE ANATOMY 101

end tip — elastic cord — end

end Section with insert — second section with insert — middle sections with inserts — no insert (just tubing) — end Section with insert

the length of a section (usually at the end).

When breaking down your tent, push poles out of their channels. Pulling invites them to separate and snag fabric, often causing foul language.

Rickety Joints

If poles feel gritty as you fit them together, clean with a dip in the pond or a blast from a garden hose, then dry thoroughly. If there's a lot of oxidation (black film that rubs off on your hands), wipe clean with a noncorrosive solvent like kerosene. Resist the urge to lubricate—that just attracts more dirt.

Really tight joints are often the source of a break and are bound to give you grief in cold weather when your fingers are fumbling. Check the connections for roundness. You may be able to squeeze squashed pole ends back into shape with Vise-Grips or pliers, but go easy!

Burrs can be toned down in the field with a stone or scrap of fine sandpaper, even the file on your multitool. Burred poles rip tent fabric and skin indiscriminately and are often harbingers of a fracture.

The male end of a pole joint may occasionally loosen and slip partway onto its pole section. You can usually pull a slipped ferrule back out by hand—compare it with another section to see how much to expose. This is a manufacturing defect and should be replaced. Superglue from your kit will work to secure the ferrule temporarily. Dave adds a hard-won tip here: don't try to secure slipped joints with a squeeze from your pliers—you'll just split the delicate tubing and make a worse mess.

Loose End Plugs

End plugs holding the shock cord can loosen, pull out, and cause cracks. This type of plug can be replaced with the solid "new style" plug, which offers a tighter fit. With this type, cord is knotted, then stopped by the end ferrule, fitted with a Shok-

lock rather than the plug itself. A loose solid plug can be (carefully) ticked with a center punch to fit snugly into the pole. The notched variety is valuable for cinching-up tired cording in the field and is worth carrying in your stake bag. Ask the manufacturer for a few spares.

Some "self-locking" end plugs incorporate a rubber gasket, which makes the pole end less likely to slip out of the tent grommet during assembly, making setup much easier for a solo camper. These make a neat update to older, non-locking-tip pole sets. Look for replacement locking tips at better outdoor shops or repair centers.

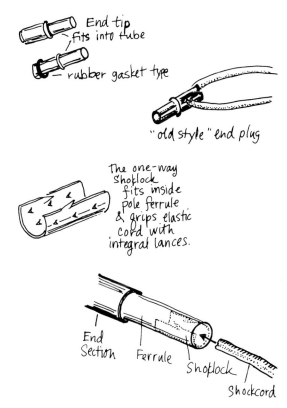

End tip fits into tube

rubber gasket type

"old style" end plug

The one-way Shoklock fits inside pole ferrule & grips elastic cord with integral lances.

End Section   Ferrule   Shoklock

Shockcord

Stretched-Out or Broken Shock Cord

Severed cord is usually caused by a splintered pole section. Smooth or tape any rough spots to protect the cord from abrasion. The rubber core of elastic shock cord does fatigue and lose its stretch, especially in very cold weather. Join all but one end section, pull the cord snug, and tie off. Remove the plug from the end section—if it's the notched kind, you're in luck. Fit the last section, cinch up the cord (allowing about 2 inches extra per section), and cut off the excess. If you have a solid plug, follow instructions for shock-cord replacement.

A stretched-out cord makes for the insanely tedious task of feeding a disjointed snake of pole sections through sleeves. If you're suffering this malady, take extra caution to be sure the joints are all fully engaged, or you may splinter some pole segments.

Most manufacturers will happily restring your tent poles for little or no charge using specially designed and formulated elastic. If you're in a time crunch or on a long trip, you may wish to rethread your own. Pull the end plug with pliers— if it's tight, tap the section end gently with a hammer to loosen. Cut the cord on the ferrule end of the section, then use a narrow rod or coat hanger to push the old cord out the open end. Follow the sequence shown to rethread the shock cord.

Splinting a cracked tent pole.

splints include hose clamps, half-moon stakes, aluminum flashing (see pages 145–47), or the Ramer ski pole patch. On long trips you may want to bring two splints. Once home, send the broken part to the manufacturer—many offer unconditional guarantees on poles.

If your tent poles never made it back from Bolivia, or you require the services of a tent pole expert, try TA Enterprises in Vancouver, British Columbia (see appendix F, Directory of Repair Services, beginning on page 232).

STAKES

Whatever type of stake you prefer, be sure to carry several spares. Consider using beefy nylon I-beam stakes for securing tent corners and key guylines, especially in high winds. Use lighter-duty stakes for secondary points. Half-moon aluminum stakes are great because they double as emergency splints for repairing poles of any type.

The High-Stakes Stake Bag

Besides stakes, here's where to stash extra widgets and spare whatnots for complete tent field repair. This kit may win you big points with friends when their tent gets hammered in a storm.

Pole Splints

Pole fractures are easily splinted in the field since most tents come with an alloy repair sleeve in the stakes bag. You will need duct tape to hold the splint in place, however. Other potential pole

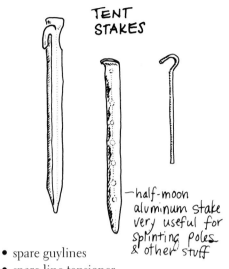

TENT STAKES

—half-moon aluminum stake very useful for splinting poles & other stuff

- spare guylines
- spare line tensioner
- roll of nylon repair tape
- pole splint
- extra zipper slider
- spare pole end plug—notched type

WHAT A GREAT GUY!

On a correctly pitched tent you can pluck a guy-line like a banjo string and bounce pebbles off the stretched and shapely rainfly. Guylines significantly enhance the weatherproofness and durability of your tent. Tent guy-out loops and grommets are often premounted on a rainfly by the manufacturer. If all guyline points are not prestrung, make a point of doing so. Coil up guys when storing and they'll be less likely to ensnare every available obstruction when you're setting up camp in the face of big weather.

loop-&-stick eases tension on grommets

tie off with simple hitch

stone tied to a tarp corner substitutes for a grommet

Sierra Designs GripClip adds unbreakable guy point

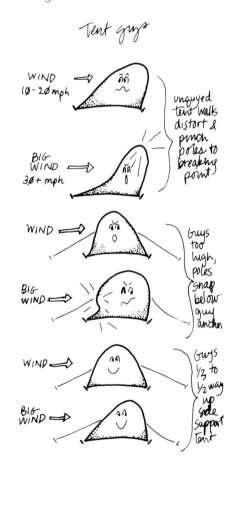

Tent guys

WIND 10-20 mph

BIG WIND 30+ mph

unguyed tent walls distort & pinch poles to breaking point

WIND

BIG WIND

Guys too high, poles snap below guy anchor

WIND

BIG WIND

Guys 1/3 to 1/2 way up side support tent

Aluminum or plastic line tensioners allow easy adjustment without fumbling with a knot. Buy a handful from any outfitter and slip a few spares in your stake bag.

line tensioner

If your guyline loop or grommet is damaged, you can easily create an alternative with a stone (see illustration, page 53). Another nifty option is the Grip Clip from Sierra Designs, a secure, temporary guyline fastener that can also be attached to a pole.

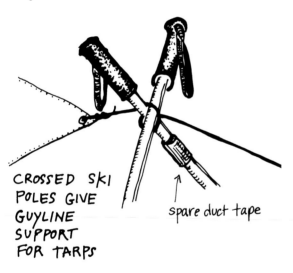

CROSSED SKI POLES GIVE GUYLINE SUPPORT FOR TARPS

spare duct tape

> The men who had been relieved groped hurriedly among the soaking sleeping bags and tried to steal some of the warmth created by the last occupants.
>
> Explorer Sir Ernest Shackleton, after the wreck of the *Endurance* in the Antarctic

Sleeping Bags

See also chapter 1, Essential Techniques, and chapter 2, Fabrics and Insulations

INSULATION

Unfortunately, sleeping bags do not provide warmth by themselves. Bag insulation simply slows the transfer of heat from your body to the air around it. This is the role of loft. The challenge of sleeping bag care is to sustain the insulation's ability to loft after countless compressions in a stuff sack. Regardless of its origin—fowl or crude—insulation should be treated delicately. As your final refuge from tempests and consciousness, your fleabag's filling is your outdoor kit's most crucial element—everything else supports it. Equally crucial is how you store the bag (see page 59).

Down Fill

Down plumules have a natural oil coating that keeps each fiber supple and resilient. Heat, chemicals, dry cleaning, and even body oils will strip this protective coating and cause loss of loft. Good preventive maintenance means keeping a down bag's lining and shell as clean as possible.

Down may shift to one side of a sleeping bag; often this is a design feature so that you can load the down to the top surface, depending on conditions. To redistribute down, lay the bag open on a flat surface, then pat, push, fluff, and cajole the fill where you want it to go.

Clumps—collected piles of down—result from compacting a wet bag or from incomplete drying after washing. If you've stuffed a wet bag in your pack, remove it as soon as possible. With your fingertips, work along the shell, baffle by baffle, and break up clumps by pulling them apart carefully. You should do this several times during the drying process.

Are special, wash-in down treatments worth the

bother? The jury is still out, but Nikwax offers water-based Down Proof, which coats fibers of down (and outer fabric) with a polymer/wax finish to repel moisture. While this may make sense for an older bag, consider that a treatment may make your bag shell less breathable too. Better-quality down is carefully processed to ensure a proper acid/oil balance anyway, so the best treatment you can give your bag is gentle care. The best case for a wash-in treatment is if you know your down bag has been dry-cleaned. In that case, the down would benefit from some protective coating.

Synthetic Fill

Believe it or not, man has yet to develop an insulation as resilient as down. Synthetic fills lose their ability to spring back after compression much sooner than down, so the requirements of down care go double for synthetics. Most people choose a synthetic-filled bag for use in potentially wet conditions. When the bag does get wet, handle it tenderly to avoid tearing the batts (do not wring). NEVER dry-clean a synthetic bag. Always keep synthetic bags away from intense heat—as in the trunk of your car—to which the fibers are most vulnerable. Use machine dryers only at the lowest heat (see pages 58–59).

Baffles and Shingles

Poor-quality bags have **sewn-through construction**, which parts the insulation so that air can blast through the stitch holes onto your huddled form. The only thing you can do to improve this chilling situation is seal the outer lines of stitching.

Most down bags employ a baffling system to regulate fill. Without baffles you'd have a cold heart and hot feet. Baffles are usually constructed of nylon mesh, which is strong and very light. These humble cells endure endless abuse as they are twisted and wrenched and yanked, and they deserve respect. Be mindful when removing your bag from its stuff sack. Inspect rows of stitching

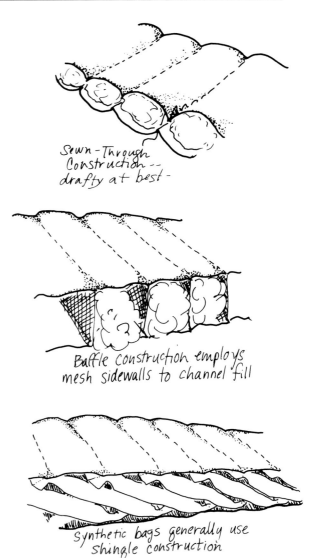

Sewn-Through Construction — drafty at best

Baffle construction employs mesh sidewalls to channel fill

Synthetic bags generally use shingle construction

both inside and out; even a few pulled stitches should be caught early. Baffle damage is most likely to result from careless handling of a soaked bag. Lift a bedraggled wet bag as if it were made of tissue paper; let excess water drool out gradually—do not wring. Hang-dry lengthwise on a line.

Synthetic batts are typically layered as **shingles**. Sheets of fibers are sewn directly to the shell and lining and are as vulnerable to twisting as down baffles.

The simplest thing we can say about the complicated subject of choosing a sleeping bag is, "They don't make 'em like they used to."

And for that, we say, "Great!" Modern sleeping bags are warmer, lighter, cozier, and more versatile than ever. It's just that they're, well, kind of confusing to figure out.

Finding the right bag involves a string of personal decisions—more than any other piece of gear, except maybe boots—based on your anticipated needs, budget, and personal metabolism.

- **Hating the ratings?** Don't despair, you're not alone. No single factor creates more confusion than manufacturers' temperature ratings. Ratings correlate reasonably well between different models in one maker's line but relate in only the most general way between different manufacturers. Fine-tuning the choice depends largely on your personal thermometer. If you're a cold sleeper, opt for a bag rated one class colder (for lower temperatures); hot snoozers can get away with one class warmer, saving some weight in the bargain.

For general three-season backpacking in temperate climes, a 20° bag is a solid all-around choice. Fair-weather campers or those in the southern regions can probably opt for a 40° sleeper. Fall or spring use in the mountains means you'll need a 10 to 20° bag; deep winter use means 0° or well below.

- **Down is lightest, lasts longest.** Mother Goose figured out how to sleep toasty eons ago. No synthetic fill is lighter, warmer for its weight, or lasts longer. We are committed down-bag fans; our matching down bags (wedding presents) are still going strong after more than 10 years and untold hundreds of sleep-outs. The downside of down is that it loses 50 percent of its insulating power when wet. If you're careful (and/or choose a waterproof-breathable shell fabric), this dread scenario is less likely than you'd think.

- **Synthetic, no longer pathetic.** You may remember old-style synthetic-fill bags from summer camp: dogs-n-ducks flannel lining and drafty rectangular shape, all rolled up like a giant cinnamon bun that dangled from your backpack. "Well," as one of Dave's climbing buddies likes to say, "not no more!"

The latest generation of miracle-fiber, better-living-through-petrochemicals bags have nar-

SHELL AND LINING

Among your sleeping bag's enemies are body and hair oils, salt, sunscreens, spilled tomato soup, and insect repellents. All these acidic substances work through the shell to decompose down and reduce insulative performance of any fill. Your bag will work longer if you keep both shell and liner clean. Don't get naked in your bag! Even in summer, bring a light cotton shirt for sleeping.

Try a cotton, polypro, or silk liner between you and your bag. One terrific version is the Cocoon, a shimmery silk sleeve that weighs just a few ounces and feels fabulous. During summer, it's a cool, clean alternative to a hot, sticky bag; come winter, the silk adds insulation.

Winter campers or those on long alpine expeditions may want to consider a VBL—vapor barrier liner—to keep nightly body perspiration out of the down fill. As you sleep, your body heat and respiration (if you're a burrower) condense inside the bag, gradually penetrating the liner, dampening the insulative capacity of the down, and adding weight to the whole shebang. Arctic travelers have seen their bags gain several pounds on a two-week trip from this phenomenon—a convincing case for VBL use.

Depending on quality, some down fills contain

rowed the gap considerably. Compared with down, a top-quality synthetic bag now only exacts a pound or three weight penalty, depending on the temperature rating. Compressibility is much more equivalent as well. And no down bag sleeps as cozy after two weeks in the drooling Alaskan bush as even the most lowly synfill sleeper.

- **Love yer mummy.** Forget the heavy, bulky rectangular bags of yore (the ones that always ended up as quilts on the camp couch); slim, trim mummy bags rule. Squirmy sleepers can't even complain about mummy bags any more: bagmakers now incorporate elastic knee panels, shaped foot areas, and wider shoulders.
- **Dodge the draft.** Make sure that the draft tube backing the main zipper is attached to the top of the bag, and not the bottom. This way, gravity helps the draft tube do its job.
- **Hoods in the woods.** The snug, wraparound hood on a good mummy bag keeps you cozier than a fat cat draped around your neck. The neck collar also keeps you from "submarining" down into the bag, where your breath condenses and soaks the lining.
- **Girl bags.** (Annie, being female and all, speaks with certain authority here.) With more babes in the backcountry than ever, manufacturers are eager to cash in on this "new" product niche. Research shows that women lose heat at the extremities 15 to 20 percent faster than dudes; thus, women's sleeping bags generally feature more fill, specifically around the footbox and torso. Cutwise, traditional mummies have proved too big at the shoulders, too tight at the hips. Although bags have been available in varying lengths for years, the average 5-foot, 4-inch woman ends up heating a fair amount of empty space in a standard-issue sleeping bag. Should you buy it? Annie's a winter camper and likes stashing clothes and boots in the bottom of her "male" fleabag.
- **Mating.** A coupla thoughts: Two bags zipped together makes for a thoroughly toasty nest. If you're planning for two, be sure you buy a right- or left-side zipper, depending. As far as the act goes, it's your call; just remember that a bag lasts longer with fewer launderings.

a certain volume of feathers. Poorer-quality fill can contain up to 18 percent feathers, the quills of which can poke maddeningly through shell fabric. Your best and most satisfying bet is to pull the offenders out (they offer no insulation) and make sure the hole heals itself. If a small puncture hole remains, add a drop of urethane adhesive or a nylon adhesive patch.

ZIPPERS

The most common sleeping bag zipper is a No. 7 coil, which works well around bends and is unlikely to damage fabric caught under the slider.

Usually there is an insulated draft tube to block airflow along the zipper's length. Make sure that this does not get stuck in the coils. (See also pages 10–15.)

If you've ruled out all possibility of zipper repair and have decided replacement is in order, you can send your sleeping bag to the manufacturer or repair center for painless professional service or you can replace it yourself. Before attacking the stitching, carefully determine if the zipper has been sewn into the seam—otherwise you'll have an instant roomful (or lung full) of down. If the zip is sewn into the seam, run a line of stitching behind the zipper to seal the down cells before removing the zipper stitching. Another tip: fill a pump spray bottle with water and lightly mist the surface where you're opening baffles. The dampened down will stick to itself rather than to everything else in the room.

CLEANING

Attending to stains soon after they occur is an easy way to keep your bag clean and postpone the need for a complete washing. Use a vinegar–liquid soap or lemon-borax solution to scrub away any oil or food stains (see appendix B, Low-Tox Cleaning Solutions, beginning on page 216, for cleaning recipes). For more tenacious tar or tree sap, you can employ a little kerosene—be sure to follow the illustrated procedure, because the solvent may also harm insulative fibers. After scrubbing the spot, you might consider treating that area with a durable water-repellent spray.

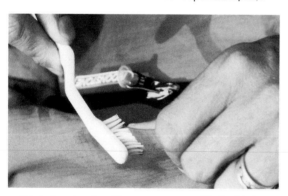

Spot-clean insulated bags or garments: lift the fabric away from the insulation before scrubbing.

Carefully lift the stained area of the shell away from the insulation (if it's a down bag, shift down away from the section you're treating). Fold in half through the stained area; gripping the fold, spritz cleaner or solvent on the spot and scrub with a soft brush. The cleaner will soak through to the other side of the fabric without penetrating the filling. Clean the opposite side of the fold, then rinse with water.

No matter how you clean your sleeping bag, you'll break down some of the insulation. However, laundering restores loft; dry cleaning does not. Even if your bag says to dry clean, don't. Often a "Dry Clean Only" label is placed there as a deterrent—a warning to treat the product gently—to prevent the bag from being washed carelessly at home. Dry-cleaning solvents can destroy insulation (solvents strip natural oil from down and can distort synthetic fills). Beyond that, inhaling residual solvents has been known to cause allergic reactions, which cuts into the fun of your wilderness encounter.

No dry cleaning!

Air-Drying

Let your sleeping bag get fresh air and sunshine during trips to make sure it's dry before stuffing. (This is the only time you should expose your bag to UV radiation.) On a sunny day you can dry your just-laundered bag outdoors just as easily as you can in a machine, or use a combination of both methods. When hanging the bag from a clothesline, support the bag along its length rather than hang it from one end.

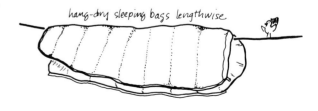

MACHINE-WASHING

Once fabric starts to take a sheen, or if your bag is starting to lose loft, it is time for a wash. If you have a big investment in a high-quality, high-loft down sleeping bag, you might consider sending your bag for a professional groom by its manufacturer or a repair service center (see appendix F, Directory of Repair Services, beginning on page 232). Otherwise you can wash your synthetic or down sleeping bag by hand (best) or use a commercial, front-loading washing machine only (see page 35).

If you use a machine,

- Use a gentle, nondetergent soap. Feathered Friends, manufacturer of premium down products, recommends using a soap especially formulated for cleaning and restoring down.
- Apply soap directly to soiled areas.
- Soak 15 to 60 minutes (important).
- Wash on the gentle cycle using cold water.
- Wash a second time using no soap.
- Lift the wet bag carefully to protect baffles.
- Dry as recommended below.

Machine-Drying

"Under ideal conditions," says Bob Upton of Rainy Pass Repair, "drying a sleeping bag takes 1 hour, 40 minutes." So line up your quarters and plan to carefully monitor the drying process—as often as every 15 minutes. The bigger the dryer, the better. Drop directly affects drying time: if the dryer is too full, there's less drop, thus less drying. Inside an overpacked dryer the air can reach temperatures higher than the assigned setting (hot enough to melt insulation or zippers). If the fabric is hot to the touch, remove the bag from the dryer to air.

If there's plenty of room, add a few dry towels to the dryer to absorb moisture from the bag.

Remove wet towels at the first check and replace with dry ones. Putting a tennis shoe or ball in the dryer to "fluff up the loft" will do more harm to the insulation than good.

Periodically remove the entire bag and check for clumping insulation. Down clumps should be gently worked apart so they'll dry evenly. Synthetic batts should not be broken apart; try to shift them without too much tension at stitch lines.

STORAGE: SAFE SACKS
Compressing

Never store any sleeping bag in its nylon stuff sack—use that for short-term, on-the-road storage only. When storing under compression (in a small stuff sack or pack), stuffing is better than rolling.

Step on a bottom corner of the stuff sack while you grasp the mouth in one hand. With your free hand begin stuffing the bag, starting with the bulky foot section. Press down often to compress the insulation as you stuff your way, accordionlike, to the hood section.

Long-Term Storage

A bag should rest fully lofted. If you have closet space, suspend the bag from its end loop or drape it over a hanger. The most popular method recommended by manufacturers is to store a bag in a large, breathable cotton storage sack, which allows the bag to breathe and loft.

Always store bags in a cool, dark, dry place, away from likely sources of mildew. Don't expose your sleeping bag to heat of any sort—even from sunlight—unless you're drying it.

Sleeping Pads

Sleeping pads provide more than comfort to your weary bones. A pad helps protect your sleeping bag insulation from being compacted excessively under your weight, so loft is maximized. A pad also provides insulation against the cold ground. Both functions help you sleep warmer.

There are basically two types of sleeping pads: closed-cell foam pads and self-inflating pads.

CLOSED-CELL FOAM PADS

Evazote, Ensolite, and other polyurethane foam pads are superlight, bulky, and so inexpensive they're often considered "disposable," even though they last virtually forever. Indeed, old foam pads never die—they can become cup or bottle insulators, kneepads, backrests, or paddle floats or perform zillions of other custom functions. Closed-cell foam pads are ideal for outfitting canoes and kayaks and should never be discarded lightly.

The big advantage of durable, closed-cell construction is that it doesn't absorb water like open-cell foams (a.k.a. sponges). However, the foam does compress over time and loses its insulative capacity. Store your closed-cell pad flat, if possible, or loosely rolled. Storing bound by tight straps or bands will compress and deform the pad before its time.

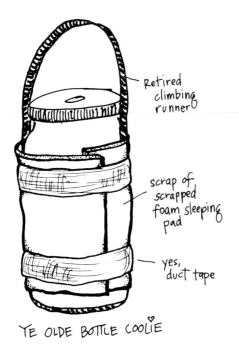

Retired climbing runner

scrap of scrapped foam sleeping pad

yes, duct tape

YE OLDE BOTTLE COOLIE

OPEN-CELL, SELF-INFLATING MATTRESS

Open-cell foam works just like any other insulation, offering the most protection when expanded to its maximum capacity. Although naturally puffier than its closed-cell counterpart, open-cell foam requires inflation with air to sustain its loft under weight, and it must be protected from water. Therefore, open-cell foam is bonded to an air- and watertight envelope of urethane-coated nylon fabric with heat-welded seams and is inflated by means of a valve.

Mattress foam has a memory. If you store your mattress tightly rolled, the foam will forget everything it ever knew about loft and hold the compressed, flattened shape. Always store your sleeping mat unrolled with the valve open to facilitate maximum loft. Compacting the pad temporarily for trips does not damage the foam.

Preventive Tips from the Pros

While there are now several brands available, Cascade Designs's original Therm-a-Rest mattress irrevocably altered perceptions of backcountry comfort and remains today the most popular of all self-inflating mattresses. Innovative from the word go, Cascade Designs has been an industry leader in the quest for greener production standards, aggressively promoting warranty and repair policies and constantly developing new repair techniques—the patching process described here is their very latest recommendation.

Diana Eken, Therm-a-Rest repair specialist, sees as many as 7,000 mattresses a year in her lab; about half are cheerfully replaced under warranty even though many are battered, grimy veterans suffering from years of neglect. Diana laughingly assesses each mattress and efficiently effects hundreds of repairs per week. She has developed the patching process to a fine art and offers these commandments.

- Always store your mattress clean, dry, and unrolled with the valve open.
- Dry out your mattress between trips to prevent mildew.
- Keep mattress away from DEET, sun, and any heat source.
- Keep mattress away from pets.
- Use flexible urethane adhesives (e.g., Seam Grip or Urebond) for repair.

Coated Fabric

Mattress fabric coating bears the dual tasks of holding air inside the mattress while keeping moisture and debris out. When your self-inflating mattress springs a leak, it's probably the fabric that's punctured, torn, abraded, or otherwise damaged. Keep the mattress clean and free from sand, dirt, and sharp objects such as crampons, sticks, and sundry spiny things. Stray campfire sparks are common causes of leaks large and small. Direct heat from a stove can cause blistering and delamination of the fabric.

The seams of a self-inflating pad are radio-frequency-welded, bonding the urethane-coated fabric panels together without actually melting the material. Damage to or near the seams usually spells factory repair.

As with any synthetic, the surface fabric (as well as the foam underneath) is especially vulnerable to DEET, solvents, oils, and even sunscreens, which can melt, damage, and delaminate the coating. Never use any petroleum-based solvent to remove spots from your mattress. A quick scrub with soap and water or a citrus or vinegar cleaning solution is your best bet. Close the valve when washing.

The slippery, coated fabric of a sleeping pad often causes dreaded *Gaposis*—your equally slippery nylon sleeping bag has no purchase on the surface of the pad, and you wake up shivering on the tent floor. This can be addressed with Cascade Designs's Slip Fix, a urethane spray that gives a little textural resistance to the fabric. You might also try applying zigzag beads of urethane seam sealer on the mattress surface.

Valve

Open-cell mattresses "self-inflate" because an opened valve allows passage of air into the mattress as the springy foam regains its loft. Once the valve is closed, air is trapped within foam cells to provide firm support and displacement when weight is applied to the mattress.

Valves are seated in a stiff, urethane-reinforced corner of the mattress using a urethane adhesive. On Therm-a-Rests, old-style metal valves occasionally bind and malfunction due to grit. These should be replaced with the newer nylon valve—available anyplace that carries the mattress. A surprisingly common problem is that puppies and other creatures will chew the valve and puncture the airtight mattress coating.

Valve Replacement

Remove the old or damaged valve with pliers. Pull straight out—don't rock or twist, or you may enlarge the molded valve seat. Apply a thin bead of urethane adhesive to the barbed end of the new valve, taking care not to let glue enter any part of the valve. Press or screw the valve into the molded hole, then wipe away excess adhesive.

Pull the faulty valve straight out from the seat with pliers.

Inflation: Breathing Lessons

The best way to inflate your mattress is to exercise your patience: unfurl it, open the valve, and let it naturally loft while you go about setting up camp. Close the valve just before lying down. This is what "self-inflating" means. In very cold temperatures the inflation process will be slower. Some people carry the pad against their body (inside a pack) to keep it warm for quick inflation.

A new mattress has been completely compressed for packaging purposes and requires an initial breath inflation to restore its loft. Blowing air into your mattress will provide firm support and increase its loft, especially in cold weather. However, if you do a lot of winter camping, breath inflation is not such a hot idea — moisture from your own hot air can accumulate, condense, and freeze inside the mattress. Any residual moisture in warmer temperatures can cause mildew and hasten the demise of your sleeping pad.

Don't inflate your mattress with a high-pressure pump; this risks maxing out the seams. Likewise, don't leave an inflated mattress sitting in the hot confines of your car on a sunny day, or you may be taken for a terrorist.

Eew, Mildew

Mildew is caused by storing the pad in a damp, warm place or with the valve closed or by storing a dirty pad. Moisture and dirt invite mildew to grow and deteriorate the fabric's airtight urethane coating from either inside or outside. Avoid mildew by keeping your mattress clean, and always store it dry with the valve open. If your mattress is wet, try squelching mildew by leaving it in the sun for several days with the valve open before storing. Extreme cases of mildew require drastic measures (see sidebar, page 26).

Field Repair

Annie's first Therm-a-Rest was slashed by an errant ice axe. After a cold night, she gave it up for lost and sold it to a friend for a dollar. The second was skewered on our honeymoon by a porcupine-fish spine, dampening nuptial comfort. Both incidents could have been avoided with mindfulness. Punctures are easily field-repaired; lacerations can be surgically corrected at the factory.

Duct tape works fine temporarily but tends to leak slowly. The tape also leaves a nasty sticky residue that attracts dirt and renders a permanent repair almost impossible. If you enjoy your self-inflating pad, carry a patch of nylon repair tape — better yet, bring a repair kit containing a urethane-coated fabric patch and urethane adhesive, like Shoo Goo or Freesole. A regular bicycle tube patch kit sometimes works; Cascade Designs offers a compact repair kit.

I Think It's Leaking . . . But I'm Not Sure

Roll up the mattress according to the deflation technique described above. Close the valve and leave the mat overnight. If your pad self-inflates, you have a leak.

Locate the Leak

Finding a slow leak in the field is difficult. If an inflated pad doesn't hiss, carefully roll it to increase pressure; listen with your face close to the pad to catch the sound of any emissions.

If that doesn't work, immerse the inflated pad (valve closed) in a bathtub or quiet pool and watch for a telltale stream of bubbles to lead you to the leak. If you know generally where the leak is, you can pinpoint it by misting that area of the inflated pad and watching for bubbles. The valve will typically emit a few bubbles, but if it's not a continuous flow, the valve is fine. Once you find the leak, mark it clearly. Don't forget to check for more than one hole!

If you know the pad has a leak but are completely stymied as to its whereabouts, don't feel inept. Mere humans cannot breath-inflate a self-inflating mattress to more than 1 psi (pound per square inch). At the factory service center a special, precise machine will pump exactly 3.5 psi—the maximum pressure—into the offending mattress.

A leak within an inch of the edge of your pad is pretty difficult to patch effectively and should be sent for factory repair. If that's not convenient, goop a bunch of urethane adhesive (Freesole) to create a patch.

Patching in the Field or at Home

- Clean off any tape residue, sunscreen, or DEET with soap and water, then rinse thoroughly. Allow to dry. For best patch adhesion, clean with alcohol to remove any lingering soap or oils.
- Use the deflation technique to squeeze as much air out of the mattress as possible. Close the valve.

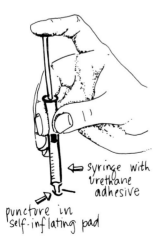

⟵ syringe with urethane adhesive

puncture in self-inflating pad

- A small puncture can be healed by working a small amount of urethane adhesive into the hole. Add a drop of glue to the top of the hole too. Allow the adhesive to cure completely before inflating.
- Large punctures and tears require a patch. Cut a patch at least ½ inch larger than the hole, making sure to round the edges. Position the patch on the deflated pad, then trace around it. Follow the field triage patching instructions (page 64).
- If your patch is not a self-adhesive, coated material, you must also apply a thin coat of adhesive directly to the patch. Do this before coating the damaged mattress so that the patch surface will be tacky but not wet when you apply it.

AIR MATTRESSES

Punctured air mattresses can be treated as any inflatable. Most air mattresses are made of vinyl or plastic, so any glue you use should be formulated accordingly. Vynabond and PVC (polyvinyl chloride) cement are popular options.

Pin-Sized Punctures

To fix a small puncture wound in your air mattress,

- Locate and mark the puncture as you would for a self-inflatable.
- Deflate the mattress.
- Prep the area with a swab of alcohol.
- Apply repair glue to the tip of a toothpick and insert into the puncture.
- Repeat.
- Apply a small bead of glue to the top of the puncture.
- Allow to cure completely (according to glue specifications).

Patches

Air mattress tears or punctures can be repaired by following the triage patching instructions, or try a bicycle tube patch kit.

FIELD TRIAGE PATCH

1. Thoroughly soak the puncture area with clean water. Rub water into the fabric fibers briskly until the area turns dark. Wipe off excess drops.
2. Boil a liter or so of water in a flat-bottomed metal pan.
3. While you wait for the water to boil, generously inject Seam Grip directly into the puncture.
4. Use the applicator nozzle to work Seam Grip thoroughly into the wet fibers and up to ½ inch (3 mm) away from the center of the puncture. Keep the coating even and about 1/16 inch (1.5 mm) thick.
5. Squeeze out an additional ¼ inch (6 mm) of Seam Grip onto the puncture to purge the nozzle of contaminated adhesive. Don't work it into the fabric—let it bead up on the fabric's surface.

6. When the water boils, cut out the patch, remove the backing paper (if any), and place the patch on top of the puncture.
7. Set the pan on the patch.
8. Lift the pan from the patch. Check to make sure no Seam Grip has exuded from underneath the patch. Wipe off any excess.
9. Replace the pan on the mattress and allow it to stand undisturbed for an hour. The mattress will now be ready to use.
10. To check your repair, pressurize the mattress by folding it with the valve closed. The patch should not show bubbling leaks when wetted. If leaks occur, remove and discard the patch, then repeat the repair procedure allowing extra cure time.

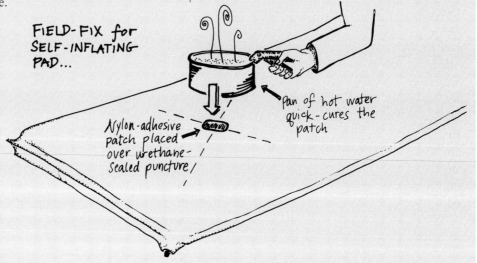

FIELD-FIX for SELF-INFLATING PAD...

Nylon-adhesive patch placed over urethane-sealed puncture

Pan of hot water quick-cures the patch

CHAPTER 5

Packs

Ach du lieber!
... und how long
haf you carried
all dis schtuff?

PACKING ANGST

I love to go a-wandering
Along the happy track
And as I go, I love to sing
My knapsack on my back

"The Happy
Wanderer"

A Cautionary Tale, or, Quasimodo's Revenge

Dave's worst experience with a pack (and as a career backpack tester, he's had some doozies) came on an abortive climbing trip with a gang of college chums to Mount Louis in the Canadian Rockies. The kind of trip you have nightmares about: horrid weather, heinous bugs, endless bushwhacking on the wrong side of a river. Their chosen route turned out to be a frightful pile of limestone rubble scantily bound together with moss. Fortunately it rained for three days, so no one was tempted to do anything silly. The lads finally conceded defeat and started hiking out.

Barreling down the mountain, fueled by visions of overdue burgers and beers, Dave suddenly felt the entire shoulder harness come adrift. A key buckle had popped, no way to fix it, and the only way he could carry the monster was bent over like Quasimodo. Seven miles of staggering and snarling followed.

What really hurt was that the pack had had the same failure factory-"repaired" just before this very trip. Once home, he attacked it with a Speedy Stitcher, and that fix was still holding strong when he yard-saled the pack (along with real bell-bottoms and his 1967 bus) ten years later.

The Five-Point Pack Check

The moral of our story: before you head out, take time to inspect your pack. Check out the zippers, straps, fasteners, fabric, and seams. Spend a few minutes peering over your pack to get psyched for the upcoming trip, and maybe find (and fix) a cracked buckle that could well have ruined it.

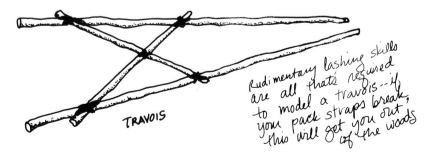

TRAVOIS

Rudimentary lashing skills are all that's required to model a travois—if your pack straps break, this will get you out of the woods

1. ZIPPERS

Modern pack zippers tend to be so huge that you can't possibly break them, right? Well, most of the time. Usually zipper problems are slider-related (see pages 12–14); you should always carry a spare slider if you use a panel-loading, zipper-dependent pack. This is less of an issue with top-loaders.

If, after replacing the slider, you determine that the zipper needs replacement, send the pack away! The tedious, technical task of replacing a pack zipper requires heavy-duty machinery and experience to match. If you insist on replacing the zipper yourself, consult Sumner's *Sew and Repair Your Own Outdoor Gear*, and prepare for an adventure in stitchery.

Any snagging fabric threads? Clip back and heat-seal with a lighter or soldering iron as described later in this section. Use a garden hose with a powerjet attachment to clean out any grit, or try a stiff brushing in the tub or sink. Use a soft brush, like a toothbrush, on the coated side of the packcloth. We don't recommend using soap on the coated side, either.

2. STRAPS

Straps rarely break, but they often pull out from their seams. Watch for any cuts or abrasions that may cause a failure. If an important strap does break, try to cannibalize another from your pack (a compression strap, for instance) and splice it in by stitching or with ladderlock fasteners from your repair kit.

Reattaching a Blown-Out Pack Strap

Use the sewing awl in your repair kit. Start from the outside to determine the correct placement. Pin the strap to secure the proper angle—if in doubt, look where the same strap attaches on the other side of the pack. Carefully turn the bag inside out to expose the seam, clip away the protective seam binding tape, then close with several lines of stitching. If there's enough length, anchor

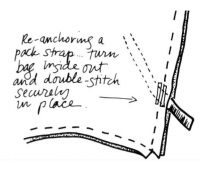

Re-anchoring a pack strap... turn bag inside out and double-stitch securely in place.

the pack strap tail to the body of the pack for added security.

3. FASTENERS AND HARDWARE

With the myraid straps and polycarbonate flim-flam on packs, Murphy's Law insists that failures be fairly common. Especially vulnerable is the female side of a 2-inch hipbelt buckle. UV, cold, and/or advancing age makes plastic parts brittle, so if they get stepped on or tossed onto a rocky surface, *hasta la vista*, baby. You may be able to keep the buckle functioning with a wrap of duct tape to hold the split together. For that matter, consider protecting the hollow half with a duct-tape jacket before it breaks. Always pack matching spares for crucial parts.

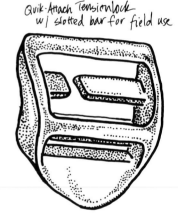

Quik-Attach Tensionlock w/ slotted bar for field use

A terrific innovation is the Quik-Attach Tensionlock, with a slotted bar that allows you to replace any tensioning fastener without having to unsew the webbing loop it's attached to. No field repair kit should be without one.

4. FABRIC AND COATING

Look for signs of abrasion, punctures, fading, stains, or mildew.

Abrasion usually occurs along the bottom of the pack, especially on climbing rucksacks that

Eke a few more miles outa ye olde rucksack...

...duct tape the bejeepers outa this area

get hauled a lot. If there's wear in a specific location, you can add a patch of nylon tape on the inside and a swatch of PVC-coated stuff on the outside to create a protective, slippery surface. We've seen pack bases completely mummified with duct tape, the ultimate waterproof, coated surface. You may reserve such treatment for your more tattered models.

Punctures are typically the result of ice tools, slices from ski edges, center-punching a sharp branch, or an overstuffed pack's getting dragged or shipped by air. Packcloth likes to unravel around tears, so catch holes while they're small and easy to patch with urethane adhesive. Neglected holes soon need larger fabric patches (see pages 7–10).

Fading is usually due to excessive UV exposure, though heat doesn't help packs over the long haul. Heavily faded areas mean the fabric is

PACK FITTING TIPS

Sizing a pack is sort of like buying expensive shoes. Finding the right fit often means you have to work closely with a salesperson; if they can't talk turkey on pack fitting, you'd best keep shopping.

- **Torso length.** The most critical pack measurement, the correct torso length ensures that the relationship between the hip belt and the shoulder straps is right for your body. If the pack is too long or too short, no amount of fiddling can fix it. Annie's pet peeve: a too-long pack that towers overhead and restricts headroom, enforcing a subservient hiking style.
- **Waistbelt.** This term is actually something of a misnomer since this key feature needs to cradle your hips, not encircle your waist. Better packs offer interchangeable sizes here; the goal is to have the belt wrap snugly around your hips with no gaps or wrinkles. Allow for extra clothing layers.
- **Shoulder straps.** Sizing rules here too. Look for interchangeable parts, smoothly contoured foam padding, and an adjustable sternum strap.

For a proper fit, the padded part of the strap should end a few inches below the armpit; if the strap is too short, it'll pinch, and longer straps chafe like the devil. Women can now find shoulder straps contoured to fit around ample breasts instead of squashing them.

- **Load-lifters.** These straps adjust the tension on top of the shoulder straps and are perhaps the least understood and most misused part of any pack. Adjust the shoulder straps first, then tug on the load-lifters to snug an unruly load against your back. Loosen them a bit for more upper-body freedom of movement. Use your load-lifters to add or subtract headroom.

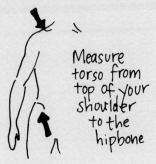

Measure torso from top of your shoulder to the hipbone

fatigued, and you should be prepared to patch it at any time—resign yourself to replacing the whole thing before long. Consider spraying the fabric with 303 Protectant.

Stains are part of the customized patina any well-used pack develops. However, certain types of gunk can prematurely age the packcloth or damage the coating. Pack your stove fuel carefully, because gas and kero are pack-eaters. Double-check seals on the fuel bottle and store it in a sturdy (and sacrificial) stuff sack. Any sticky stuff on the outside of the pack (like klister wax from skis) should be removed as soon as possible, or it will attract dirt and, ultimately, mildew.

Mildew destroys fabric and its coating. Always allow your pack to dry thoroughly, and brush off dirt and grime before storing. A lot of pack damage starts from the inside when food or fuel spills are left unattended and cause deterioration of the coating. Food spills also attract nibbling creatures. Turn your pack inside out and clean it every now and then.

5. SEAMS AND STITCHING

Individual stitches stretch only so many times before they fatigue and break, especially if you typically stuff your pack near to bursting. Look at all visible stitching on the main pack body to check for any broken stitch lines—touch these up immediately with your hand awl. If there's a spot of stitching that's getting abraded for some reason, run a bead of urethane seam sealer along the stitches to protect them.

Turn your pack inside out, brush grime from the seams, and check for frays. Loose threads should be clipped and heat-sealed. This is more of a problem with older packs. New packs of good quality usually have taped or bound seams that survive harsh use much longer than plain seams.

It's really not worth the time and effort to seam-seal your pack when a a 10-cent plastic trash bag will keep water out much better. Line your entire pack with a clear bag, and pack your gear (especially food) in waterproof stuff sacks (Annie always uses a super lightweight dry bag for her sleeping bag). A raincover is worth the investment to keep your pack clean and dry—wonderful when you'd rather *not* stash the pack in your tent.

Pack Rats
PUBLIC PACK ENEMY NO. 1

Canada's infamous Bugaboo Range "snaffle-hounds," or pack rats, taught Annie the single most important preventive maintenance tip for packs: Never employ your pack for overnight food storage! Use something relatively expendable, since conniving rodentia delight in outwitting even the most ingenious food-hanging rigger.

Stealthy snafflehounds perforated Annie's favorite old 5,000-cube hauler, suspended from an overhanging boulder with thin cord. Ravenous rats

then munched their way through one side and crunched out the other, leaving a few crumbs and many substantial holes in her trusty Gregory. Our rigging system became increasingly elaborate until finally the food bag hung between large swiveling foils 30 feet from anything. A couple of nights later, a succession of holes marked the path of hungry visitors through our group's last unchewed rucksack. Our normally serene Buddhist friend ended up trying to skewer a bold little varmint with his ice axe.

Use a heavy stuff bag (bring plastic garbage bags to waterproof if necessary) for hanging food. If rain is likely, consider a paddling dry bag for food storage. These PVC or urethane-coated bags have a watertight seal that keeps animal-attracting smells in and at least the less determined rodents out. Animals are also attracted to sweat and body salts that accumulate on pack straps and on the back panel; discourage this by regularly rinsing your pack with fresh water.

PUBLIC PACK ENEMY NO. 2

There's a reason why airline ticket agents often make you sign a waiver when you check your backpack—something about these rugged carryalls brings out the aggressive nature of some baggage handlers. Between check-in and the time you pull your tattered pack from the bag-claim carousel, any number of goons have grabbed, hurled, lurched, wrenched, and wrestled with whatever strap dangled near. After a string of airline-altered pack straps, we developed a sure-fire binding technique that leaves only one handle available—the one designed to lift the pack.

Idiot-proof your pack for travel by burying breakable and hard-edged items like tent poles or cook kits deep within the beast, generously padded with soft stuff. If you're not keen to sit on the pack from any angle, start over. Do not load anything on the exterior: it will just catch on baggage belts, rip the pack, and then disappear forever. Cinch down

This rucksack is battened down and ready for travel; note that the hip belt is fastened forward around the pack body.

all compression straps, and carefully weave dangling ends out of sight. Tighten shoulder straps to their shortest length, also tucking loose ends away. Wrap the hip belt forward around the pack body to achieve a smooth, round profile. Run the belt through ice-axe loops too so it stays wrapped. Make sure the bag-claim tickets get wrapped around the grab loop—a little flag that says nicely, "Lift me here."

Of course, the simplest way to avoid airport mistreatment of your pack is to envelop it within a big duffel bag lined with a foam sleeping pad. If you're shipping ice tools, definitely use foam pads or stiff tubes slipped over the picks and spikes, unless you prefer to risk multiple puncture wounds in all your other gear.

Patching

See also Fabric Patching, beginning on page 7

The holes you're most likely to experience are due to animals—*Ursidae, Canidae, Rodentia*. The type of patch you'll need depends on the hole size and

Take one look at the multifarious packs displayed at your local outdoor store, and most pack buyers blanch. Where do you start? Take heart, finding the right pack isn't as hard as the number of options might make it look.

- **Define your needs.** Know before you go what you plan to do with the pack. If you're just going on day trips or overnights, there's no need for a full-on load monster that would support you on a two-week solo adventure to Mount Stupendous. If you're unsure about your intended uses, err on the small side. Maybe it's premature to buy a pack; renting a pack is as easy as renting a car these days, and by trying different models, you'll get a clear sense of what you want.
- **Internal versus external.** Make this choice based on where and how you intend to travel. Internal-frame models typically offer greater load stability and freedom of movement. Choose an internal if you're planning to hike rough trails, climb, ski, or bushwhack. The trade-off is greater expense and more involved loading and unloading. External-fame packs carry better on decent trails (though not on rough ones) and offer better cooling against your back, easier loading and unloading, and better gear organization in multiple pockets. Externals can also haul ladders, tripods, or hardside coolers, no worries.
- **Top-loaders versus panel-loaders.** Top-loading packs offer better load control, more ease of movement, better weather resistance, and increased load security (i.e., less chance of things falling off the outside). Zip-open panel-loaders are beloved of travelers for their suitcaselike ease of packing; however, those long zippers are like rain gutters straight into your sleeping bag. Make sure any panel-loading compartment has backup straps in case of a zipper blowout.
- **Size guidelines.** Resist the urge to carry too much stuff—after all, you are carrying your possibles bag, right? Pack capacity is rated in cubic inches. Here's a rough outline of which size fits which uses.
  - Up to 2,000: Basic daypack size, superlight overnights
  - 3,000–3,500: Weekend trips, equipment-intensive day trips like climbing or winter sports
  - 4,000–4,500: Most backpacking trips of up to a week
  - 5,000 or more: Load monster, best for guides, parents, masochists, and extended backpacking adventures. Add another 1,000 cubes or so for winter gear.
- **Bells and whistles.** Pockets let you organize supplies efficiently without resorting to packing in 21 separate stuff bags. Make sure the pack has compression straps to squeeze the load into a manageable bundle or adjust the shape according to the activity. We prefer a sleek, simplified pack profile; specialized accoutrements like ski pockets, shovel flaps, daisy chains, and tool holsters are just so much claptrap if you don't really need them.

level of damage to the pack. Most chewed-up packs come out of the woods with duct tape or adhesive nylon patches affixed, but these are almost certainly temporary, since they are neither structural nor waterproof.

Small, bite-sized holes or punctures can be cured either with urethane adhesive or by heavily overstitching the area with a packcloth swatch for backing.

A fist-size or larger patch probably requires

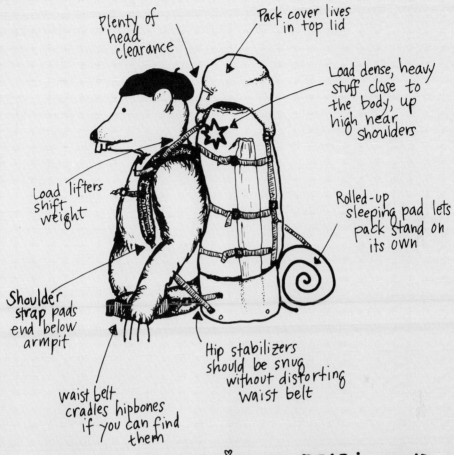

Plenty of head clearance

Pack cover lives in top lid

Load dense, heavy stuff close to the body, up high near shoulders

Load lifters shift weight

Rolled-up sleeping pad lets pack stand on its own

Shoulder strap pads end below armpit

Hip stabilizers should be snug without distorting waist belt

waist belt cradles hipbones if you can find them

PACKFiTTiNG DETAiLS to BEAR in MiND

- **Weight-watchers beware.** Weight counts, but don't shortchange your comfort. Packs designed to haul big loads are not going to be light: figure on roughly a pound for every 1,000 cubic inches.

- **Raingear for your pack.** Don't forget to spring for a pack cover; your sleeping bag will thank you.

deconstructing seams and splicing in new fabric. Most home machines can't handle layers of heavy packcloth; for a really bombproof, durable patch we strongly recommend sending the job to the manufacturer or a repair center (see appendix F, Directory of Repair Services, beginning on page 232). If you're heading on a long trip, be sure to bring an awl, heavy-duty thread, and a few squares of packcloth so you can effect a rudimentary rodent-iary repair.

A few weeks before setting out on a Canadian river trip, Annie decided to give our well-used Duluth pack a makeover. The packcloth's interior coating had been disintegrating for some time, leaving whatever was stored in the bag festooned with bits of cruddy brown gunk. Turning the pack inside out, she used a stiff brush and warm water to scour away any lingering coating.

The next step was to trim away all the frayed

Cut away fraying threads along the seams and zipper track.

Heat-seal raw seam edges with a wood-burning pencil or soldering iron.

fabric edges along interior seams, which tended to catch in the zippers. She sealed the raw edges by running them along a heated soldering iron held stationary in a vise.

Turning the pack right side out, she waterproofed the clean, dry cloth using Thompson's Water Seal in a handheld sprayer; she began by spritzing all the seams, then saturated the pack body. Proving the treatment was as easy as tossing the pack out into a rainstorm: drops of water beaded up reassuringly on the fabric surface.

All this preparation was worthwhile, since it rained for most of the trip. However, Annie's attention was so focused on rewaterproofing that she forgot to check a very basic, essential element: the pack straps' attachment points! The stitching held just until the last mile of the last (and longest) portage. A simple enough field repair, but avoidable had someone done the Five-Point Pack Check.

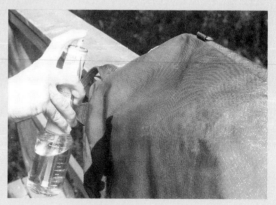

Use a Preval sprayer with Thompson's Water Seal to re-waterproof fabric, paying special attention to seams.

External-Frame Packs

Externals require the same Five-Point Pack Check, with a few extra considerations. Shoulder straps are usually connected to the frame (rather than the pack body) by a grommet, clevis pin, and retaining ring. If your external's shoulder strap blows out, it's usually caused by the fabric's tearing away from the grommet. You can repair this in the field by heating up your knife awl and punching it or a red-hot stick through the strap about an inch away from the original grommet. Make sure the new hole's edges are heat-sealed to prevent tearing, then insert the pin/ring. Carry a spare pin and ring too. Once home, order a replacement strap from the manufacturer.

The other problem specific to an external-frame pack is failure of the frame itself. This is usu-

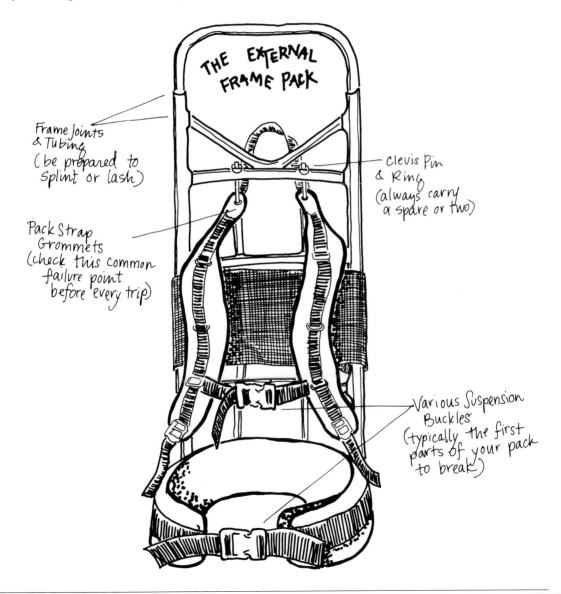

THE EXTERNAL FRAME PACK

Frame Joints & Tubing (be prepared to Splint or lash)

Pack Strap Grommets (check this common failure point before every trip)

clevis Pin & Ring (always carry a spare or two)

Various Suspension Buckles (typically the first parts of your pack to break)

ally due to Public Pack Enemy No. 2 or to sitting or falling on a frame in such a way that it bends the tubing and substantially weakens the structure.

Correct the bend with a splint from parts in your repair kit—a section of split tubing, a soda can, or aluminum flashing can be bound with hose clamps. Of course, a stick and bootlace make an equally suitable splint. (See sidebar, page 146.)

Pack tubes rarely shear, but if they do, plug the tubes with a green stick, then splint as suggested above.

If the frame is welded, it may well break at a joint. If that's the case, splint and lash the frame as best you can and tell lies about it later.

The Tumpline

If you find your pack straps straining under a full load, or if they suffer suspension failure, try a tumpline to relieve the stress. On a film adventure deep in the jungles of Belize, Dave found that the local Mayan guides carried the largest camera cases with only a tumpline. This device was nothing fancier than a strip of special bark, something their forefathers had used for centuries.

This primitive load-haul technique has yet to be improved upon for simplicity: A single strap serves to correctly balance a load over your skeleton, so that you have more energy to walk and chew gorp at the same time. The headpiece fits at the junction of your forehead and crown, thereby lining up your vertebrae in a proper load-carrying position.

For some reason, most people who write about the tumpline spend too much time talking about the pain of maladjustment, but we'll leave that to individual experience. Most Duluth-style packs come with a tumpline, or at least with attachment points, but one can be rigged to any pack or odd-sized load with practice. Try to affix the ends at or near shoulder height, using whatever attachment points are available—compression straps, frame stay, what have you. Knowing how to rig a tumpline can prove in-valuable if you blow a pack strap on a long trip, or worse, if your partner blows a knee and you have to wrangle his load.

Traditional Duluth Pack rigged with a Tumpline

The Tortuga Principle: Gear chosen for any trip will expand to fit available space

Therefore, smaller is better, faster, safer!

PART 2

Footwear

There's man all over for you,
blaming on his boots the faults of his feet.

Samuel Beckett, *Waiting for Godot*

A Tale of Two Cobblers

HOW THE 1980S NEARLY CLAIMED KOMITO

If any one person awakened Annie to the idea of repair as an honorable profession, it was Steve Komito, in Estes Park, Colorado. His shop served as a sort of climbers' bistro during the heroic days of free-climbing, and Komito himself is a classic climbing character. His vocation as cobbler the perfect complement to his avocation as skier and climber, Komito delivers pithy wisdom and good-hearted gossip with every resole. Just about everyone knows somebody who's bivouacked on his deck, yet despite his generosity and enthusiasm, Steve nearly called it quits a few years back.

What almost killed his business was the disposable 1980s, when people started buying lightweight, inexpensive "sneaker boots." In the good old days, climbing and hiking boots were expensive—an investment that required reverential care.

Enter the recent surge in rock climbing and telemark popularity, and a new generation of footwear whose price renders boots once again worthy of repair. "Hundred-and-fifty-dollar rock shoes were the best thing that ever happened to me," Komito says. Now his shop boasts an 800 number.

NET FIT

"Since Jesus' sandals, footwear was all made the same way," waxes Dave Page, cobbler, during a visit at his Seattle neighborhood hangout, Still Life with Coffee. "An upper was stitched to a slab of sole, then trimmed to fit. Now the trend is for *net fit*, where a finished sole is pressed on with adhesives—no stitching, no trimming, no smoothing. We no longer resole, we *re-bottom*."

This trend toward adhesion of molded, cemented soles rather than an externally stitched welt can be traced back to the first lightweight fabric-and-leather hiking boots, which employed running-shoe construction methods to create a lightweight boot that required virtually no break-in. Unfortunately, like other conveniences of our time—diapers, lighters, dinner out—those first-generation fabric boots became disposable.

Happily, bootmakers responded to pleas for more substance and drier feet without reverting entirely to the heavy, stitched-sole clunkers of yore. Today's hybrids combine leather uppers with a molded footbed, and not only are they more durable and weatherproof but they can be re-bottomed by select cobblers like Page, whose Italian deep-cavity press is literally deus ex machina. Both cobblers celebrate better boots; we celebrate their craft. (See appendix F, Directory of Repair Services, beginning on page 232, for a listing of specialty cobbler shops.)

DAVE PAGE'S MANTRA FOR FOOTWEAR LONGEVITY

1. Clean after use.
2. Waterproof in moderation.
3. Keep away from heat.

CHAPTER 6

Weatherproofing Boots

See also Seams and Seamsealing, beginning on page 20; and appendix A, Adhesives

Keeping Water Out

Boot maintenance centers on one thing: keeping water out. The less water absorbed by your footwear, the longer it will last. You can accomplish this in several ways: by treating the leather, by carefully drying after use, by wearing vapor-barrier liners, and by using gaiters whenever possible. Think of gaiters as little tents for your boots, protecting both the leather and your efforts at leather treatment. (See pages 42–43 for more information about gaiter care.)

SEAMSEALING BOOTS

Generally, fewer seams equal dryer boots and a lesser likelihood of a catastrophic blowout. Improve wearability and weatherproofness by caulking all external seams—especially where the boot upper meets the sole. A thin application of urethane sealant on clean, dry seams *before* weatherproofing does the trick.

First, clean along the seams with water and a stiff brush (an old toothbrush is ideal). Once they are dry, buff the seams with denatured alcohol to remove any residual oils and ensure a successful bond. Be sure to allow time for the alcohol to evaporate before applying sealers. The best way to achieve a clean, consistent bead of sealer is with a syringe. Allow full cure time before applying additional waterproofing treatments.

TREATING LEATHER

Leather is hydrophilic; it will absorb most any wet stuff like a sponge. Once leather becomes wet, moisture quickly travels from pore to pore by a pumping action (as the boot flexes) and from fiber to fiber by wicking, or capillary action. Wet leather is extremely heat-conductive—your body heat passes through faster than you can gobble a Power Bar.

Even though leather is one of the most durable and resilient materials known, once wet it stretches and weakens; as leather dries, it shrinks and becomes brittle. Leather is skin, plain and simple. Unlike skin, however, your boots don't possess a steady supply of natural lubricants and protective coatings—unless *you* supply them, that is. The key to long life for your leather boots is to maintain the leather's natural equilibrium with lubricants that provide water-repellency.

Use a syringe to apply seamsealer along stitch lines—neat & precise

BOOT GOOPS

While it is difficult to differentiate among the zillions of leather products available, Komito insists that as long as you use *something*—anything, even basil-infused olive oil—to waterproof your footwear, you're on the right track. However, since most boot treatments fall into the following general categories, you can make an educated choice for treating your own boots.

Fats or Greases

Fats or greases such as tallow—historical standbys—offer only the shortest-term protection against moisture. These coatings also contain contaminants that will invite mildew and other cooties to roost inside the leather and may also attract nibbling varmints. Best leave "bear grease" to the bruins, eh?

Oils

Oils quickly penetrate pores to soften leather and are a good choice if you're faced with stiff, beastly boots that chew your feet to shreds while you're out trying to have a good time. Oil provides breathable weatherproofing because it coats individual leather fibers; however, oil also permits the fibers to stretch, thereby weakening the overall strength of your footgear. Oil treatments are best reserved for breaking in new boots, softening the odd hot spot, or reconditioning old, brittle leathers. Use any penetrating oil, including mink oil, very infrequently because such dramatic softening capabilities may result in premature loss of fit.

Waxes

Waxes work best on leather surfaces with a smooth finish. Waxes by themselves have a hard

> ## BEESWAX
>
> Sweet milk and gratitude
> as fingers by the fire
> rub warmth and glow
> into cracked leather toes
>
> They had traveled far
> to bathe in honey
>
> A.G.

time penetrating leather; they work by clogging pores to create a waterproof, nonbreathable barrier. Slathered-on wax tends to float on the leather surface, forming a thick skim coat that abrades or cracks off. However, several very thin coats of wax applied to warm (not hot) leather and allowed to cure thoroughly between applications will form a tough, flexible, weatherproof shield. There's no need to heat wax before applying it; you can generate adequate heat by rubbing in the wax with your fingers.

Silicone Treatments

Silicone treatments, especially spray types for fabric and leather boots, are popular for their super-hydrophobic, lubricating qualities. Breathable silicones also repel stains and soils, but they don't offer much durability. As with adhesives, silicone leather treatments don't form a chemical bond with leather fibers and tend to dissipate quickly. There is also the argument that a silicone treatment may penetrate existing adhesive bonds and inhibit future adhesives. The best use for silicone or polymer spray treatments is on suede or nubuck leather uppers.

Dave Page warns that waterproofing can actually speed up deterioration of your boot's construction; treatments can migrate into the seam between upper and sole, penetrating and damaging adhesive bonds.

The waterproofing Caveat: treatments may penetrate adhesive bond between upper & sole.

BOOT TREATMENT TIPS

The type of leather conditioner you choose is less important than how you apply it. Simply slathering on boot goop won't protect your boots. A great amount of damage occurs when wax is applied over dirt, which gets worked into pores and weakens the leather. *Thorough leather treatment begins with a clean boot.* A stiff brushing under the faucet will remove old wax and dirt. Jeff Grissom, a cobbler at Page's shop who apprenticed with Morin Custom Boots in Colorado, contends that Woolite is the best boot cleaner available. "Wash both inside and out before conditioning," he says.

- Break in new boots slightly before treatment (see page 81).
- Boots should be very dry before conditioning (unless you're applying a water-based treatment).
- If you plan to seamseal boots, do so *before* waterproofing the leather and allow the sealer to fully cure before treatment.

- Remove the boot laces and meticulously work in the dressing with your fingers, paying special attention to overlapping seams, lacing eyelets, and folds around tongue gussets, where most water penetrates.
- Allow the dressing to fully cure, preferably overnight, before wiping off the excess with a lint-free cloth (chamois or PakTowl). At this point, depending on the condition of your boots, you may wish to apply a second, thin coat of goop.
- Set the freshly treated boots in a sunny window or apply moderate heat (from a woodstove or hair dryer) to warm and soften the conditioner. Then polish or buff the boots to seal the dressing—that is, to create a hard, smooth finish.
- If the boots feel sticky even after 24 hours, the dressing has not cured and will pick up dirt rather than protect the boot against it. Rewarm and buff the boots until any excess conditioner is removed.

Water-Based Polymer Coatings

These coatings carry a certain proprietary mystique—no manufacturer will tell you *exactly* what's in his brand—but they function somewhat like DWR textile treatments by bonding to individual leather fibers without softening them or altering their integrity.

Different types of water-based treatments are available for smooth-finished leathers, suede or nubuck leathers, and fabric-and-leather combinations. The suede types are particularly nice because they minimize the color change and darkening of rich leathers that result from the treatments.

Water-based polymer coatings are excellent for field use (as on a long trek) because they can be applied to a wet boot; in fact, these treatments actually work best on wet boots because moisture

in the leather draws the active ingredients deep into the pores. As the water evaporates, polymer residue clings to leather fibers, forming a thin, breathable, water-repellent coating when fully dry. Of all the various boot goops we've tried over the years, these have proven the most effective over time for leather footwear. On long trips you may use them in the field. Just try to clean the slime off your boots first.

FABRIC-AND-LEATHER CONSIDERATIONS

Fabric-and-leather boots require just as much treatment as leather boots do if you want them to last very long. Treat the leather sections by following the guidelines for leather boot care. The fabric sections merely need an occasional application of a spray water-repellent treatment (see Fabrics and

Insulations, beginning on page 25). Apply the treatment to clean, dry fabric *before* waterproofing the leather.

Boot Linings

Your feet crank out pint-loads of moisture during a hike or ski tour, which transfers from socks to boot linings and may result in mildew and a less-than-subtle fragrance. Since the bulk of foot perspiration is through the bottoms of your feet, the most expedient drying method involves removing insoles or inner boots after wearing and allowing the linings to air. On a trip, take a minute before turning in to *wring* the moisture out of your inner-soles—you'll be amazed at the volume! Hang-dry the liners in your tent or lay them out on a sun-warmed rock; both boot and footbed will feel drier in the morning.

VAPOR BARRIER LINERS

Vapor barrier liners (VBLs) will do a lot to preserve the integrity of your leather boots and make them considerably more comfortable during long trips. Vapor-barrier socks are like coated nylon foot jackets: worn over your socks, they keep moisture from penetrating outward into boot linings. Feet have their own nifty little thermostats to regulate perspiration, so you won't overheat.

This "closed system" created by the VBL actually reduces the loss of body heat. Your socks get wet, but you can easily dry them overnight or change them and eliminate the discomfort and danger of donning frozen, saturated boots on a winter climb or ski tour. Heavy-duty plastic bags (like bread bags) work fine but aren't as durable as those sewn from coated nylon. VBLs are commercially available and easy to sew at home.

Drying Boots

Leather is skin, after all. *The same amount of heat that would burn your skin will just as quickly damage leather.* Keep boots away from intense heat unless you prefer warped, shrunken, and hardened leather uppers and midsoles. Heat also will damage glues that bond sole layers together, causing delamination. So don't cook your boots around the campfire! On a dry day in camp remove the laces and liners, then rack the boots on branch stubs. Alternatively, dry them on a warm boulder in the sun with tongues held open to promote air circulation. In winter, sleep with your boots inside your tent or even in your sleeping bag to prevent them from freezing overnight.

If you're not worried about freezing and can't imagine sharing a small chamber with your odorous boots, set them upside down on a pack or stuff sack to keep the dew out. Beware of salt-sniffing, gnawing creatures who might find your sweaty boot far more attractive than you do.

At home, or during a motel break from the trail, remove insoles, stuff wet footwear with newspaper, and change the paper every few hours. Those skimpy little motel towels work wonderfully as boot dryers. Stuffing boots with newspaper during off-season storage is also a good way to prevent mildew from invading (or to deter creatures from filling your ski boots with acorns).

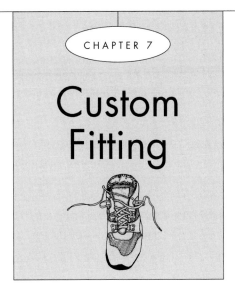

CHAPTER 7

Custom Fitting

If the shoe fits . . .

Anonymous

When it comes to foot health, Americans stand on decidedly shaky ground. Foot ills among shoeless peoples affect perhaps 3 percent of the population, versus some 70 percent of shoe wearers in the United States—who spend a staggering $28 billion annually on foot health care.

It's easy to blame such widespread foot complaints on the dumb shoes people tend to wear on the street: vicious spike heels, pointy Guccis, wobbly platform clunkers. Even so, hikers' supposedly sensible trail boots inflict more than their share of misery on recreating tootsies. It's not surprising if you consider that each time a backpacker's foot strikes the ground, the load is equivalent to about twice the guy's weight.

Since each foot bears its own unique history, it is no small success to find a durable boot that fits both your needs *and* your crooked left metatarsals (see sidebar, page 82). Once you've found the right pair to fit your weirdo feet, a little time spent customizing each new boot to its intended foot will truly enhance comfort and performance.

BREAKING IN

A confession here from Dave, longtime professional boot tester: "I heartily dislike boot testing—brand-new boots wreak entirely too much wear and tear on my precious feet." In test after test, stiff new boots killed much of his enjoyment of the trips involved. On recreational outings he grabs his old faithfuls, a bit down at the heel perhaps, but the hot spots have long since softened up.

You can best coax leather boots into the shape of your particular feet when the boots are a bit wet. Don't fill them with water—you'll invite mildew—but do take them for several rainy-day strolls or meanders through morning dew. Damp leather gives up its own shape and assumes your contours much faster.

You should wear new boots around before attempting to weatherproof the leather for two reasons. One is to break in both uppers and midsole partially before softening the leather. The other is to clean off any lingering tanning resins, which prevent sealants from bonding to leather fibers. A stiff brush under a running tap will also help to remove tanning resins.

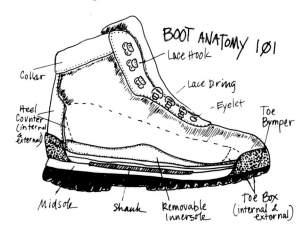

BOOT ANATOMY 101
Lace Hook
Lace Dring
Eyelet
Toe Bumper
Collar
Heel Counter (internal & external)
Midsole
Shank
Removable Innersole
Toe Box (internal & external)

Boot-Fitting

INSOLES

Perhaps the simplest way to adjust boot fit is with insoles—trimmed to fit your needs exactly. Anatomically shaped aftermarket footbeds such as Superfeet add arch support and shock absorption, not to mention warmth. Insoles also come in varying thicknesses to adjust fit tighter or looser; thinner insoles give feet more room, while thicker ones snug-up a loose boot.

You can craft your own insoles from a thin sheet of minicell foam—just copy a pair of running-shoe liners. Annie cannibalizes old liners to fill in for her notoriously short toes. Wool (felt) liners take up a lot of space initially but pack down in time. They are breathable, absorbent, and very warm. (A spare pair of felt liners on a long pad-

---

BUYING BOOTS THAT ACTUALLY FIT

Careful boot shopping pays big dividends down the trail. You may even miss out on the blistery joys of break-in entirely. Well, almost. Our hard-won tips for buying the right boots for your particular feet:

- **Measure your dogs.** Sounds simple, but it's amazing how few people really *know* their foot shape. Measure the overall length, of course, but equally important is the ratio of overall length to arch length. Short-arched folks may need to size down a half- or full size from the overall length, and vice versa for long-arch types.
- **Match boots to your intended use.** Unless you live in Chamonix, there's no need to lug around weighty crampon-compatible mountain boots to hike local footpaths. On the other hand, don't shortchange yourself: an avid backpacker might trash three or four pairs of light fabric-and-leather "trail sneakers" in the time one pair of midweight leather hikers would last—and your feet would be far happier and drier in the bargain.
- **Avoid ordering by mail.** Hear this, catalog freaks: save yourself lots of pain by shopping in person. There's no substitute for trying on all the boots you can find.
- **Drive the salesperson nuts.** Don't let yourself be rushed while trying on boots. The main difference between various boot brands is the "last," or general foot shape they'll fit best. Just because a salesperson loves her Acme Trail Trompers doesn't mean they'll fit you. Try on all the boots the shop carries in a particular category, then focus on the pair that feels best on first impression. If you find a patient, informed boot fitter, tell everyone you know about the shop—it deserves the support!
- **Use the right socks.** The thickness and number of sock layers makes a big difference in how boots fit. Most people prefer a thin liner and a midweight boot sock to minimize chafing. Dave likes a single midweight sock; Annie loves a thin wool liner and a fuzzy outer sock. Make sure your stockings have smooth toe seams and don't wrinkle or bind at the ankle. Forget cotton—go with synthetics or wool blends only.
- **Leave yourself some wiggle room.** Hard working hikers' feet may swell a full size on the trail. Jam your toes against the front and make sure there's at least a thumb's width of room at the heel. Conversely, make sure your heels won't swim around—nothing eats up feet faster.
- **Lace boots snugly, then walk up- and downhill.** In case you hadn't noticed, the outdoor world is not flat, so test new boots on the incline. Better boot shops now feature inclined, faux-stone ramps to test boot fit. If your toes jam on the downhills, look for a larger size now, before it's too late.

---

dling trip is Annie's secret weapon—thanks to this trick, she's able to smile pleasantly even before the morning's first hot cuppa.)

If your boots feel *okaaay* but still squeeze your foot here and there, trimming innersoles can yield surprising comfort. Cut away gradually where you require more room, and make sure to bevel the edge so you don't feel a ridge underfoot.

For boots that feel loose around the heel, try a pair of Sorbothane heel plugs from the boot shop—or in a pinch, a matchbook—wedged under the innersole; snugging up this area helps prevent chafed heels (which, incidentally, are easy to further defrictionize with a patch of duct tape).

MORE SOLE THAN YOU CAN CONTROL

External examination of a worn outersole reveals a lot about your gait. A little wear to the inside or outside of the heel is normal; extremely irregular wear will shorten sole life and may need to be corrected with orthopedic inserts, available through a podiatrist. Correctly fitted inserts can also improve stride efficiency.

HOT SPOTS

Don't ignore hot spots: attack them before they develop into full-fledged blisters. They usually don't go away, so stop where you are, take your boot off, and attend to the offending area. Cobblers have a secret tool called a *rubbing bar* that burnishes away irritating contact points. You can use the butt of your Swiss Army knife to solve this fit problem: Apply pressure and rub the hot spot to smooth and soften the leather. Your feet will be pleased with how well this works.

Lacing Tips and Tricks

- Nylon laces last forever, or at least until they become tent guys, sunglass retainers, or the makings for a game of cat's cradle.

- Flat, braided nylon laces don't work well in lace locks (those flat, double-riveted hooks usually placed over the instep) but are easy on the fingers. Some claim that these stay tied better than round laces, but we disagree.
- Cotton or rawhide laces weaken when wet; once sodden or frozen, they're next to impossible to untie.
- For winter campers: spritz a little silicone treatment on laces to prevent them from icing up.
- If you trim and heat-seal lace ends, make sure the lace will still run through your boot eyelets—you may need them for prusiks!
- Watch out for el cheapo hardware with sharp edges that will fray laces. Chintzy plastic eyelets on some fabric-and-leather lightweights are prime offenders, but so were the metal lace eyes on Annie's new $350 Italian telemark boots. Dave employed a small round chainsaw file to smooth out the sharp edges.
- Occasionally shift laces to and fro so they don't prematurely wear in one spot and break.

Mountaineer's Lace

Prevent laces from loosening with the *mountaineer's lace*. Simply change the direction as you wrap laces around hooks so you're threading from the top down. The lace wraps over itself, providing extra friction, so it's less likely to shift under pressure on the trail.

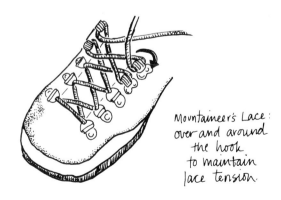

Mountaineer's Lace: over and around the hook to maintain lace tension.

Double-Hitching

Maintain precise lace tension with a double hitch. Wrap the laces around each other a few times and cinch, creating a stopper. This trick lets you leave the toebox loose yet cinch the ankle snug, for instance. Use a double hitch before making a bow, and the laces will stay tight even if the bow becomes untied.

Skipping Eyelets

Have a niggling high instep? It's definitely legal to skip eyelets. Tension-off lower laces with a dou-ble hitch. Skip eyelets over the problem area, then crank another double hitch and finish lacing. If boot tops bark your shins, leave the top pair of eyelets undone. Dave often skips the top two pairs of eyelets when trail-hiking in stiff mountain boots, then ties 'em back up for the climb itself.

Z-Drag

Direct and maintain tension with a mini Z-drag, which lets you pull your heel tighter into the boot's heel pocket.

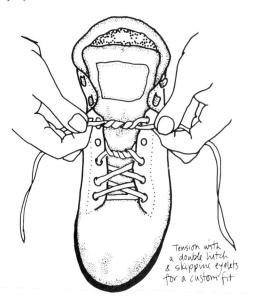

Tension with a double hitch & skipping eyelets for a custom fit

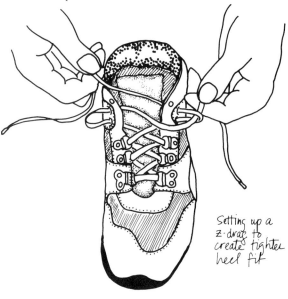

Setting up a z-drag to create tighter heel fit

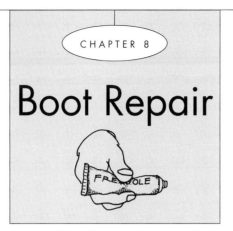

CHAPTER 8

Boot Repair

The climbing shoes were made as follows: First we unravelled some sisal bags, obtained from the kitchen for a few packets of cigarettes. The threads were twisted together into a rope which was soaked in water, beaten and straightened between two poles of our barbed-wire fences. Finally they were sewn together in the shape of a sole. The uppers were cut out of a square yard of old tarpaulin.

Felice Benuzzi, *No Picnic on Mount Kenya*

Midway through a ten-day hike deep in the jungles of Belize, our friend Darryl was horrified to discover that his right boot sole was flapping like a fishwife's tongue. Umpteen stream crossings and razor-sharp limestone trails proved too much for his aging fabric-and-leather hikers.

These tired old boots are ready for retirement . . . but what stories they could tell!

A rough wrap of duct tape was all he could do, but it did little to allay his fears about no spare footwear to get him out of the bush and past creepy-crawlies the likes of which he'd never seen. He wished he'd worn sturdier boots, even after good old duct tape saved his butt.

Typical Repairs
TORN LEATHER

Leather tears may be traced directly to three likely causes: lack of maintenance, a-a lava, and puppies. If you fail to weatherproof your boots, they'll either be too dried-out and brittle or too sodden and pliant to withstand abuse. A small tear is correctable with urethane adhesive, provided you've carefully prepped the area and cleaned any lubricants off the leather surface. Puppies are another story; they'll probably pick your new telemark boots for teething. If this happens, a consultation with a cobbler is in order. (And don't be too hard on the dog.)

SMALL HOLES

Patching quarter-sized holes with urethane adhesive in a fabric boot is no problem. Just keep the boot level as it dries. (See pages 7–10.)

SOLE RECLAMATION

If your boots have a stitched (Norwegian) welt, rejoining the upper to the sole is better left to a cobbler. Most light- and midweight hiking boots sport a bonded sole with a rubber toe bumper or

REGLUING A SOLE

- Regluing any major boot part is essentially a surgical procedure—cleaning and prepping are key. Wash the boot with soap and water. Once it is thoroughly dry, lightly sand the gluing surfaces. Wipe down the clean, dry boot thoroughly with denatured alcohol before gluing. (See appendix A, Adhesives, beginning on page 212.)
- Stuff the boot with paper to provide structure.
- Use contact cement (Barge brand is the most popular footwear adhesive). Spread a thin layer of adhesive on each prepared surface and let them rest until almost dry.
- Align and mate the parts carefully—you only get *one* chance with contact cement.
- Clamp the parts together with a C-clamp or wrap tightly with strong tape, and let dry. Secure clamping is important to the success and life of your repair.
- Finally, seal the joint with seam sealer.

Gluing toe & heel bumpers or sole, then clamping & taping

rand to shield the joint, and these are easily repairable at home. Sole replacement, however, is the cobbler's bread and butter.

BLOWN SEAMS

In the field, a few turns of duct tape or a twist of baling wire will hold your blown-out boots together temporarily. If you have a little time, you might be able to restitch an opened seam with the awl in your sewing kit (the sailmaker's palm is ideal for this). Seamsealing will help lengthen the life expectancy of fraying stitches.

Ski Touring and Telemark Boots

Backcountry skiing involves a good deal more walking—a.k.a. *slogging*—than most "pinheads" would ever care to admit, and it's bloody hard work. Snow is wet and feet sweat, so regular boot maintenance is crucial. You can delay waterlogging somewhat by wearing gaiters and VBLs, but don't neglect leather treatment and seamsealing, particularly along the welt and around the toe area, where constant contact with bindings really abrades the boot construction. If your toebox area is chewed up and torn as a result of unenlightened care, send the boots to a mountain-boot specialist for rebuilding.

Note: most of our tips date from prehistory, when all tele boots were retro and leather. Yah, we love our carefree T2's, but nothing beats leather for touring.

REINFORCING THE TOE WELT

Protect the vulnerable toe welt of your touring boot with a coating of—you guessed it—Seam

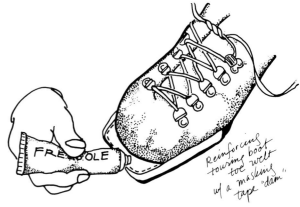

FREESOLE

Reinforcing touring boot toe welt w/ a masking tape "dam"

Grip or Freesole urethane adhesive. Clean and prep the upper and welt, then make a masking-tape dam around the toebox edge. Apply the adhesive and set the shoe in a level position for the full cure time. Don't use for at least 48 hours.

PINHOLES

Aside from water damage, the most common back-country ski-boot disorder is a cracked or broken sole under the toe, usually centered around the binding pinholes. This can be prevented by regular inspection, but if it happens in the field, three-pin bails alone will not hold your boot. In the field, jury-rig a cable binding with a nylon cord, bungee, or wire. Once home, commit your boots to the clinic for a resole operation—when it's time for resoling, you can specify your desired midsole stiffness for a truly custom boot.

Good news for the spatially challenged: if the toe of your sole is riddled with divots from mis-stepping, you needn't race off to have a metal pin-plate mounted. Those extra holes are cosmetic damage to the outsole; the "real" holes have metal eyes imbedded in the rubber to catch pins. Warns cobbler Komito, "Repair pinplates are put on with screws drilled through both sole and mid-sole, creating a weak spot that's bound to fracture. The cure is worse than the disease." You can avoid this problem entirely by using a pair of cable bindings or by simply being more mindful when stepping in.

SUPERGAITERS

If gaiters extend the life of your ski boots, then supergaiters can render them nearly immortal. Well, not really, but the protective properties of supergaiters are worthwhile insurance for pricey tele boots. These insulated boot parkas have tight-fitting rubber rands that surround the boots at the sole, so virtually no snow (i.e., water) can penetrate the uppers. The only problem is keeping rands from slipping off the smooth, contoured leather.

Solve this by applying a skim coat of ski binder wax to the leather or by spreading a thin layer of Freesole around the sides of the toebox, providing a stickier contact for the rands.

Warning: Our skiing buddy John Harlin tossed his tele boots into the closet one spring with tight-fitting supergaiters still attached. When he retrieved them the next winter, his boot soles were warped like bananas. Though we believed them to be wrecked, Dave Page the cobbler says they might be cured with a resole job that includes a new midsole.

Harvey Page has earned a mountainous reputation for leather "fitting" and rebuilding. Here he remounts tele boot buckles at brother Dave's cobbler shop.

Plastic Mountain Boots

Paul "Punisher" Cleveland, a peripatetic tramper, ski tourer, trail-maintenance guru, and wilderness EMT who *uses his gear up*, tried as hard as he could to think of an unusual repair situation. Paul finally recalled the hinge on his plastic double boot cuff that popped. Although this minor failure didn't require field triage, a 33-cent stainless rivet from the hardware store proved a viable replacement.

Other than regular air-drying of the inner

boots and obvious hardware failures like busted buckle systems or popped lace eyelets, there's little to attend to with plastic boots. Plastic doubles can be successfully resoled and reranded by any mountain-boot specialist. Also, if you've heard about custom-fitting or stretching the plastic shells by applying heat, don't. This should be handled by a mountain cobbler or ski shop, by a skilled, competent boot technician who knows the subtleties of heating and stretching various expensive plastics.

Rock Shoes

THE CINDERELLA SYNDROME

The more ambitious the route, the tighter the rock slipper, right? We've been forced to trade away more than one pair of shoes when this principle proved podiatrically unsound. The fact that rock shoes stretch constantly complicates this sizing dilemma.

Annie's latest pair of Cinderella slippers proved excruciatingly tight on early outings. She tried to speed up the stretch process by softening the uppers. Rather than soaking the leather in water, she wiped the shoes down thoroughly with denatured alcohol, then wore them until they were dry. The dampened uppers formed right to her little paddle feet as the alcohol evaporated. Fair warning—this treatment may speed up break-in, but it may also hasten the separation of rubber rands and sole edges. An oil treatment will do a more radical job of softening but may overstretch a light leather upper.

We've heard of convincing slippers to fit by hammering the sole or driving cars over the last, but this will damage a board-lasted boot beyond repair by fracturing the midsole, heel, and toe counters. Consider this method a last resort.

DELAMINATION

The sole of a climbing shoe is bonded to rand and last with heat-sensitive adhesive and is designed to be easily removed for resoling. This means that any excessive heat source—like a campfire or, most likely, the trunk of your car on a hot summer day—will activate the glue and delaminate soles, rands, and other key parts. If you continue to climb on delaminated soles, you're likely to damage the rand, not to mention the rest of your body. You can try to reglue and clamp the delam, but the bond is likely to be sketchy—you're better off with completely new half soles.

HOLY SOLES

When to resole? Most penny-pinching climbers wait too long before considering a resole job. New soles or half soles will adhere much better if you haven't completely worn through the original rubber in any one place, including the edges at the toe. A good goal is to *try to preserve the rand at all costs*, since this part of your boot largely determines your edge control.

Climbers generally find half soles to be the most viable resole operation, since most wear occurs near the toes and the ball of the foot, rarely at the heel (unless you're an off-width masochist). Slippers and slip-lasted shoes can handle just one or two resoles before losing their integrity, but other, more substantial boots may be successfully resoled several times. Home resoling is both straightforward and economical. Your rock shoes set you back at least $100, so a $20 repair kit makes sense.

However, it may be well worth your while to spring for a professional resole, which runs about $50. The cobblers recommended in appendix F, Directory of Repair Services (beginning on page 232), use machinery designed to re-create the original fit of your shoes, and their expert gluing and grinding methods minimize the risk of delamination (a likely result on a home job, especially your first one).

THE HOME RESOLE

Order a kit (see appendix G, Materials Resources, beginning on page 236) containing directions, glue, and enough rubber to make two pairs of half soles or one set of full soles, plus instructions and a tube of adhesive designed for bonding footwear. Sheet kits give you more options than precut kits. *Home resoling is really a two-person operation*, since there are moments when it helps to have at least three hands.

A *Surform tool works to prepare gluing surfaces and custom-shape new rubber soles.*

A recently introduced Aqua-Stealth sole kit allows you to resole your favorite old river sandals with sticky climbing rubber following a procedure much like redoing climbing shoes.

If the rubber left on your old shoe is superthin but still well attached, you may consider applying a new sole directly to the old one. This popular solution adds stiffness and durability to slippers. Use the thin rubber kit for this, and sand or grind the original sole as thin as possible.

Cutting

Cutting a blank sole from the thick rubber slab is awkward at best; use a utility knife with a fresh blade or a very sharp, thin knife. The easiest way to slice the rubber is to have a friend spread the rubber apart as you cut.

Grinding

Resoling calls for a fair amount of grinding, which can be accomplished in a number of ways. The easiest way is with a belt grinder or sander. Lacking that, you can use a coarse, 3-inch grind wheel (about $3 at your local hardware store) on a power drill. If you're in the manual mode, spring for a Surform tool, which will work fine to both prep and shape the rubber.

Remove old sole over hot burner

Remove the Old Sole

- Remove the old sole, or the front half, as shown. Heat the rubber over a red-hot electric stove coil until it's hot to the touch (about 3 to 5 minutes). Do not let the rubber get so hot that it smokes.
- Use Vise-Grips or needlenose pliers to peel away the sole. If the rubber doesn't peel easily, continue to apply heat to the opened area and separate the layers with a knife.
- Be careful not to tear away any of the rand or midsole, or you'll have to repair those gouges (by filling with Freesole or Aquaseal) before applying a new rubber sole.

If You're Adding Half Soles Only

- Don't heat the whole boot—just the part you want to replace.
- Slice off the peeled section and bevel the edge of the original rubber at the instep to create a larger gluing surface.

Cutting New Soles

- Use the old sole as a pattern.
- Trace around the sole, allowing plenty of room between boot patterns.
- Cut the patterns into separate, rough-shaped soles, leaving plenty of room (¼ to ½ inch) for the final trim.

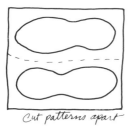

Cut patterns apart

Gluing

See also appendix A, Adhesives, beginning on page 212

- If you've accidentally ripped out any sections of the midsole, fill with urethane adhesive and allow to cure completely before gluing the sole.
- Make sure the rand edge is as square as possible. You may wish to build up the edge with urethane (making a masking-tape "form"), then trim or sand it square once cured. This square edge is important for adhesion and later performance.
- Prep the surfaces to be glued by sanding, then brushing away any dusty residue.
- Clean the gluing surfaces with denatured alcohol. Do not touch the cleaned surfaces with your fingers.

John Buckner traces around a rock shoe to pattern the new sole.

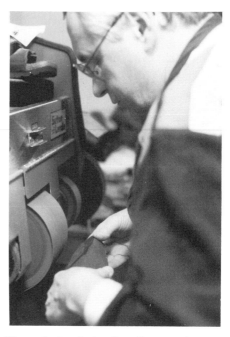

The professional edge: Dave Page grinds a new half sole to like-new performance.

- Apply a very thin coat of contact cement (Barge brand is most recommended) to both surfaces. Wear a rubber glove to spread the cement into a thin, smooth layer.
- Allow the cement to dry completely—at least 2 hours—before joining the surfaces.

Sole Mates

- Stuff the boots with newspaper to add structure to the form.
- Heat both glued surfaces over a red-hot electric coil for no more than 30 seconds, making sure the rubber surfaces (or your hands) do not begin to smoke.
- Carefully align the surfaces, starting at the beveled edge, then roll the sole toward the toe, firmly squeezing along the contour of the boot.
- Hammer along the edge of the bond to further convince mating.

Ensure a solid bond by hammering new rubber sole with a wooden mallet before trimming.

- Allow the glue to cure completely, preferably 48 hours.
- For a bomber resole on slippers (not board-lasted boots), *Climbing* magazine (no. 101) offers this slick trick: Carefully position the front wheel of your car onto the *front section only* of the shoe and park the car overnight. Retrieve the flattened shoe and knead it to restore the shape.

The Final Trim

- Trim away any excess rubber with a utility knife.
- Use a vise or get a friend to help you separate the rubber for smooth slicing.
- Be conservative, since you can fine-tune the trim with a grinder.
- Grind the edge to your favorite angle.
- For small sections of delamination along the edges, the sticky-rubber supplier Five Ten Company recommends filling with Freesole or Aquaseal.

Rubber Boots

L.L. Bean built an institution on customer service, including a fine boot-repair facility to which Annie's late grandfather sent his Bean boots for rebottoming every umpteenth year. Her brother still wears those boots—the original tops must be sixty years old! Granted, both men qualified as fanatics when it came to taking care of their stuff, always treating the leather uppers to generous waterproofing each spring.

Before treating the leather on your Beans or Sorels, apply a little urethane sealer around the stitching that joins the leather upper to the rubber bottom to help keep water out and protect the individual stitches.

Rubber waders or Wellies begin to suffer tiny cracks as the color starts to fade. Keep the material supple longer with regular applications of 303 Protectant. (Don't get any on the bottom, or you'll wipe out.) Typically, the rubber will crack where the boot flexes as you walk. If leakage is a problem, consider gooping on a little Aquaseal. Take time to let the liners dry out after wearing—remove any insoles and set the boots in a cool place to allow canvas to dry without mildewing. Make sure you don't shorten your beloved Wellies' life span by storing them folded over, sitting in the sun, or next to the ozone generated by a large electric motor.

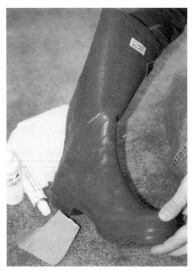

Rubber boots may fatigue and crack where boots flex.

Prepare the area by sanding, then cleaning with denatured alcohol.

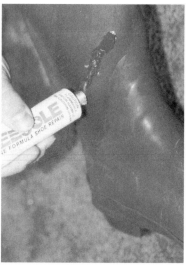

Apply urethane adhesive to caulk the leak.

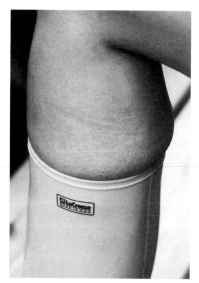

Problem: rubber boot tops are too tight for gnarly calves.

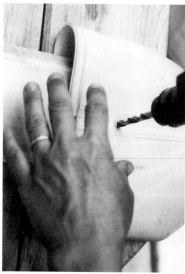

Solution: drill hole about 2 inches from the boot top; this stops the slit from tearing further.

Slit the boot top down to the hole; now the calf won't whimper.

PART 3

Hardware

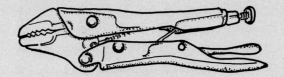

The Rewards of an Inventive Nature

A visit with Win Ellis always leaves Annie with an original perspective on some everyday object or method. Ask Win, the quintessential inventor, about most any topic, and he'll respond slowly, "Well-l-l . . . I really don't know much about that, but I imagine . . ." and then continue with logical rhythm to explore the territory in question.

Win makes a living fabricating unique, techy yacht fittings and manufacturing and marketing his own ingenious gadgets (like the Windspeed kayak spinnaker rig and rechargeable headlamp battery packs). He seems perplexed by the fact that most people are content to leave the thinking to somebody else. "Those weekend warriors who buy all their gear at an outdoor store are letting someone else have all the fun designing and problem-solving."

Win waxes poetic with tales of his own resourcefulness: "Years ago in India, I had some time on my hands, but no money, and I decided to make a backpack frame from bamboo and a little parachute cord. I braided the cord for straps, then padded them out with strips from an old Army blanket. That lashed frame was totally flexible and rugged—you could've strapped a car to the thing.

"Another time, walking through Nova Scotia in terrible weather, I made a fine lean-to shelter shingled with fish bags I'd found washed up on the beach. Any beach has all matter of goods for repairs or innovations: bleach bottles, floats, nets, potwarp, flip-flops. . . . Say, an old flip-flop is the ideal fan to coax a smoldering fire into action."

Win speaks warmly of everybody's favorite repair essentials, including duct tape and dental floss: "Our first night out on Baffin Island, our tent vestibule blew off in the horrendous wind. We secured it with dental floss the next day, and it held up excellently."

Win's ingenuity with found objects serves to acquaint you with the skills required in this section. If something breaks on a trip, keep your eyes open and your brain in gear, and you may well surprise yourself by solving the problem at hand.

CHAPTER 9

Stoves and Cookware

Yet, instead of going out at once with the begging-bowl, he stayed his stomach on slabs of cold rice till the full dawn.

Rudyard Kipling, *Kim*

Annie and Kristin were somewhere off the back side of Alaska's Wrangell Range, a five-day hike from the nearest anything; the bush plane wasn't due for another eight days. The trip progressed famously through vast treeless tundra, absolutely stunning, exactly what they'd come for. So why were they spittin' mad on a gorgeous evening? One word, five letters: stove.

The wretched thing was gasping and converting copious amounts of precious fuel into little more than black crud on the pot bottoms. Not much firewood around, so it looked like raw oatmeal and, worse, no coffee. Their chagrin centered around the folly of being capable gourmet gals in remote backcountry with two backpacks full of cookable food and a solitary, sickly cooker.

Fortunately, a tip from the first edition of this book bailed them out. They field-stripped the stove, lit a feeble fire of willow twigs and beaver sticks,

PROTECT YOUR FOOD, SAVE YOUR GEAR

Wild creatures habituated to human food can be pesky nuisances, especially around campgrounds or the bases of popular climbs. Think about it: anything humans eat is bound to taste better than an animal's natural diet (Annie knows from experience that pasta primavera is far superior to uncooked beetle larvae and urchin roe). Cunning marauders are hardly slowed by a few millimeters of nylon, and nothing short of polycarbonate barrels will deter a bear. By protecting your food, you'll spare your favorite pack and help protect the natural habits of wild species.

- Store and hang all food in stout, waterproofed stuff sacks. Do not leave them in your pack or tent, even if you're off on a day hike.

- Separate your cooking area from your tent site.
- Regularly rinse pack straps, hip belt, and back pad with fresh water to remove accumulated body salts.
- Keep food residue off all fabrics—clean up spills immediately.
- Use a bear-proof container, as required in several national parks.
- Treat anything with a scent—garbage, toothpaste, first-aid ointments—the same as food.
- Hang your food (there's no excuse for a climber with a load of hardware not to set up an animal-proof system).
- In treeless areas, stack rocks over the food-bag—to deter coyotes, coons, and porkies but not mice, bear, or ravenous through-hikers.

managed to heat up the generator tube, and then plunged it, red-hot, into frigid creek water to break up the accumulated carbon deposits. The stove relit on the first try, roaring like a little furnace. The prognosis for the trip improved dramatically. (Just don't ask Annie about the pepper-spray incident.)

The Crankiest Item in Your Pack

A camp stove is probably the most intricate, fiddly piece of equipment you're ever going to haul around in the wilderness. Yet, if you're like most rugged individualists, you've never even glanced at the operating instructions.

"Reading the instructions is the single most important step for smooth operation of any stove," says Mike Ridout, MSR's tech lord and repair specialist. "If more people read their instructions, I'd probably be out of a job." Ridout also emphasizes that there's no quicker way to ruin your stove than to loan it to a friend.

This section is less about repairing specific stove models than about how to care for camp stoves in general and what sort of performance you might expect from the different types. With more than 50 packable stoves available on the market, to dissect each unit here would be more painful than simply reading your particular stove's instructions.

Stove Types

ALCOHOL
Alcohol burners sport the fewest parts of any liquid-fuel stove and are therefore among the most reliable; as long as you have fuel, you're able to generate BTUs. Silent but slow, an alcohol stove requires more fuel and more time to produce the same amount of heat as a white-gas burner produces, so expect your tea breaks to take a little longer. A windscreen and a well-fitted cook set are vital to obtaining reasonable boiling and cook times. Denatured alcohol is renewable, burns without pressurization, and offers low volatility, making it a favored cooking fuel for enclosed spaces like boat cabins and tiny tents.

BOTTLED GAS
Probably the most convenient and least troublesome cooking option for average above-freezing conditions, butane, isobutane, and butane/propane stoves are sort of like giant Bic lighters; unfortunately, they are almost as disposable. Spent fuel canisters are not yet refillable, though some brands are now at least recyclable. Whatever the brand, if a bottled-gas stove malfunctions, your only option is to "fix it" by purchasing a new one, so you'd best carry a spare unit on a long trip. Still, these stoves simmer like crazy, and, because of their simplicity, they are popular with high-altitude climbers. Bottled-gas stoves generally work great down to +40°F; below that, they become increasingly inefficient.

WHITE GAS
Additive-free white gas (Coleman or MSR fuel) is the cleanest-burning and most popular fuel for all-season use in North America. These stoves pressurize liquid fuel in a small tank by pumping or heating. The fuel is forced through a vaporizing jet to a flame spreader or burner, producing fast, hot, economical BTUs. This type of stove has a lot of crucially integrated parts—most field disasters and makeshift repairs relate to white-gas or multifuel stoves.

MULTIFUEL
Multifuel stoves are essentially variations on the white-gas theme, with jets designed for burning alternative fuels, such as unleaded auto gas or kerosene. While the care and maintenance are generally the same, you must clean the burner jets on a multifuel stove more often because the less-

refined liquids (especially kero or diesel) tend to clog parts. Be sure to filter the fuel, too, and don't store any of these fuels in the stove. Solvents and detergents in automotive gas are especially prone to solidifying and gunking up your rig.

Pressurized Liquid-Fuel Stoves, Simplified

Despite myriad spinoffs and innovations, most liquid-fuel stoves still function along the same lines as the first-generation MSR X-GK or Svea 123 (many of which continue to fire faithfully thanks to diligent, maintenance-oriented owners). Liquid-fuel stoves all share the same general parts.

GENERIC GAS STOVE ANATOMY

1. The **fuel tank** is pressurized in one of two ways: by compressing air in the tank with a hand pump or by "self-pressurizing" when heated (fuel vapors expand inside a warmed tank). Tanks can be damaged by corrosion, by storing fuel inside, and by a faulty seal (usually caused by stripped threads at the filler cap, pump attachment, or other orifice).

2. A **control valve** allows pressurized fuel to travel through a fuel line to the jet and burner. The control valve may be damaged by heavy-handed treatment (i.e., by overtightening the knob, you lout) or by a cracked, worn O-ring seal.

3. In the **jet vaporizer** or **generator assembly** pressurized fuel passes through a smaller-than-pin-sized hole, which converts the liquid into a superfine spray that burns hot with a blue flame. The brass jet is the greatest troublemaker of all stove parts, bar none. Lighting and extinguishing the stove cause carbon buildup that clogs the jet from the inside, while the orifice is under attack from outside dreck like dirt, oatmeal, and boiled-over Ramen noodles. A dirty jet means poor fuel flow, a sputtering yellow flame, blackened pots, and generally poor results. Many stoves now offer a self-cleaning jet—really just a built-in stainless steel needle that pierces the jet—activated by fully opening the control valve or by tipping the burner upside down. Older styles require hand-pricking.

4. The **burner cup** and **flame spreader** disperse fuel so that it burns cleanly and evenly. Although this is the least-troublesome part of your stove, the flame spreader may expand and distort over time; check to see that the spreader is recessed from the burner cup (it should be).

PRIMING IS EVERYTHING

No matter what brand of liquid-fuel stove you use, priming and preheating the unit are the keys to both short- and long-term performance.

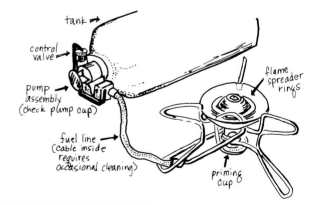

replace generator tube when clogged

pressure pump

control valve

Do not store fuel long-term in gas tank

tank

control valve

pump assembly (check pump cup)

fuel line (cable inside requires occasional cleaning)

flame spreader rings

priming cup

With self-pressurizing stoves, dribble an eye-dropper of fuel into the spirit cup only—don't douse the tank, as some crag-crazed dudes are wont to do. Some people prefer the control and cleanliness of priming paste for this job. As the paste or priming fuel burns, the flame preheats the fuel jet and pressurizes the tank. The priming flame also preheats the fuel vaporizer tube, so when you open the control valve you get a fine mist that burns blue rather than a smoky blast of yellow flame from raw fuel.

Don't leave control valve key on stove while burning

flame spreader

Priming a self-pressurizing stove ... fill the spirit cup only. Don't immolate the entire stove.

A stove with a remote, air-pressurized tank first requires pumping to compress the air in the tank, then priming and preheating the generator tube assembly, fuel vaporizer, and jets.

Allow the primer flame to burn down to candle-flame size, then open the fuel control valve to start the stove. If the flame goes out, open the valve about one-quarter turn and relight the stove. Do this quickly, before the preheated parts cool off; otherwise, you're likely to relight a hissing spray, which will be followed by a huge flare-up that will burn down your vestibule.

Once you've made it this far, you're in the pre-heat phase. Allow the stove to burn at its lowest level (with a blue flame) for one or two minutes before increasing the flame for full-blast cooking.

General Stove Maintenance

Whether you use your stove frequently or occasionally, it's essential that you follow the recommended maintenance procedures, particularly if your stove has a remote, pump-pressurized tank. Field "repairs" are more often just field cleanings, done much more easily at home on a sunny deck than in a howling wind with fumbling, cold fingers and a growling belly.

Tools for stove maintenance and replacement parts are tiny, virtually weightless, and essential to peace of mind on an extended trip. Carry your little bag of stove parts right in the sack with your stove, because sooner or later you are going to need them. Tape the jet-cleaning tool to your fuel bottle so it's always handy.

Annie adds one other, hard-learned tip: double-check the thick O-ring seal on fuel bottles too. Being a rocket scientist and all, she noticed Coleman fuel leaking from her spare fuel bottle (hey, at least she'd stowed the fuel separate from her food, so it wasn't gas-flavored rice that caught her attention). This should have been an easy fix, except that she was kayaking 50 miles out of Sitka, alone. She nursed the balky bottle a few days further by carefully carrying it upright, eventually transferring all the fuel to her stove's integral tank.

MAINTENANCE TIPS

- When assembling your stove, always lubricate the connecting parts with a little saliva or lip salve so you don't tear any tender O-rings.
- Whatever you do, do it gently, gently! Do not use excessive force to seal connections. You'll have a hard time separating the parts; you may even weaken them.
- O-rings act like the head gasket on your car. Replace them as often as once a year, since UV and penetrating solvents in fuels will dete-

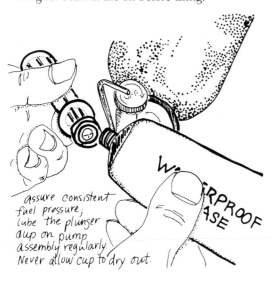

fuel tube cable *(handwritten label)*

Lubricate fuel cable with saliva before fitting into pump/tank. *(handwritten)*

riorate rubber compounds, increasing the fire hazard during stove operation.

- Oil the pressure-pump plungers as often as possible.

Dry, mangled leather pump cups produce no air pressure and slide with no resistance when you stroke the pump. You can use any light-grade machine or cooking oil; in a pinch, use lip salve, rubbing it in until the leather becomes soft and pliable. In the field, you can fashion a new pump cup with a swatch from the top of a leather boot tongue. Soak in the oil before using.

assure consistent fuel pressure; lube the plunger cup on pump assembly regularly. Never allow cup to dry out. *(handwritten)*

- Inspect the vaporizing jets regularly. The jet-pricker or cleaning needle in your stove's repair kit is made of stainless steel, while the jet itself is soft brass. The harder metal of the needle can enlarge the jet hole and cause flare-ups and irregular fuel flow. You may need to replace the jet at any time, so carry a spare in your repair kit. If carbon buildup is significant enough, your jet-pricker simply shoves a chunk of carbon back into the body of the jet rather than breaking it up. Remove the jet and hold it

up to a light to inspect; clean from the inside or replace.

- Use a Scotch-Brite pad to scour the flame reflector, fuel cable, or any other rusty or carbon-coated parts. Sometimes a generator tube will become sticky with fuel deposits. Clean these by soaking them in white gas, then scrubbing with the abrasive pad.

If you've cleaned the jet & still get sputtering flame... try heating the generator tube, then plunging into cold water. this breaks up carbon deposits *(handwritten)*

- Compressed air (the canned kind, used for blowing dust out of a computer keyboard) is also effective for removing grit from inside a fuel tube or other hard-to-reach parts.

- One of the best metal-cleaning compounds we've found is something sitting in your refrigerator: ketchup. The combination of vinegar and acidic tomato paste polishes tarnished brass, copper, and stainless steel to a high luster. Slather on a coat of ketchup, let it sit a few minutes, then burnish with a clean cloth. The hardest part is convincing bystanders that you are merely cleaning the stove, not preparing to eat it.

Cleaning tarnished brass with ketchup: slather, rub and rinse. When you see how shiny the stove comes out, will you ever put this stuff on a tofu-pup again?

TROUBLESHOOTING: LIKELY STOVE PROBLEMS

Insufficient priming. Burn performance is directly related to priming and preheating. An erratic or yellow flame is a telltale sign that your stove is too cold and cranky.

Fuel system leak. Air or fuel is escaping somewhere between the tank and jet.

For fuel leaks:

- Check all fuel tank orifices, including threads that may be stripped.
- Inspect connector seals and O-rings for damage, dryness, or decay.
- Examine the pump valve and seal for damage.
- Look to see if the jet hole is enlarged.

For air leaks:

- Make sure the pump is completely threaded into the fuel bottle.
- Check the pump assembly for cracks, a dry pump cup, fatigued seals, or damaged O-rings. Perform the pump test (see page 100).

Jet malfunction. A jet may be clogged by carbon or other debris. An enlarged jet (from aggressive cleaning) can allow too much fuel to pass, resulting in intermittent flare-ups. You may be using a jet designed for another type of fuel. Look carefully at the jet itself: kero jets are usually stamped with a tiny K. A gasping jet may simply be telling you that the tank is empty—check the fuel level or pump more air pressure.

Contaminated fuel. Fuel additives, condensation, and just plain sand in the tank will clog the fuel path and obstruct jets, resulting in an unreliable flame at best. Peer carefully into the empty fuel tank; if you see water droplets or sand particles, swish a little clean fuel around inside and discard (*not* into your auto tank—a new stove costs $50, while a new SUV runs five digits). Allow the stove tank to dry completely with the cap off before storing.

CAVITY CLEANER

Chris Townsend, Scottish author and inveterate backpacker who once hiked the Continental Divide from Canada to Mexico, offers this account:

"During a December crossing of the Cairngorm mountains in Scotland, my soup boiled over and blocked the jet of my camp stove. After I discovered I'd forgotten to bring a jet pricker, I tried various alternatives but they were all too thick. Blowing down the fuel line didn't work. Not far away was a small bothy (a simple mountain shelter) into which I'd seen two walkers enter. I made my way there to ask if they had a jet pricker. They didn't, but suggested trying a toothbrush bristle. I did, it worked, and it saved my trip."

DEFENSIVE OPERATING TIPS

Don't get your stove confiscated at the airport. Ticket agents often quiz backpack-toting travelers about their camp stoves. A stove in your luggage is subject to seizure unless the fuel tank is separated from the stove and is absolutely empty of fuel—no fumes allowed. Do not expect to dump fuel down the airport bathroom drain if a ticket agent calls you on this subject. Propane or butane canisters are subject to a blanket ban, and vigilant Euro X-ray baggage scanners *will* spot cans you thought were hidden. Bring the stove head and plan to purchase fuel cans after you arrive. If you have any doubts at all, call ahead and ask about the airline's policy.

Protect your stove from impact and set up your camp kitchen away from the traffic zone. The first day into a two-week river trip is no time to stomp on the burner.

No Substitutions! Do not substitute another manufacturer's tank; use only parts designed specifically for use with your stove model.

Don't overfill the tank. Fill to manufacturer-suggested levels always; overfilling can result in pressurization problems and dangerous flare-ups during priming. A too-small air space will cause the pressure to fluctuate excessively over a short period, resulting in an erratic, surging flame and requiring constant adjustment of the control valve.

Check for leaks with every refuel. With all valves shut off, turn both the tank and the burner upside down and watch for spreading gas at connecting points or dribbles from any orifice. If you spot a leak, do not use the stove. Repair it or munch cold oats.

Prime time is precious. Be mindful as you prime and preheat your stove. This is when most flare-ups and accidents occur, and it is crucial to the smooth operation of your burner. Follow instructions exactly.

Filter your fuel with a small, felt-lined funnel (available where you purchase your Coleman or MSR fuel). This screens out water and debris that will bedevil you sooner or later.

Strive for a blue burn. If you can't achieve a blue flame after a minute of operation, shut down the control valve on your stove and reprime it. Inefficient yellow or orange flames produce jet-clogging soot.

PUMP TEST

- Empty the fuel bottle. Screw the pump onto the empty bottle. Open the control valve and pump the plunger to empty any remaining fuel.
- Close the control valve and pump the plunger about 50 times to develop air pressure. You should feel resistance—if not, oil or replace the pump cup, then resume the test.
- Remove the plunger assembly at the bushing.
- Submerge into tub of water and watch for a steady stream of bubbles to spot the leak. Minor

initial bubbling at orifices is normal, but a steady stream indicates a poor seal.

Fuel Conservation
TRY A WINDSCREEN

Windscreens can conserve up to 50 percent of your fuel. Use a wraparound foil windscreen (available wherever you purchase a camp stove, or make one at home with heavy-gauge aluminum foil or flashing). Make sure the windscreen allows some ventilation, or your flame may sputter and die. Sometimes windscreens work too well, reflecting heat down to overheat tanks and fuel lines. Always monitor the temperature of your fuel tank—if it's hot to the touch, open the windscreen or turn off the stove for a few minutes and reorient your windscreen.

BLACKEN YOUR POTS

You might be employing fuel-saving cookware without realizing it. Simply using a lid decreases radiant heat loss, while a blackened pot accelerates heat absorption (see page 103). Another fuel economizer is MSR's Heat Exchanger, a corrugated aluminum band that fits around your cookpot to channel hot air around the sides.

SIMMERING HINTS

Simmering is notoriously difficult for a liquid-fuel stove with a control valve located tankside rather than at the burner. The steady, low flame required to simmer tends to flutter and sputter, clogging parts and generally frustrating the chef.

One method for simmering is to start with low fuel pressure (fewer strokes of the pump) or begin with a half-full fuel bottle. This means you'll compress a larger air space; as the fuel is depleted, the extra compressed air prevents the internal pressure from fluctuating (and the flame from sputtering), so you'll face less control-valve adjusting.

To extract a passable simmer from its blow-

A fire-blackened coffeepot heats faster, making this crucial beverage in record time.

Cold-Weather and High-Altitude Operation

At high altitudes or in wickedly cold conditions the temptation is strong to cook in your tent—something every stove manufacturer explicitly warns against. Peter Hickner, of Feathered Friends, tells about a nameless climber whose stove melted through his bag, sleeping pad, tent floor, and a good bit of glacier before wheezing to a permanent halt.

If conditions force you to cook inside a small space, do so in a firepit dug just inside your tent vestibule, so you can kick the thing out the door before your entire tent poofs. If using white gas, be especially careful not to spill any supercooled liquid gas on bare skin when refueling. The resulting instant frostburn is incredibly painful, not to mention dangerous. Likewise, liquid fuel can blister or permanently contaminate your high-tech tent and clothing fabrics, so refuel outside your tent. Always check for leaks by turning the fuel tank upside down before priming and lighting the stove.

Insulate your fuel bottle from snow with foam or a mitten. Impurities—especially the paraffin in kerosene—can freeze and inhibit fuel flow to the burner.

torch-like stoves, MSR recommends operating the burner at a high rate for about five minutes, then slowly adjusting the control valve to simmer. MSR-challenged Dave recommends his own trail-tested simmering technique: fire up the stove to red-hot, then turn the fuel valve off and back on every few seconds. We've found that the easiest way to slow-cook a cheese fondue is to insulate the cooking pan with a metal spacer or a *plaque radiant* designed to diffuse heat or to partially fill a larger pan or skillet with water to act as a chafing pan/double boiler.

Use a skillet to insulate your cookpot

Small-Space Safety

Alpinists often rely on nonpressurized alcohol stoves as the only safe alternative to butane canisters. Alcohol's low volatility and quick evaporation when spilled make this type of stove a certain, if slow, choice for cooking in a tent, snow cave, or boat cabin.

Faster boiling times make bottled-gas camp stoves more desirable than alcohol-burners, and the canisters actually become more efficient at higher altitudes (above about 15,000 feet), since lower atmospheric pressure allows the gas to vaporize at lower temperatures.

However, insulating the canister is the key to efficient cooking in cold temperatures at lower altitudes. Efficiency drops considerably as the fuel (and pressure) is depleted, so warming the bottle is necessary to keep the stove burning hot. Isobutane seems to offer more consistent fuel delivery than butane or butane-propane blends, but it pays to follow a few warming tips if you're using stove cartridges.

To insulate and increase the efficiency of your bottled gas,

- Use a foam beverage insulator for the fuel bottle (or make your own with a piece of an old foam pad and duct tape).
- Boost the flame by holding the gas cartridge in your hands to warm it.
- Sleep with the canisters in your bag, and carry them next to your back in the pack.
- Wrap a band of copper flashing around the canister, pointing the tail end to the stove flame.

To boost fuel pressure, dip butane canister in warm — never boiling — water.

Hand-warm butane canister to increase fuel pressure

Butane canisters need a little help from their friends for more efficient operation in cold weather or high altitudes.

Transferred heat can be insulated with foam padding as suggested above.

- Hold the fuel can over heating water, even dipping it into the warming — but never boiling — liquid.
- Windscreens are crucial in the cold — a windbreak of snow or rocks will go a long way toward making your stove work more efficiently.
- Carry a firepan or nonflammable base to insulate the stove burner from the snow. Pan lids and old license plates are popular, and so is the scrap of aluminum flashing from your repair kit. Some stoves offer suspension kits so you can hang the rig from a ledge, or — *gasp* — inside the tent (but you didn't hear it from us).
- When you're melting snow, start by melting just a handful to liquid, and only then fill the pan with snow. The liquid helps the snow melt faster and keeps a hot flame from scorching your pan before there's any water to cool the metal. Mound snow in the middle of the pan, don't pack it up the sides — you lose too much heat that way.

PACKING UP

- **Blow out the flame** after you've closed off the gas rather than allowing it to flicker and die. Once the flame is out, the lingering raw gas fumes will cleanse the jet.
- **Release the fuel pressure** in the tank before packing. Do this only when the stove has fully cooled. This minimizes pressure and the likelihood of leaks in transit.
- When dismantling your stove, **wipe off any fuel dribbles**, and carefully store your fuel bottles away from any food. An isolated, outer pack pocket is ideal.
- **Freshen your fuel.** Long-term stored fuel suffers from condensation and leaves a junky residue, and your stove suffers in turn. Pour off any unused fuel before storing or shipping your stove. Swish a few tablespoons of clean gas around inside the tank, then drain it off. Leave the cap

off and allow any remaining drops of fuel to completely evaporate. Screw the cap back on loosely.
- Store the stove and the tanks in a **cool, dry place**.

Get the Most from Your Cookware

- Rounded sides heat (and clean up) more efficiently than squared-off corners.
- Blackened pans deliver heat more evenly and even save a little fuel. If your cook set is shiny new, you can cheat a little by purchasing some black, heat-resistant stove paint at the hardware store and coating the outside of your pots. Heat up several rounds of water in the newly painted pots before using them for cooking. You can also blacken pans by filling them with water and setting them on red-hot coals. The water prevents the metal from overheating and losing temper.
- Nonstick coated pans equal easier cleanup, less waste, and better sanitation.
- Never plunge a hot pan into cool water (likewise, avoid pouring cold water into a really hot pan) or you risk ruining the pan's temper.
- Always scour gunky stuff from pan bottoms immediately with a scratchy pad, sand, or fire ash. Even stains left from cooked-on food can cause irregular hot spots that cause later creations to stick and burn.

Cast-Iron Cookware

Bargain barns and secondhand tool shops abound with iron treasure. Our corn-pone biscuit mold and mini Dutch oven were rescued from a forlorn state and now serve paddling appetites with dignity. A thin film of rust marks a pot worth saving; if the pan in question is pitted or flaky with rusty scales, don't bother.

Most rust can be worked off with steel wool or a wire "toothbrush," but the easiest way to prepare the pan for seasoning is with oven cleaner (see appendix B, Low-Tox Cleaning Solutions, beginning on page 216). After removing as much rust as possible, evenly coat all surfaces of the pan with the cleaner. Wrap inside a plastic bag and allow to sit overnight. Wear rubber gloves to scrub away the grime in a sink or on newspaper. Clean thoroughly with the hot water method (*below*) before seasoning.

SEASONING

Despite their weight, cast-iron skillets and Dutch ovens remain staples for backcountry chefs who like to cook over an open fire or for groups. Unfortunately, the secret to seasoning these beasts nearly disappeared with the last sourdough trapper, and many wannabe traditionalists are stumped by sticking, rusty pans. To season new or salvaged cast-iron cookware,

1. Start with a clean, dry skillet, pot, lid, muffin pan, etc.
2. Coat the inner and outer surfaces lightly with mild cooking oil.
3. Place the pan in an oven preheated to 350°F and heat until the oil just begins to smoke.
4. Remove and allow to cool slowly.
5. Rub the entire pan with a soft, lint-free cloth.
6. Repeat the procedure three times to achieve a darkened, seasoned, dependable, nonstick pan.

CLEANING CAST IRON

It's true: you shouldn't use soap to clean your favorite cast-iron cookware. Heat an inch or more of water to boiling in the offending pan to draw out any lingering flavors. Scour with plain steel wool (not a presoaped pad) or synthetic scratchy pad. For nasty, gummed-on chili, scrub gently at the spot, using baking soda as a last resort. Rinse with clean water and dry immediately with a soft cloth. Check scrubbed spots that may have been stripped of seasoning and reoil if necessary.

CHAPTER 10

Water
Filters

The bottle had a fitting for a filter in the screw-cap. We made a filter but it proved to be the only item of our whole store which was definitely useless. It consisted of two pieces of wire gauze found in the famous rubbish-heap near the camp but boiled and otherwise disinfected, containing layers of compressed powdered charcoal and dressing muslin.

Felice Benuzzi, *No Picnic on Mount Kenya*

A two-week paddling trip into the galactic beaver country of Ontario's James Bay lowlands quickly exposed the limitations of our group's water filters. The river ran rich from lodges and leaves, full of tannin and the murk of the northern forest. After a few days the task of pumping 6 liters per pit stop became, well, a real pump—hardly a rest for cadence-weary canoeists. Peter, who had filtered his way through Pakistan without straining a vessel, was amazed when his trusty filter functioned only a few days before choking.

An equally frustrated Tom, our resident engineer, tinkered with his filter on a windy beach. Soon he bounced up the bank with a pail of water. "I've figured it out," he beamed, "you just remove all the elements and the pump works great."

Pump water filters, notoriously finicky widgets even under the best conditions, are a testament to the advantages of boiling. However, scant or nonexistent fuel—usually in the very places where you need water treatment most—makes filters essential traveling gear.

Most filters provide physical, rather than chemical, treatment. A filter that also "purifies" implies germicidal action, usually with iodine, in addition to physical filtering.

Unfortunately, filters often do their job a little too well, as in Tom's case, and clog. Ceramic filter elements offer the longest service life of filters on the market today, but other types combining activated charcoal, iodine resin, or microporous membranes are affordable and viable options. While effective, certain of these Johnny-come-lately filters have more parts, require more care, and—curse Murphy—tend to break down frequently. Others are designed with less mechanical complexity and longer element life for easier maintenance.

No matter what they're made of, all pump filters will clog over time—if they don't, how can they be doing their job? The key to satisfactory performance is to reduce the amount of sediment pumped through the unit. Conscientious use, frequent cleaning, diligent storage habits, and periodic replacement of filter

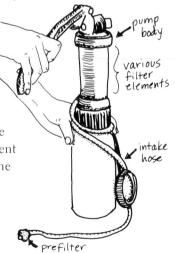

pump body

various filter elements

intake hose

prefilter

- Allow water to settle in a bag or pail before filtering; draw breakfast water the night before if possible. Silt that settles out won't clog the filter.
- Use a prefilter. These are usually sponge-type strainers that intercept big particles that would quickly clog the main filter element. Easy to clean, a prefilter postpones inevitable dismantling and is well worth its modest additional cost.
- Pump from still pools, not swift-running streams. Moving water suspends more stuff that'll clog your filter before its time.

- Pump the unit dry after each use; shake out the hoses.
- Carry the filter in a mesh storage bag that allows moisture to evaporate.
- In freezing temperatures, sleep with your filter (sealed in a plastic bag) to prevent moisture from icing inside the elements. Though freezing does not hurt your filter, ice crystals will slow down its operation considerably.
- Discard the first few cups of water coursed through your filter with every use. This flushes out any debris from the outlet, as well as stale flavors.

elements are the price of no-worries drinking water.

Filter Field Care

Regular attention in the field ensures that your filter operates smoother and longer before the inevitable clog. As with stoves, it is *essential* that you read your filter's operating instructions and follow them religiously. If pumping becomes difficult, stop and clean the filter elements. Wash your hands thoroughly with soap and filtered water before and after cleaning.

If you own a ceramic filter, you're in luck—cleaning is dead-simple: remove the cylinder and wipe dry. Sometimes really dirty water will leave a film that's easily scrubbed off with a stiff brush.

To clean a depth filter with variable elements (the most common type currently available), don't try to forcibly remove any parts. Some filters require only that you swish the cartridge in clear water and then rinse the pump body. Gently scrape, brush, or flush any removable mesh screens. If a screen appears stained or changes color, replace it. Scrape carbon cartridges clean with a knife.

Some pump filters feature a pressure-relief valve that bypasses the filter element when clogged. This protects delicate filters from being punctured by the pump's high water pressure, which would then blast untreated water straight through the unit. If your filter starts squirting water out of the pressure-relief port, it's time to clean it.

Most manufacturers suggest sanitizing a filter once you've handled the separate elements. Do this by dropping the filter into boiling water or by flushing with a bleach solution, as described here.

Carry a small bottle brush to keep your water filter clean in the field

Ye Olde Bleach Flush

Running a weak solution of bleach through your filter after a trip and before long-term storage is a good practice. The diluted chlorine ensures that any hang-dog protozoa won't colonize inside your filter elements.

1. Mix 1 quart water with 2 teaspoons household bleach.
2. Remove the prefilter and soak in the solution.

3. Pump to cycle the bleach solution through the filter.
4. Pump the filter 10 strokes to remove any lingering stale water.
5. Dry the filter with a soft cloth, then allow it to air-dry overnight.
6. Do not store in a sealed container.

Didn't Clean Your Filter before Storage?

You're guilty. You came home from that last trip and just stuffed your pump into a drawer. Now you're leaving for the mountains and the filter smells like a science project from your refrigerator. Heck, it *is* a science project—full of mold and bacterial growth. Is there any hope?

The answer depends on your filter type and, as always, on the manufacturer's instructions. For the typical depth filter, there's a chance that Ye Olde Bleach Flush, above, will bail you out. For some ceramic filters, you can just pop the unit apart and dunk the ceramic element in boiling water to kill the cooties.

In any case, wash the entire unit—all parts, hoses, etc.—in hot water and dish detergent, then rinse and drip-dry, like you'd wash the used camping dishes after a trip (you *do* wash the dishes, don't you?). Some makers recommend boiling filter elements even during a trip—again, check your owner's manual. For others, there's zero hope once the filter's contaminated. Just bite the bullet and buy a new element on your way to the trailhead. But cheer up, you won't neglect the storage-cleaning ritual again.

CHAPTER 11

Knives and Multitools

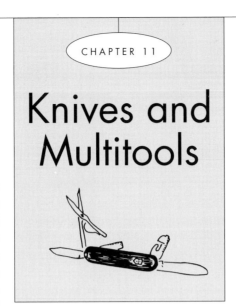

Annie's first knife was a Swiss Army Spartan, a present from her dad. That simple but versatile knife stayed with her for a dozen years before slipping from an aerie into a jumble of boulders. Our friend Liz didn't skip a beat. "I'll make you a present of mine," she volunteered, "they're cheap in Germany" (where she lives)—thereby sparing Annie a sentimental loss by an equally sentimental gain. A rawhide umbilical cord now secures her well-worn German Swiss Army knife to rucksack or belt loop.

Part of the survivor's ten essentials, and certainly a pivotal repair tool, your knife serves a hundred purposes and asks little in return. For some, honing their constant companion is an important ritual; others break down and attend to their knife only when it's so polluted with peanut butter and packed with pocket lint that it refuses to fully close, or to open at all.

Cleaning

During college, Annie often whiled away boring lecture hours with that godsend, the Swiss Army toothpick, meticulously removing crammed crud from the slots and recesses of her Spartan while daydreaming of wine-and-cheese repasts high and far away. She'd picked up basic blade-honing skills years earlier from Uncle Herb, the family chef and connoisseur.

Though cleaning a folding knife is certainly a fine pastime for long layovers, this task is made supremely simple by dropping a fully opened knife into your dishwasher or into a pot of just-boiled water for a minute or so. Extended boiling risks turning your knife into a Dali-esque thing with drooping plastic handle. (If you've made this error, send the knife to the manufacturer, who will replace the handle, no questions asked.)

Myriad shapes (left to right): Lockback folding hunter; Swiss Army; one-piece sheath knife; Scottish "skean dubh" dress knife; French folding picnic knife; traditional 3-bladed pocket knife; compact locking pocket knife with serrated blade—emergency harness knife for climbers and paddlers.

A quick boil also invites long-stuck knives to loosen up, so you can get at a corroded blade or joint. Cleaning can be done in the field, of course, but if you expect your knife to fix, slice, pare, whittle, punch, or bore, you'll need to clean it at home.

Once you've removed the fetid detritus with an old toothbrush, work the blades or tools in and out. If you use your knife a lot, chances are the oils from your hands have kept the appendages in good working order. Otherwise, apply a little light-grade machine or cooking oil to the hinges; work back and forth, then wipe off excess oil.

In the field, scour a stained, rusty, or gummed-up blade with wood ash from your campfire. (The wood ash is mildly abrasive; it also works great for scrubbing your cook set.) For fun, try ketchup; it's highly acidic and de-grimes a blade in nothing flat. This is a fun campfire trick to show your buddies that rarely fails to impress someone so much that he or she swears off eating the red goop for life.

RUST NEVER SLEEPS

Dave oiled his leather belt sheath before heading off on a paddling adventure where, on the first day, he dumped. Even though the exterior of the knife sheath was oiled for water repellency, the inside was not; his sheath remained damp for the duration of the trip, spawning a thick coat of rust on his prized multitool.

Treat the inside of a your knife sheath with an aqueous leather treatment or heat a small amount of beeswax and pour it into a warmed sheath—work it in using a toothbrush. Excess wax certainly won't harm the knife, but it could make for slippery handling. For trips where you're certain to get wet, consider switching to a quick-drying nylon sheath.

Some knife manufacturers combine stainless steel blades with a weight-saving aluminum body. Left unused, or aided by exposure to salt water, the dissimilar metals will corrode by galvanic action, manifested by a furry, white film on metal surfaces, especially at hinge points. This type of knife requires regular lubrication to maintain easy operation.

DISCOLORATION

Really hard steel blades will darken with a blue patina as they age. This natural rust-proofing should be allowed to remain. High-acid fruits may leave stains on softer, carbon steel blades—nothing to worry about.

STICKY LOCKBACK

Wood-handled lockbacks (knives with blades that "lock" in the open position)

Toolbox in your belt: modern multitools now compete with your favorite Swiss Army. All those appendages need regular maintenance.

are known to swell with humidity, making it just about impossible to extract the blade with your fingers—such knives are best left at home when you go on a saltwater voyage. Other lockbacks may stiffen in a similar curmudgeonly fashion. The French knifemaker Opinel recommends using the Savoyard Knack to open the lockback: grasp the hinge end, blade side down, and give the opposite end of the knife a sharp tap against a hard surface. The blade tip will pop out.

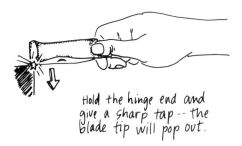

Hold the hinge end and give a sharp tap -- the blade tip will pop out.

DON'T PRY

Your knife is not a crowbar, screwdriver, or hammer. Asking it to perform these functions will certainly endanger the blade. More than one innocent bystander has been nicked by the soaring, sheared-off tip of a prying blade.

Storage

Storing it in a damp sheath is the most destructive act you can perpetrate against your trusty blade. Fabric or leather sheaths draw and hold moisture, which translates to rust. Store your knife unsheathed, or consider this option: thoroughly clean and oil the knife, wipe it dry, then sprinkle it with wood ash and wrap it in a soft cotton cloth.

Gaining an Edge

Whenever we're cooking in someone else's kitchen, we can always count on one thing: the knives will be dull! A sharp knife is easier to handle and is vastly safer than a dulled, nicked blade. A dull blade means you have to rely on force instead of finesse to cut. There's nothing more frustrating and painful than slicing into your knuckle instead of a crusty boule.

One dazzling July day Annie was happily frying up some quesadillas on a Maine beach while her ten-year-old charge was gathering driftwood. She looked up to see young Master Will standing before her, gull-white, then saw why: he'd nearly sliced two fingers off with his dull jackknife. As recognition dawned, she was oblivious to the fact that the sizzling skillet was branding her thigh. In this case, two serious first-aid incidents could have been avoided if she'd checked the condition of the lad's knife.

Many people are stymied by the process of knife sharpening, probably because it's so simple. Although there are many ceramic sharpening gadgets available, nothing gives an edge like a stone. A sharpening steel may work well for skilled blade

As your grandpa always warned, "Nuthin's more dangerous than a dull knife or a blunt axe!"

mystics, but anyone with a large stone can sharpen any steel tool, including scissors, chisels, axes, or machetes. Sharpening a serrated blade requires a special file and patient practice.

Learning to hone blades on a stone is a matter of determining what sort of edge you need and applying even pressure at a controlled angle. A narrower angle means a more delicately finished blade.

STONES

A rectangular honing stone can be purchased at a hardware store or from most fishing outfitters. A small, thin, 3-inch stone isn't a bad choice for field use when skiing, ice climbing, or fishing. Large stones usually have a coarse side for working out burrs and roughening the blade and a fine side to achieve a sleek, finished edge.

The Stone Is Too Dry, Dear Liza

If you never got it from the folk song "There's a Hole in the Bucket," a honing stone should be

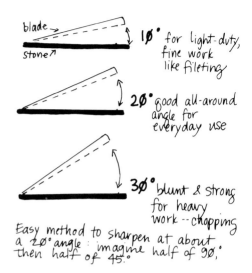

SHARPENING ANGLES

blade →
stone ↗

10° for light-duty, fine work like fileting

20° good all-around angle for everyday use

30° blunt & strong for heavy work -- chopping

Easy method to sharpen at about a 20° angle: imagine half of 90, then half of 45.

lubricated with oil or water before you begin sharpening. This gives the stone a film that protects it from grit and metal shavings and reduces friction.

THE STROKES

Shaving Stroke. Elementary and effective, this is the stroke to teach a young person. Pretend you're slicing a thin layer from the stone.

Circular Stroke. This is best for large, long blades. Begin at the point and work toward the tang.

Figure-8 Stroke. Advanced only. This stroke requires focused attention to pressure and angle, but the alternating licks ensure even treatment to both sides of the blade.

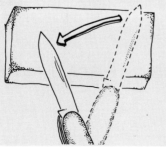

The shaving stroke. Draw the blade toward you

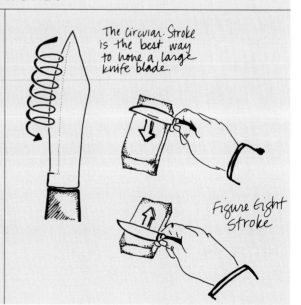

The Circular Stroke is the best way to hone a large knife blade.

Figure Eight Stroke

Hudson Bay Camping Axe

Hudson Bay Kindling Axe

Sharpening Tips:
How to Get Way Honed

- Keep your fingers clear of the honing surface!
- For a truly sharp knife, start with the coarse surface of the stone, always using an equal number of strokes on each side of the blade. Touchups require just a few strokes on the fine surface.
- Stainless steel blades may take twice as long to sharpen as carbon steel blades, but even then the process shouldn't take more than a few minutes.
- Steady, even pressure on the stone is key. Never push so hard that the blade takes a bend. Ease the pressure with successive rounds and finish with a light touch.
- Count your strokes out loud, or establish a 5- or 10-stroke pattern.
- Wipe off the blade each time you start another round of strokes.
- Test the keenness by dragging the blade lightly across the back of your thumbnail to produce a thin shaving of nail. Apply no pressure—just the weight of the knife is plenty. For the squeamish: the knife should slice smoothly and effortlessly through paper.

Test a blade edge by dragging gently across your fingernail.

AXE SHARPENING

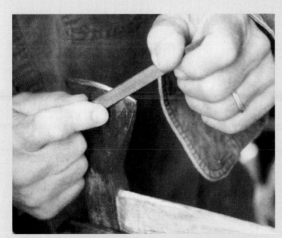

Step 1. Clamp the axe firmly in a workbench vise for the best finger retention. Work the file along the blade at the angle matching original edge. You don't want it too thin.

Step 2. Touch up the edge with a whetstone to remove filing burrs and "hone 'er sharp as a fishwife."

BLADE SHARPENING: KEEN AND CLEAR

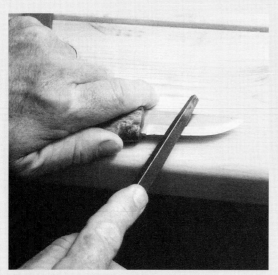

1. Remove nicks and burrs first with a file. Continued filing restores the desired blade angle.

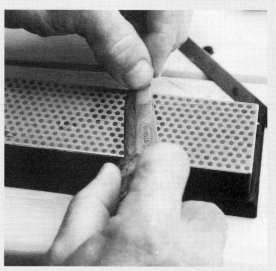

2. Hone the edge on a sharpening block lubed with light oil or water. Carefully match the blade angle established with the file.

3. Strop the knife on a wide leather belt, working the blade back and forth with even pressure

4. With a knife this sharp, you're ready for the next great blackout—who needs an electric razor!

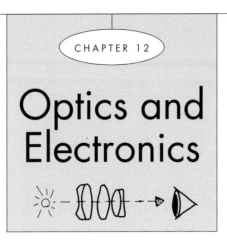

CHAPTER 12

Optics and Electronics

"Everyone should have his own point of view." "Isn't this everyone's Point of View?" asked Tock, looking around curiously. "Of course not," replied Alec, sitting himself down on nothing. "It's only mine, and you certainly can't always look at things from someone else's Point of View."

Norton Juster, *The Phantom Tollbooth*

Scotty Simper, redoubtable soundman for PBS's *Anyplace Wild* film crew, was in a definite pickle. Scotty is a wizard at keeping electronics alive despite the most trying outdoor conditions, but during this January ice-climbing shoot on New Hampshire's Mount Washington he was losing the battle.

His sound gear runs on a passel of batteries, and he'd carefully surrounded his sound mixer and wireless audio transmitters with chemical heat packs to keep everything crankin' warm. Trouble was, wind-driven snow kept filtering into the sound bag, melting on the warm black boxes and one by one shorting them out.

At camp that night Scotty dried everything with his last stash of heat packs, then allowed it all to go stone cold, which wasn't difficult since the temperature was a rosy –14°F. The next day the chilled gear all worked fine, though his battery life was much reduced. By day's end spindrift once again coated the black boxes, but since they were at "room temperature," the snow didn't melt, the electronics kept working, and our ice-climbing episode had terrific audio.

When you bring specialized instruments into the backcountry, you challenge fate. Wet weather, knocks, and rocks don't mix well with lights, binoculars, laptop computers, GPS units, walkie-talkies, still cameras, and video camcorders. Yet for many travelers the experience just wouldn't be the same without the advantages of their cherished widgets: light after twilight, magnified vision, permanent memories on film or tape.

When we asked regular backcountry lens and electronics users what their favorite repair item was, without exception the answer was a tiny screwdriver—a jeweler's or eyeglass screwdriver, like the little screwdriver that slips into the corkscrew on a Swiss Army knife. The next favorite tool: plenty of fresh batteries. After that, consensus held that there's not much a layperson can do to repair electronic or precision equipment. Long equipment life in the field really depends on preventive maintenance and cultivated rituals for use, with particular attention to dry, shockproof storage and transport and careful weather protection while the gear's in action.

Binoculars
GENERAL INSPECTION AND CLEANING

Inspect lenses regularly—dirty optics directly affect binocular performance. Fingerprints, grit, and lint all contribute to fuzzy images and, if left unattended, to scratched coatings and lenses. Keep debris from collecting on lenses by storing your binoculars in their case with dust covers on.

The outer, glass-to-air lens surfaces of better binoculars have one or more antireflective coatings, which act like sunglasses to reduce glare. If left uncleaned, fingerprints and skin oils can permanently damage this coating and your views. Clean lenses as recommended in the sidebar on page 118.

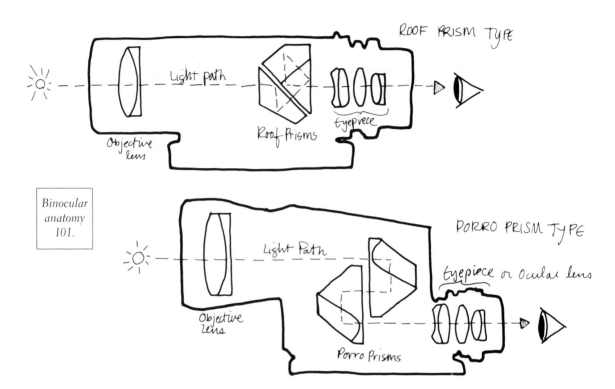

Binocular anatomy 101.

Fold eye cups back to access lenses.

A very light application of silicone will condition the cleaned fold on eye cups.

Brush or swab any grit away from rotating parts.

Quality binoculars have an aluminum body with some sort of rubber or plastic armor that provides shock absorption as well as weather protection. Usually this armor extends beyond the body to shield objective lenses and to form eye cups—channels where grit, salt, and moisture like to deposit themselves. Use your lens brush to remove any loose dust, then clean with a cotton swab moistened with a little clean, fresh water.

Eye cups, which fold over like turtlenecks for use with eyeglasses, tend to crack with age. A little silicone lubricant or 303 Protectant applied with a cotton swab will keep them supple, but take care not to get any silicone on the lens. Wipe off any excess lubricant and allow to air-dry thoroughly before storing or using.

Center-focus knobs and barrel hinges that seem too stiff for easy operating can also be spritzed with a little lubricant—TriFlow, with the directional straw fit into the spray jet, is ideal for this. Apply a few drops and work the mechanism back and forth, then clean off any grit and excess lubricant with a toothpick or the corner of a cloth. Lubricating the diopter ring is not recommended.

WATERLOGGED

What's the last sound your binoculars ever make on a paddling trip?

Ploop.

Most binocular troubles are water-related, caused either by the insidious enemy—condensation—or by the obvious threat of a complete submersion.

If your lenses appear blurry but aren't fogged on the outside, hold the binoculars at arm's length and look through the objective lenses (never into direct sunlight). You can easily spot drops of moisture or crooked lenses.

The key to preventing condensation is to avoid dramatic temperature fluctuations, especially bringing cold optics into warm, damp rooms. If you enter a snug hut after a snowy ski tour, leave the binoculars in their case to acclimate gradually to the temperature and humidity. Sealing optics inside a plastic bag before entering a warm space will minimize moisture buildup. While still outside, place the binoculars or camera in a Ziploc bag, suck the air out, and seal. Once inside, condensation forms on the *outside* of the plastic barrier.

Store binoculars in their case to protect them from water and temperature extremes. For long-term storage, place binoculars in a plastic bag with a packet of desiccant or silica gel (a camera-shop item) to absorb any moisture.

Mindful storage can keep moisture from penetrating the binocular housing and staining the lenses or prisms from inside, but nothing prepares them for a catastrophic dunking. A friend who is a sea kayak guide tells an epic tale of disassembly after his father's vintage WWII binocs had endured a capsize. After careful dissection and a freshwater bath, Chess managed to replace each lens, using a fork as a spanner, to the amazement of the native population.

Nitrogen-sealed waterproofed binoculars should not be futzed with—return them to the maker for service or replacement. However, basic models can be taken apart by humans, even though no manufacturer would recommend it. If you're in the field and your lenses are clouded and useless, you may be inspired to attempt the de- and reconstruction process. *Remember the first law of tinkering: Save all the pieces, in order. Clean and dry each piece before replacing.*

DOUBLE IMAGE: IT COULD BE YOU

If you drop your binoculars or they clonk around in your truck, chances are they'll become misaligned, or lose their *collimation.* The right and left sides should be in complete alignment, or you'll experience double images, which in turn will cause eyestrain and headaches.

Many people can't tell if their binoculars are

CENTRAL FOCUS ADJUSTMENT: BINOCULARS

- With both eyes open, set the space of the barrels by moving them back and forth until you see one image circle.
- Focus on a subject about 50 feet away (don't focus through window glass, which creates distortion).
- Cover the objective lens on the side with diopter adjustment (usually the right side) with your hand. Turn the center focus wheel until you see a crisp, detailed image with your left eye.
- Lower the binoculars and rest your eyes for a moment.

- Without touching the focus wheel and while viewing the same object, cover the opposite lens, then rotate the diopter ring until you gain a sharp focus with your right eye.
- Look through both lenses simultaneously. If the two images do not produce a sharp focus, or one eye feels as if it's being "pulled," repeat the process.
- If you can't achieve a comfortable focus after several tries, your binoculars are probably out of alignment and should be serviced by the manufacturer.

Block light on diopter lens, focus with opposite lens

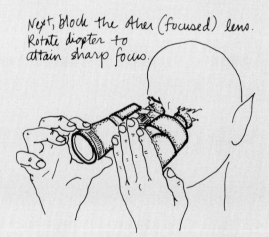

Next, block the other (focused) lens. Rotate diopter to attain sharp focus.

Custom-focus your binoculars with the diopter setting.

out of alignment because they really don't know how to regulate the diopter setting in the first place (see sidebar, above).

Still Cameras and Video Cameras

It's amazing how otherwise upright citizens can treat a camera in the most unspeakable manner, yet walk about with head up, oblivious to this cavalier, amoral behavior. Unfortunately, many of us forget that a camera is a precision instrument, to be treated gently, respectfully. No matter how little attention you pay to the mechanics of your optics, at least follow a few preventive rules. Remember, all modern cameras—still or video, cheap or expensive—require care for their electronics as well as their optics. The following instructions apply equally to still or video devices.

A skylight filter protects the camera lens from moisture, dirt, and impact.

permanently damage the seal . . . which you won't discover until you haul out a wet camera just when you most need a dry one.

Rig your camera case for comfort, safety, and quick-draw convenience during outings. Waistbelt rigging can be awkward when you set your pack down in the dust, rocks, or snow. Our pro outdoor photographer buddies almost all prefer mounting their soft camera cases in a frontal quick-draw position, clipped to the D-rings on their backpack shoulder straps.

PROTECT FROM IMPACT

There's a reason cameras come with neck or wrist straps. Shorten the strap to keep the camera from swinging into things. Use a 1-A or skylight lens filter—think of it as a $10 insurance policy for your $200 lens.

On the trail, always coddle your camera in a padded camera bag or hard-sided case. This may seem obvious to some, but we can think of half a dozen friends who toss their cameras on the car seat or in a rucksack with the attitude that a case is too much trouble, too much weight. There are hundreds of fine, streamlined, and specialized camera cases available at competitive prices. Find one that suits your style and use it: we've had particularly good luck with soft-sided cases from LowePro and Sundog.

In our film and video work we've always relied on hard-sided cases from Pelican and LowePro to protect hundreds of thousands of dollars worth of delicate (and rented) electronics in tropical heat, glacial cold, rain-forest damp, and the insidious gritty grime of deserts and caves. The key to obtaining the best performance from hard-sided cases is to make sure no grit or small camera parts (straps, buckles, etc.) are trapped in the lid's O-ring seal. If you force the case closed over these tidbits, you may

PROTECT FROM HEAT

Excessively high temperatures (such as in a car parked in the sun on a summer day) can damage a camera's internal electronics as well as cook any loaded or unloaded film. Again, the foam padding in a good field camera case helps prevent heat-related failures. This is a good argument for choosing a light-colored case, which minimizes solar heat gain.

PROTECT FROM MOISTURE

Everyone consulted for this chapter—professional photographers, lab specialists, and manufacturers—cited condensation as any camera's worst enemy in the field. When you bring your cold camera into a warm room, water vapor condenses on lens surfaces and wreaks havoc with lenses, electronics, and film. Unattended condensation may also breed fungus on internal lens surfaces and rust inside the camera body. Fortunately, you can combat the moisture menace in many ways.

Use the case. Carrying an unprotected camera inside your coat only contributes to fogged lenses as you crank out body heat and moisture. Foam padding in a hard or soft camera case insulates the camera from both impact and temperature changes. Leave the camera in its case and allow it to slowly reach ambient temperature. Treat the case with a water-repellent coating for even more weather protection. Better yet, seal it in a giant Ziploc bag or roll-top dry bag.

Here's one field professional's favorite way to **warm the camera** while minimizing the risk of condensation:

1. Remove the batteries to keep them warm and functioning.
2. Place the cold camera in a Ziploc bag, then suck the air out before sealing. Water condenses outside of the bag, not on the camera.

If you don't need to change the camera's temperature, don't. This may mean leaving the camera (in its protective case) outside or in your tent vestibule. Remember to remove the batteries to keep them warm.

Avoid heavy breathing. A rugged portage was particularly steamy, muddy, and otherwise memorable, but the photos came out entirely forgettable: Annie's elevated body temperature had completely fogged the lens. Carelessly exhaled breath and holding the eyepiece up to your eye for unbroken periods are typical causes of condensation.

Keep a silica gel packet inside your camera bag or dry box. Remember to periodically dry the silica in a low-temperature oven or on a sun-heated boulder. We've also relied extensively on commercial desiccant packs like Moisture Muncher Camera Dry—available at pro-camera supply houses—to keep electronics happy in unfriendly climes. The packs absorb up to 20 percent of their weight in water. Figure on one Moisture Muncher pack per cubic foot of drybox space. These packs, while expensive, are also rechargeable by a light baking in the oven.

PROTECT FROM DIRT AND DUST

Preserve your lens. Use a clear or skylight filter all the time, and use a lens cap. A pain, you say? Purchase a leash for your lens cap (or make your own)

LENS CLEANSE

Fingerprints will acid-etch the lens glass and coating if left unattended. Clean as soon as you spot them. Other nonadhesive substances that blur an image are dust, sand, and water vapor, all of which may contribute to corrosion and even fungus if ignored.

A lens-cleaning kit (available from any photo supply house) should include a small blower brush, lens cleaner, and lens cleaning papers. You might also include a camel hair paintbrush, reserved especially for the purpose. Find a clean, soft, lint-free cloth to use on your lenses. In the field, whatever fleece you happen to be wearing will suffice.

Optical glass is softer than ordinary glass and scratches more easily. For this reason, attempts to clean the lens in the field may damage the surface. Use a clear filter to cover your lens, and you'll only need to clean the filter.

Never use alcohol to clean any lens—it may act as a solvent and destroy coatings. Also, do not apply lens-cleaning fluid directly to the lens glass; place a little on a lens tissue, then use the moist tissue to clean the lens.

Richard Botley, at our neighborhood photo lab, insists that you should *never* clean a dry lens, or you risk permanently scratching and damaging it. Usually the fog from your breath will provide enough lubricating moisture to clear the glass. If the lens is really smudged, use lens tissue moistened with lens cleaner.

to enforce the habit. Your lenses will love you for it, and your pictures will be better.

Dust the lens and body with a blower brush each time you load film or change videotapes—especially in the field. Our comrade, adventure photographer Peter Cole, ritually brushes each spool of film to keep any dust or snow from working into the camera body. After a trip, use the

Carry a blower brush in your camera bag and use it to whisk lens, film, and any dusty surface each time you load film.

brush to remove dust, then wipe down the outside of the camera body with silicone cloth—especially if you've been around salt water, which is terrifically corrosive.

Open the rear cover and use a soft camera brush to get rid of any sand in the film chamber or videotape transport mechanism. Be judicious when using an air jet powered by canned carbon dioxide (popular with computer users) to clean the camera body or optics: You may cause damage by driving debris further into delicate internals. Nor should you touch the camera's reflex mirror, focusing screen, electonic contacts, shutter curtain, or tape transport hardware with bare fingers—oily fingerprints only attract and retain the grime you're trying to get rid of. Use canned air or a camera brush to clean away any debris.

MOISTURE PROTECTION IN USE

The diffused light of rainy days and the ethereal soft-focus world of fog provide some of a photographer's choicest moments. Trouble is, shooting in these conditions is incredibly tough on your cameras. We've collected all manner of results in this regard while shooting some 80 outdoor-adventure TV shows.

- **Bag it.** The cheapest and most expedient field rain cover is a simple plastic bag of suitable size to cover camera and lens, with a slit at one end that's taped around the lens opening. Sounds simplistic, but we've kept $80,000 Betacams humming happily through all-day downpours with nothing more than a clear plastic garbage bag draped over the top. Make sure to keep the bag's open end pointed down, and try to dry your hands off before operating key camera controls under the cover. One weakness of this method is that if you lie a bagged camera out in the sun, you'll get instant condensation.

    Various commercial camera rain covers are available, and though some work reasonably well, most of the ones we've tried are too leaky for extended use. Leakage centers around the multifarious seams necessary to craft a professionally fitted cover. The trade-off is that these more breatheable (i.e., leaky) covers aren't as prone to condensation problems during variable sun-cloud conditions.

- **Bumbershoot it.** Don't dismiss that simplest, eminently backpackable and most British of foul-weather shelters: the umbrella. A tiny, el cheapo Tote-type umbrella shelters your camera during film changes. Wedge it down behind your backpack straps or life jacket, and it keeps

mist off the lens remarkably well. Holding an umbrella is also an admirable job for your faithful camera assistant (a.k.a. trip partner).

Lens Cleaning

1. Dust the lens off with a brush.
2. Gently fog the lens with your breath.
3. With lens tissue or a soft cotton cloth, wipe with gentle, circular motion from center to outer rim. In misty conditions, swipe the lens with lint-free paper towels (we've had the best luck with Bounty). Check the cloth beforehand to make sure you haven't picked up any grit particles.
4. Remove any tough spots with lens tissue moistened with lens cleaner.
5. Repeat step 3.
6. To test the lens for clarity, slowly breathe on the surface. If moisture evaporates quickly and evenly, you're all set. If one spot holds moisture longer than the rest of the surface, clean again.

STORAGE TIPS

- Make sure your camera is clean and dry when you put it away. Follow the cleaning tips above.
- Make it a habit to set any switch options to "Off" whenever your camera is not in use. This prevents unintentional current consumption or battery discharge, which can cause corrosion as well as run down batteries prematurely.
- When transporting the camera, reverse the batteries in their compartments to avoid unintentional discharge. Just remember to switch them around before use, so you don't miss a fantastic grab shot when a rutting moose charges your canoe!
- If storing the camera for any length of time, remove the batteries entirely.
- Store your camera in a cool, dry, well-ventilated place. If you're worried about humidity, place the clean camera in a heavy-duty Ziploc bag with a packet of desiccant.
- If possible, periodically check a stored camera for moisture, exchange the silica gel, and check to see that everything still functions—just like Dave does on bleak winter days with his old sports car, stored in our barn.

Goggles and Glasses

If you wear and depend on glasses, your first line of protection should be to secure them with a strap or retaining cord. Take a spare pair with you on trips.

The most common eyeglass failure is a broken or stripped hinge. Rather than repairing it with a Band-Aid, try a fishing swivel, a pierced-earring wire, or a

COLD-WEATHER TIPS

Below-freezing temperatures take a particular toll on electronics. These tips will help you get the most out of your battery-powered gear in winter conditions.

- Sleep with your batteries but leave the camera in the cold.
- Switch your autofocus camera to "manual" to save battery drain from the autofocus motors.
- Film becomes brittle in subfreezing temperatures. Load film and advance frames slowly to avoid tearing the film inside the camera. Film should also be brought to ambient temperature slowly, inside its canister, before loading. (The same rules apply for film stored in your freezer.) Once you've shot the film, keep it free from condensation to preserve the quality of the exposed images.
- Steve Howe, wildlife photographer and writer, suggests that if you do a lot of subzero shooting, you should consider sending your camera to the manufacturer to have its normal silicone lubricants replaced with dry graphite. This decreases friction at low temperatures, where wet lubricants become stiff and sluggish.

section of monofilament line to secure bow to frame. A simple paper clip makes a slick spring-tension hinge if you thread it so that the loops are on either side of the bow. These field fixes are so effective that they may become semipermanent.

When your nylon frames become stretched or twisted, not only are they uncomfortable but the stress may cause the lenses to pop out at the most inopportune moment. Restore the intended shape of your shades by dropping them into just-boiled (not boiling) water for several minutes. This should awaken your glasses' molded memory. Remove and clean. Your neighborhood optician can also custom-fit your glasses, often at no charge.

CLEANING

Old-fashioned soap and water remains the best eyeglass cleaner. Always buff with a soft cloth; a chamois or square of PakTowl (available at outdoors stores) is ideal.

ANTIFOG TREATMENTS: DO THEY REALLY WORK?

The deal with any lens is that the surface next to your face is warmer than the opposite side—all the heat from a steep climb or hot chili escapes from your head, that great regulator. This temperature differential is what causes snow, water vapor, and chili-induced cold sweat to condense on the lens surfaces and blur your view of the tree you're about to hit.

Antifog treatments create a clear surface coating that makes water bead and roll off, rather than mist over, the lens. The best treatment is probably McNett's Sea Drops, formulated for dive masks, though even this formula must be reapplied frequently. We've had good results from Rain-X Anti-Fog on the lenses of waterproof camera housings.

Antifog applications do help dispel condensation but are by no means a cure. What you really need is better ventilation. Double-lensed goggles or face shields solve this problem pretty well, but

Ye olde matchstick and duct tape glasses repair.

For the toughest sport glasses, look for sturdy, integral nylon hinges that won't bend.

Replace a missing hinge screw with a twist tie, fishing swivel . . .

. . . or a handy paper clip. This solutions provides a spring-loaded hinge action more solid than the original!

chronically fogged prescription-wearers should think about contact lenses (but remember that lens solutions freeze somewhere about 25°F).

Compasses

There's not a darn thing you can do to fix a squashed compass; best to bone up on age-old navigation techniques using your wristwatch. Carefully protect your compass from impact, and with larger kayak types, from leakage from freezing temperatures. However, it doesn't hurt to check the compass accuracy periodically—before you set out.

Double-check a compass's accuracy with another compass. Just don't place the compasses too close together, or they'll influence each other and confuse you.

A Bit about Batteries

Most of us carry and depend on a flashlight, headlamp, or camera; some wouldn't venture far without an avalanche transceiver or weather radio. All these outdoor appliances share a common weakness: batteries. Learning to maximize the energy from each cell will spare you inconvenient failures.

One way to get the most current is simply to wipe off all the contact points on both the battery and the gadget it powers. Also, use matching batteries where pairs are called for—that is, don't use a half-charged battery along with a fully charged one.

BATTERY STORAGE

Like any chemical product, batteries begin deteriorating from the moment of manufacture. A battery's service life depends on how much it is used and how well it is stored.

Get into the habit of removing batteries from your equipment before storing for any length of time—leaking electrolyte and other gases can corrode contacts, and this oxidization causes resistance between the batteries and electronics, resulting in erratic behavior, followed by failure. Most of us have uncovered a long-lost flashlight only to find a gummed-up, miniature toxic-waste disaster inside (see next page). Regularly clean battery terminals and camera contacts with an ordinary pencil eraser to alleviate any corrosive buildup.

Batteries should be stored in a cool, dry place (though freezing batteries does more harm than good). Even a properly stored battery discharges energy over time; you'll still get the same voltage out of the cell, but for a shorter time than from a battery of more recent vintage. Try to "use up" rather than store a partially spent battery so you'll harness the most energy from it. Before an expedition, we start with all fresh batteries and relegate dubious ones to household duty.

Replace all batteries at the same time for reliable performance. Don't stuff two partly used cells along with four freshies into your VHF radio.

In cold weather, alkaline batteries lose up to half their power. Remove batteries from transceiver, camera, or what have you and carry or sleep with the batteries in a pocket close to your body. Pricey lithium cells lose very little juice in the cold and boast an extended shelf life—attractive factors for little-used but crucial electronics like avalanche beacons or your spare headlamp.

BATTERY DISPOSAL

Few communities collect batteries for safe disposal, so consumers should save spent cells at home rather than commit them to the waste stream. Store in a cool, dry spot in a well-marked container. Check with your local recycling center, dump, or town office about disposal options.

Try to limit, or at least reduce, your battery intake by conscientious use and storage, and seek alternatives whenever possible. For instance, plan a trip around a lunar calendar; try beeswax votive candles instead of a flashlight or lantern around camp. Although beeswax may seem expensive, it melts at a higher temperature than paraffin and lasts longer. Think of the sweet scent as a reward for not using a petroleum-based product. (The honey bee is the only creature utilized by man that naturally produces more than it needs, all the while propagating native plants. Support your local apiary!)

RECHARGEABLES

The more dead batteries accumulate in your home, the more likely you are to gain an interest

FAT WITH BATTS

Could it be a surprise that us fat American cats use the most batteries on this planet? And where do the 3.5 billion batteries we buy each year go? Rather than talk about heavy metals (like mercury, nickel, cadmium, lead, zinc and lithium) percolating into the stream you're about to paddle, we urge you to try to recycle your batteries. Try your local jewelers for button-style batteries. Check your local town office or recycling center for options. Contact the Rechargeable Battery Recycling Corporation to find out the nearest nicad recycling depository: 800-8-BATTERY, or www.Rbrc.com. For more information, there's also the Battery Council International, 401 North Michigan Avenue, Chicago, IL 60611; 312-644-6610.

WIN ELLIS'S NICAD LOBOTOMY

- Wear safety glasses and gloves.
- Connect an insulated wire to the positive terminal of your auto battery.
- Hold the rechargeable's negative end against the negative battery terminal.
- Quickly brush the wire across the rechargeable's positive end. You'll see a small spark. Repeat two or three times.

If the rechargeable does not respond to these ministrations, it is no longer usable. Store spent cells in a cool place until a disposal method becomes available.

Nicad lobotomy not tested on laboratory animals

in rechargeables. Once you've made the modest initial investment in a charger and batteries, you'll enjoy savings. *The caveat:* Although rechargeable batteries work in most applications, their intensity and duration are less than alkalines (to say nothing of lithium cells), so you need to pack spares. Minor variances in voltage may make rechargeables unsuited to finicky videocams and other electronics. Additionally, nicads (nickel-cadmium rechargeable batteries) contain electrolytes every bit as caustic as those in other batteries—they're just kept out of the waste stream longer.

What about the white powder that forms on top of a nicad battery? Contrary to popular myth, this does not indicate that your battery should be discarded. Potassium hydroxide (the electrolyte) penetrates seals, reacts with carbon dioxide in the atmosphere, and forms potassium carbonate (the white crystals). The crystals are harmless and may be cleaned off with soap and water. After wiping the battery dry, apply a little dot of silicone lubricant to help retard the growth of more crystals.

Not surprisingly, it is the *internal* buildup of these same crystals during storage that may cause your cell to refuse a normal charge. This battery can be saved! The cure for this memory loss, advised by inventor Win Ellis, is to pass a high current quickly through the afflicted cell. Use your car battery to fuse internal crystal "whiskers" and restore the life of your rechargeable (see sidebar, page 123). This will also make you feel like a mad scientist.

Nicads are also prone to becoming oppositely charged over time. This reversed polarity may also be cured by the zapping technique described above. They can then be recharged in the normal manner.

Note: Check out the new generation of packable solar chargers, available at most well-stocked outfitters. These solid devices weigh just a few ounces and will charge your AA headlamp batteries while you paddle or backpack along your day's route, assuming there's sun.

LITHIUM CELLS

If you're a cold-weather camper, your best bet is lithium batteries, which are superreliable and in frigid temperatures will outshine rechargeables by

Tape over the contact points on lithium cells in your headlamp to prevent draining during travel.

a factor of four. They are expensive, so it pays to cover battery contacts with duct tape when traveling or not using—nothing's more annoying than arriving in camp at dark with a $20 dead battery in a headlamp that turned itself on in your pack.

Headlamps and Flashlights

Problems with these essentials are usually battery-related. The key is to keep the lamp from turning on in a backpack—tape the switch in the "Off" position if necessary.

Flashlights and headlamps are notorious for having terrible switches. If you have one of these beasts, do yourself a favor and replace the entire lamp rather than become frustrated by a poorly placed, poorly designed switch unit. Sometimes you can temporarily fix a balky switch by bending its contacts so that they touch each other more securely.

The most trouble-free switch is the rotary type (the entire lamp bezel twists on and off), though even these have been known to discharge themselves.

Many headlamps offer a nesting place for a spare bulb; make sure you have a spare and check to see that it works.

External battery packs are a good idea if you're heading into cold, wet conditions. You can wear the batteries next to your warm body so the light will work when it should. However, the connector wires tend to pull out under tension. Prevent this by tying a knot in the wire between the connection and the housing.

DUCT TAPE BRIGHTENS YOUR DAY—AGAIN

A flashlight provides good duct tape storage: wrap a few yards of tape around the barrel.

Glow-in-the-dark or reflective tape will make your light easier to locate in the dark.

CHAPTER 13

Climbing Gear

See also part 2, Footwear;
chapter 14, Winter Gear;
Cordage, pages 18–20; and pages 34–35

Climbing hardware featured in a book about repair? Since all climbers are taught to scrutinize their gear regularly and retire it before wear becomes a danger, "fixing" is rarely an option. Here's a case where *prevention* is key. So lower your eyebrows and read on to learn how proper care and maintenance will protect an investment that protects your life.

Note: Periodic review of various climbing magazines will alert you to innovations and new technologies.

Carabiners

Carabiners are manufactured from aluminum alloy or steel to rigid specifications. While alloy carabiners offer the best strength-to-weight ratio, they are prone to gouges, dents, grooves, and, ultimately, minute cracking or stress fractures as they become work-hardened. Stainless or chrome-molybdenum carabiners are heavier, last longer, and generally more robust than their alloy cousins. Anodized aluminum biners offer more than cosmetic appeal. Anodizing prevents oxidation (the black film that rubs off on ropes and hands) and helps prevent corrosion, which manifests itself as a fuzzy white film, especially after exposure to salt water.

THE RIGHT TOOL FOR THE JOB

Most climbers get the most out of their carabiners by using an assortment of styles suited to spe-

cific functions: steel or fat aluminum locking biners for anchors, belays, rappels, first clips–ground protection; standard Ds for clipping protection; bent-gates and ultralights for clipping bolts (use bent gates *only* on the rope-clipping end of quickdraws); ovals for brake-rappels, racking gear, or hauling.

Oval carabiners continue to be popular for aid climbing and carabiner-brake rappels, but **D-shaped** carabiners offer a higher strength-to-weight ratio because their design distributes most of the load along the strong spine. **Bent-gate Ds** are just as strong but are recommended only for linking runner to your rope — never directly to protection. The bent gate facilitates clipping the rope in, but it can also facilitate inadvertent unclipping.

Asymmetrical Ds or ultralights are made with smaller-diameter rod stock, which tends to be hard on your rope as it runs over this narrow radius. These carabiners don't last as long as more substantial models, are not as versatile, and are rarely worth the weight savings.

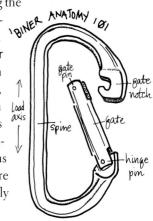

HANGDOGS BEWARE

With the advent of indoor walls and sport climbing, many people have adopted new attitudes toward falling. Even though the "controlled" conditions of clipping bolts offer a certain security, most reported carabiner failures have occurred on sport climbs, and short falls can be harder on any climbing gear than long whippers. The thin steel hangers on most bolt anchors are extremely rough on carabiners. Better-quality bolt hangers are thick stainless steel, with a rolled surface that protects carabiners from gouging. Skinny, sharp-edged hangers will stress and nick biners. So if you're a hangdog, use thick carabiners.

INSPECTION

A new carabiner should have a smooth finish and faultless gate action, with no play in the gate hinge and with a precise gate-latch or locking mechanism. Inspect the gate pin and hinge pin areas with an optical loupe or magnifying glass to spot incipient cracks and corrosion. Judge your carabiners by how much wear you see and feel, not by mere age.

Causes for immediate retirement include dropping from even a modest height (which may cause imperceptible but serious fractures in the metal) or whacking with a hammer (aid climbers, beware). Don't buy used biners or employ a found one for anything more serious than tying your dog out. If the gate or locking action feels loose (or, for that matter, very stiff), it's time for the pasture. Read the signs: nicks, grooves, drops, gouges, or corrosion around latch or hinge pins all spell *r-e-t-i-r-e*.

Load Axis

Carabiner strength is figured on its long axis. A cross-loaded biner has been substantially weakened and should be retired.

CARE O'BINERS

- If the gate latch feels sticky, you may be able to apply cross-pressure (with your hand) to the open gate to improve action.
- Lubricate gate springs and hinges with TriFlow, dry silicone, or graphite lubricant—never oil, which will attract more dirt and can weaken nylon ropes and runners.
- Clean biners by boiling, sans soap, in a spaghetti pot, or by cycling through a dishwasher (again, no suds). Wipe dry, then spritz the gate axis and latch with silicone.
- Grit can also be blasted out of a biner hinge with the powerful air hose at your neighborhood gas station, then lubed as above.
- True grit: some sources suggest soaking in a noncorrosive solvent such as kerosene, then rinsing and wiping dry before lubricating.
- Light surface corrosion can be banished with automotive metal polish. Dave has several old biners that he's polished to a jewel-like finish; the resulting glossy sheen even seems to help retard reappearance of the dreaded white corrosion crust.

Old carabiners never die—they become key rings, clothesline pulleys, dog retainers, bowline anchors for roof racking, and perform myriad household tasks. Take time to mark retired biners with paint, nail polish, or tape so there's no confusion about their history. We have one friend who nicks his retired biners with a hacksaw so there's absolutely no doubt.

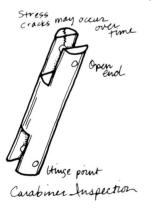

Stress cracks may occur over time

Open end

Hinge point

Carabiner Inspection

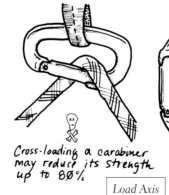

Cross-loading a carabiner may reduce its strength up to 80%

Load Axis

SLCDs, Friends, and Assorted Springy-Thingys

Spring-loaded camming devices (SLCDs) have either a rigid stem (Friends) or cable (Flexible Friends, Camalots, TCUs). All require the same inspection and care. Watch for metal fatigue (cracks); more likely, you'll spot wear on the cables, which may abrade, fray, and break strand by strand. Cables may take a twist or kink, especially in units subjected to aid climbing. You can return your worn SLCDs to the manufacturer for service and for replacement of a tired cable stem. If you notice worn or splayed cam teeth or excessive play in the head, it's time to relegate the unit to Christmas-ornament status, or use it for kayak haul-offs on a rocky shore. Also watch the nylon slings, which won't last as long as the hardware.

For best performance, clean your SLCDs as you would your carabiners. Friends manufacturer Wild Country recommends a kerosene bath for the metal parts. Wipe down, then lubricate with TriFlow—not oil, which will attract more grime.

OTHER HARDWARE

Follow carabiner procedure for inspection. Retire anything with cracks, gouges, funky springs, loose rivets, or after dropping or whacking with a ham-

Spritz a little Teflon lubricant around moving parts of clean cams.

mer. If, for instance, your ascender slips on a dry rope, that's a sign you'd be foolish to ignore.

Ropes

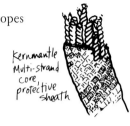

*Kernmantle
Multi-strand
core
protective
sheath*

Since WWII, all climbing ropes have been woven from nylon, or Perlon, for its durability and elastic qualities. Today's climbing rope utilizes "kernmantle" construction—a multistrand nylon core, or kern, with a braided protective sheath, or mantle. The core provides strength. The mantle holds everything together, protects the core from abrasion, and gives the rope its hand, or feel. A tightly woven mantle gives stiffer handling but is less abrasion-prone than a softer one. There are two basic types of rope: *dynamic*, with a certain amount of elasticity, and low-stretch *static* lines.

Static-rope construction minimizes stretch, a favored factor for caving and fixed-rope situations. Static rope's low-stretch construction makes it considerably more abrasion-resistant than dynamic rope; thus, it is the best choice for jugging (weighting), hauling, and handlines. There are a few things you can do to preserve the life of your static line.

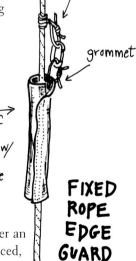

prusik

grommet

- Windproof it: A wind-tossed fixed rope is prone to shredding. Therefore, anchor it from above, below, and at intermediate stations.

Sleeve of stout canvas w/ Velcro closure

- Pad it: Any rope that runs over an edge runs the risk of getting sliced, but a fixed rope that endures

FIXED ROPE EDGE GUARD

repeated jugging is especially vulnerable. Pad the edges with a foam pad, duct tape, or your sweater. Aid climbers often devise a "rope protector" made from stout fabric and held in place with a prusik.

The core of a dynamic rope is stretchy enough to absorb the energy generated by a fall (so you don't stop with a jerk and bust a gut). Each fall reduces a rope's ability to dissipate energy. Short falls near your belayer are actually much harder on a rope than longer falls, because there's less rope to stretch and absorb energy. Ropes, anchors, and belay hardware accumulate stress with each successive fall, so sport climbers should pay close attention during inspection. If you ever "catch hard" on the sharp end of the rope and don't feel any stretch, retire the rope immediately. We have climbed several times at a gym that uses disconcertingly worn ropes. Although many people would never consider climbing at a crag with a squashed, furry rope, they seem to have no trouble dangling off a roof problem in the gym on a rope that resembles a molting caterpillar. Funny.

DRY ROPES

Dry ropes have been factory-treated with a water-repellent coating that extends the life of a rope in several ways. Ropes are usually coated with Teflon or another fluoropolymer, but some companies employ paraffin coatings, which tend to attract grit and feel sticky. Dry ropes generally absorb less water, an important consideration for alpine or ice climbers, since a wet rope will double in weight, stretch endlessly (i.e., the rappel from hell), and possibly freeze solid.

A coated mantle's slick surface is significantly more resistant to abrasion and to UV damage, both archenemies of any rope. However, a very tightly woven mantle on an uncoated rope may be just as water-repellent as a loose, coated mantle. These subtle variations may be reflected by price. Don't be cheap; be safe.

Nikwax now offers a wash-in treatment called RopeProof, which will add or restore maximum water repellency to ropes.

KINKS

Does your brand-new rope have a great hand but turn into corkscrew-pasta salad the minute you toss it for rappel? Kinky ropes are a frustrating malady, and only through trial and error with different brands and sizes will you seize upon the perfect rope for you. Softer, smaller-diameter ropes kink more readily than fat, stiff ones, and certain practices and hardware may contribute to this pesky problem.

For example, a figure-8 device is more likely to introduce kinks than a Sticht belay plate. Lap-coiling is another kink perpetrator—try the butterfly coil. Unkink your rope by passing its entire length through your hands three or four times, until the rope feels smooth again. You can also hang your rope straight down the cliff while coiling to ease the twists. Stacking your rope loosely and randomly during and after climbing (say, in a rope bag) prevents kinks from setting in.

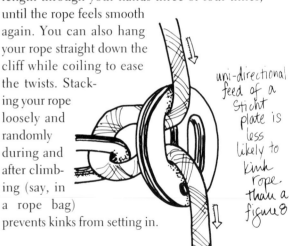

uni-directional feed of a Sticht plate is less likely to kink rope. than a figure 8

RULES OF THE ROPE

Ropes pick up a load of sand and grit with tiny, sharp edges that eventually work through the mantle and nibble at the core from inside. Keep your rope clean by stacking it out of dirt whenever possible, preferably on a rucksack or scrap of nylon cloth, then storing it in a rope bag. If your rope appears very dirty, give it a soak in the tub with a nondetergent soap (see pages 34–35), then rinse it twice. Blue Water Ropes suggests adding a fabric

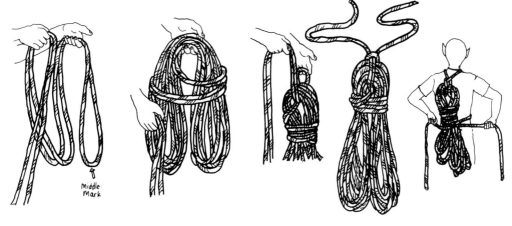

Middle Mark

a butterfly coil is less likely to cause kinking & will feed better; also, this type of coil may be carried like a backpack

softener like Downy to the first rinse to restore suppleness. *Do not* machine-wash or -dry; rather, loop the rope in a shady place to air-dry. Specialized rope cleaners are available from climbing shops or the Mountain Tools catalog.

How you transport and store a rope can also cause fatal fatigue. Auto trunks are major culprits—heat, chemical fumes, and battery acid have destroyed many ropes. This goes for your Bosch or Hilti batteries, dudes, so pack ropes separately from the dread drill. UV damage is often cause enough for retirement; faded or stiffened ropes reflect excessive exposure to sun or any heat source.

Note: At a mountain-rescue-team meeting in North Conway, New Hampshire, members conducted an eye-opening experiment: During the meeting, they soaked a rope in DEET (N,N-diethyl-meta-toluamide), the active ingredient in many insect repellents. A few hours later, they group adjourned to a tug-o'-war and broke the rope.

Stepping on a rope is bad juju, especially if you're wearing crampons, since you can easily damage the inner core without obvious wear to the mantle. Feel for soft spots or lumps whenever you

coil the rope. Avoid running ropes over a sharp edge, as when toproping. You can thread your toprope through a section of tubular webbing or over an old chunk of carpet to protect against cliff-edge abrasion. If you're hauling, consider wrapping duct tape around knots on the haul line to minimize abrasion. Use your lead ropes only for climbing.

You alone know the history of your rope; never loan it to a friend or buy a used rope for climbing.

WHEN SHOULD YOU RETIRE YOUR ROPE?

The industry line:
- Immediately after a long fall.
- If there are soft or flat spots inside the sheath.
- If the rope has a frayed or worn sheath.
- If the rope becomes stiff.
- With holiday use only: retire after four years.
- With weekend use: retire after two seasons.
- With multifall use: retire after three months of constant use or one year of part-time use.

Finish rope ends or elastic cording with a quick dunk into some tool dip. Tool dip is also useful for worn ice-axe grips.

TRIMMING

If you've damaged your rope near one end, salvage the remainder by hot-cutting the bad section. Take an old knife—even a butter knife will do—and heat to red-hot on your stove burner. Wearing mitts, slice through the rope. This works (and looks) infinitely better than melting apart with a torch or camp stove, all the while inhaling wicked black fumes. Finish the ends with a dunk into some rope sealer (see appendix G, Materials Resources, beginning on page 236) or tool dip (just the last half inch). Remember to re-mark the middle.

Marking

A taped middle mark will rarely last a week on a dry (treated) rope, and we've always heard that permanent inks are bad for the nylon. You can use adhesive tape (again and again), or you can purchase a Blue Water Ropes laundry marker designed especially for nylon. Mountain Tools also offers a whip-end rope sealer (see appendix G, Materials Resources, beginning on page 236).

Slings and Kevlar and Spectra Cord

When slings become fuzzy, abraded, stiff, or faded, replace them. Don't sew your own runners; home machines can't handle the tight-tolerance bartack stitching and heavy threads required. Send them to the manufacturer or to a credible custom sewer (before you send your equipment, ask to make sure they'll bartack runners).

Kevlar and Spectra cording are made like a kernmantle rope, though the yellowish Kevlar core does not depend on the sheath for strength. Even so, if you see Kevlar peeking through the mantle, *r-e-t-i-r-e* it. Because the Kevlar core and nylon sheath stretch differently (Kevlar doesn't stretch much), you'll have to employ a special method for trimming the ends of cut cording. Spectra cord is lighter and easier to trim, but it is prone to melting at low temperatures. *Never* use Spectra cord as a back-off loop.

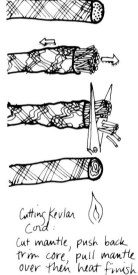

Cutting Kevlar Cord:
Cut mantle, push back trim core, pull mantle over then heat finish

Harnesses

Inspection and treatment of harnesses follow the same general rules as for ropes. Not so long ago, we argued for months over whether or not we needed to replace our harnesses. "Look at Ben," Annie insisted. "He's still alive and his Whillans is fifteen years old!"

A few calls to gear manufacturers said differently. Turns out you should retire your harness about as often as you do a rope. ("No way," Dave protested, thinking of the dozen ropes his own

Which ice axe would you rather have anchoring you to the mountain—the blunt, rounded pick in the foreground or the sharp, hooked one behind?

Whillans had outlived. "Way," say the experts.) Based on this feedback, even Ben and Dave have seen the light. They're both sporting shiny new harnesses. Dave's vintage Whillans is now part of a historic-gear display in our gear room.

Wear and abrasion are obvious warning signs. Like ropes, your harness loses strength and resiliency each time it is stressed in a fall. Clean it as you would a rope. Pay special attention to bar tacks and tie-in loops, checking for abrasion each time you use the harness. Inspect the buckle—closely—for cracks or corrosion. Also double-check any knots on racking loops—who wants to scatter pricey hardware all over the crags?

Ice Tools

Ice tools are fairly simple to inspect, since they're built stronger than you're ever likely to need. The head and spike are usually glued and riveted to the shaft and unlikely to loosen. Modular pick attachments are decidedly less foolproof; all require careful monitoring and periodic checks for fastener tightness. Maintenance involves an occasional light coat of oil on steel parts to prevent rust, filing and tuning the teeth and adze, and periodically replacing the pick.

It's a good idea to carry a wrench of the correct size whenever you carry your ice gear; always be prepared to tighten bolts, but be careful not to overtighten and strip threads. No need to carry spare parts for a day's ice climb—bring a spare tool instead. Bring a small fishhook file or snapped-off section of a regular metal file to remove burrs and touch up edges in the field.

SHARPENING

Always hand-file your axes and crampons; a machine grinder can overheat and ruin the temper of the metal, weakening it. Before attacking your axe with a file, determine what shape you're trying to achieve, and work on tools clamped firmly in a vise so you can carefully aim for that shape. General-purpose or mountaineering axes should have a negative-clearance pick so the pick isn't too grabby during self-arrest. Techy ice

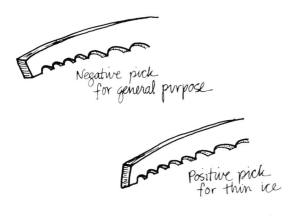

Negative pick for general purpose

Positive pick for thin ice

climbers prefer a positive clearance for better hooking on thin placements.

Malcolm Daly, veteran Colorado ice climber and head of Trango USA (climbing gear imports), offers this method for sharpening the teeth of a technical ice tool:

- Use a 12-inch mill bastard file.
- File the end of the pick so it is parallel to the shaft of the tool.
- Shape the end of the pick, beginning with the side bevels. The two sides should form an 80- to 90-degree angle. Any sharper and the pick will dull easily and cut (skin, packs, outerwear, ropes) more eagerly. The bottom bevel of the last tooth is critical to a pick's hooking ability. If the angle made by the flat bottom of the last tooth to the point where your weight hangs off the shaft is less than 90 degrees, the pick will slip as you attempt to hook. If the angle is slightly more than 90 degrees, the tool will hook well. Too steep and the point becomes fragile and tough to remove.
- Slightly bevel the top edge of the pick if necessary (most come from the manufacturer this way). The top bevel aids in removal.
- Bevel the underside of the secondary teeth so the pick won't stick frustratingly in deep placements.

Note: Malcolm warns that this technique results in a less durable pick; if you bash a lot of rocks, you'll file more often and wear out the pick sooner.

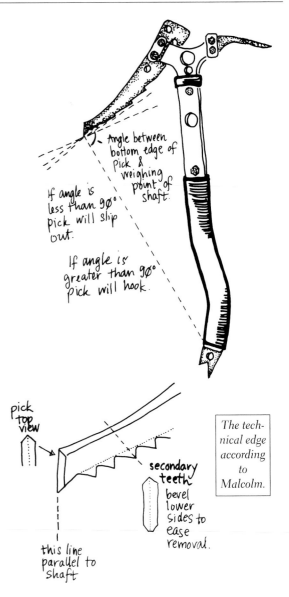

Angle between bottom edge of Pick & weighing point of shaft.

If angle is less than 90° Pick will slip out.

If angle is greater than 90° Pick will hook.

pick top view

secondary teeth

bevel lower sides to ease removal.

this line parallel to shaft

The technical edge according to Malcolm.

Crampons

Whether you use rigid or hinged, straps or step-ins, most crampon inspection centers around the front points. Tiny stress cracks like to form just at the base of these two teeth. Other problem areas to watch: the base of upright side posts, hinge areas, and the crossbar between front points. Newer

Crampons—point, counterpoint (left to right): chisel points and V-points, both ideal for snow; modular dual points (best for steepest ice); modular mono point (intended for thin ice and steep mixed ground).

Step-in bindings vary by manufacturer, but all have a retainer strap for the heel clip. Make sure all parts are in working order, tighten all screws, and bring baling wire for field repair. A little Loc-Tite on screws at the beginning of the season isn't a bad idea.

Front points should generally extend at least ¾ inch but not more than an inch ahead of your boot toe. Always follow the original design of the point when sharpening. If the points are so dull that you can't tell, shame on you. Chisel-type points should be sharpened from the top down, while V-shaped points should be evenly refiled from each side. The latest modular crampons' dual- or mono-points often bristle with

modular crampon designs have introduced the nightmare of myriad fasteners holding multiple parts together; due diligence here involves regular checks for fastener integrity and tightness.

Strap-on crampons should be fitted to the boot snugly so they will cling to the boot even when the straps are not secured. Check strap rivets and buckles, and carry a spare crampon strap. Straps are made of neoprene-coated nylon; melt back any frays with a lighter.

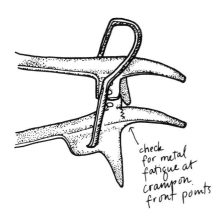

check for metal fatigue at crampon front points

Lots of gear means lots of inspections: carabiners, wire nuts, harness webbing, etc.

Two types of crampon points—identify yours before sharpening: V-shape on left, chisel shape on right.

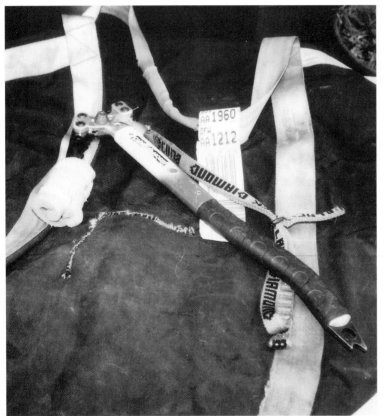

For travel, wrap ice-tool picks with foam protectors so they won't ventilate your packs and duffels. This big rip came courtesy of the pictured North Wall axe and nameless airlines. Annie neatly repaired the duffel with dental floss—it's still holding strong.

teeth like miniature ice-axe picks; these may require careful tuning, much like the technical axe-sharpening tips above. As with ice axes, hand-file only.

Crampons suffer from balling up in soft snow. Avoid this problem with a light coating of silicone on the metal as well as on any moving parts, hinges and strap buckles included. Another trick to prevent snow from sticking is to stretch a piece of pantyhose over the base of the crampon, punching teeth through the mesh. Commercial anti-balling plates are available for most modular designs; the added weight seems a worthwhile trade-off to avoid desperate scrabbling on the descent, after you *thought* the hairy part was over.

In transit, crampons cause more damage to body parts, packs, tents, and miscellany than just about any other type of equipment. Store them in their own rugged stuff sack on the outside of your pack. Armor your crampon sack with sheets of stiff plastic scavenged from an old sheet-rock-mud bucket.

Ice Protection

The trouble with ice screws is that the times when you want the protection most is on thin ice, where the screws tend to bottom out on the rock. The result? Frazzled nerves and bunged-up ice-screw teeth. There's not much to be done about the former, but the latter is most definitely fixable. Sharp screws can be placed faster and with less effort, so you have more arm juice left to finish the climb.

Clamp the screw carefully in a vise (don't crush or distort the tubing) and use a short (6 inch) mill bastard file to bring dull teeth back up to snuff. If the teeth are actually bent over and not just blunted, you're probably out of luck. Clean up burrs inside the screw tube with a circular file, like the

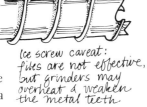

Ice screw caveat: files are not effective, but grinders may overheat & weaken the metal teeth.

type used to sharpen a chain saw. Just swipe away any burrs—don't round off the screw's inner edge, which is carefully sized so that the core of ice left inside the tube can be more easily removed.

Most ice screws are made of hard chrome-moly steel, so sharpening will take time. If you try to hurry the process with a bench grinder, you'll probably just ruin the metal's temper. Contrary to popular belief, titanium screws aren't more brittle than steel screws; the exotic metal is actually a bit softer than steel and takes a keen edge with less elbow grease.

Helmets

Ooof. Here's a topic Annie can address with distinct authority. She's a hardheaded lass, to be sure, but her stoicism has been rattled along with her brains during a few too many high-velocity wipeouts. Annie is a veteran of four concussions over the years, the repercussions of which include head, neck, and back complaints and an expensive relationship with a neuromuscular therapist.

A few years back she swore never to take up new sports that required a hard hat, but we still have quite a collection from old habits: bicycle, kayak, and climbing helmets are stacked in our gear room. Recently we found ourselves shopping for (ach!) ski helmets. Skiing isn't exactly a new sport in our household; then again, neither is crashing headfirst into trees.

Until recently there has been no clear standard for helmets, but now all sports helmets sold in the United States must meet federal safety criteria mandated by the Consumer Product Safety Commission. Additionally, climbing-specific helmets, like ropes and hardware, must pass rigid UIAA (Union Internationale des Associations d'Alpinisme) specifications.

Besides regularly checking our head rigs (admittedly difficult due to Dave's compulsive sticker collection), we give the salty straps a rinse and occasionally spritz the helmets with diluted vinegar to vanquish any microbial freeloaders.

Make sure your climbing helmet adjusts to fit over a warm hat.

SELECTING A HELMET

- Any helmet is better than no helmet.
- Determine intended use. Tough polycarbonate climbing helmets are made to withstand falling objects and leader falls but not high-speed impacts. Alternatively, ski and bike helmets are constructed primarily of impact-absorbent expanded polystyrene foam, while their thin sheet-plastic outer skins won't likely absorb a kilo-sized chunk of ice dropped out of the sky.
- Check the fit. You'll only actually wear the dang thing if it fits you, so spend some time trying on different brands. An ill-fitting lid is uncomfortable and less protective. The helmet should ride snug, level, and low on the forehead. If you can wiggle it more than an inch in any direction, add fit pads, tighten the straps, or find a different model. Various brands suit differing head shapes.
- Make sure your helmet accommodates a hat and whatever eyewear you favor. Don't forget to try goggles with a climbing or ski helmet.
- All helmets will crack or deform after a major blow. After a big wreck, retire your crash hat. Remember, it just paid for itself by saving your noggin, so enshrine it next to the broken skis. Do not give it to Goodwill or sell it in your yard sale.

Winter Gear

He carried his snowshoes and a blanket and the Blessed Sacrament on his back, and I carried the provisions—smoked eels and cold grease—enough for three days.

Willa Cather, *Shadows on the Rock*

Temperature-impaired seasonal skeptics like to argue that the best gear for surviving a long, cold winter is a house in the Bahamas. As committed New Englanders, we prefer to deal with winter more directly, choosing gear carefully to keep us warm, dry, and mobile despite the wicked weather.

Whether you're striding snow-sparkles on skis, stomping deep tracks through puckerbrush on snowshoes, or crunching along some high, wind-raked ridge, winter gear does something precious: it gets you off the couch and into fresh air. Better yet, it gets you out at a time when you'll see far fewer people, even in popular summer hot spots.

To truly savor the (admittedly perverse) joys of winter adventures, you need gear, lots of it—mobility gear (skis, snowshoes, sleds), warmth gear (puffy coats, hats, mitties, boots), and shelter gear (stout tents, ingenious igloos, snug huts with woodstoves). And the more gear you need, the greater the chances for equipment failure. But we look at the bright side of this equation: more failures equal more chances you'll have to fix something!

Touring Skis

Track or backcountry—the beauty of cross-country skis is that the essential forms are little changed from their Scandinavian ancestors (although performance certainly has changed, thanks to modern materials). No matter what type, age, or condition, your skis require the same general care. Make ski tuning and prepping part of those fall get-ready-

SKI CARE

These are the best ways to ensure a long relationship with any skis, according to shop lord Tom Dolliver at Swallow's Nest in Seattle.

- Regular hot-waxing with base prep will both protect and enhance the performance of the skis. All skis have a porous base that can dry out.
- Wipe off and dry your skis after each use, especially after they've been for a glide on your roof rack. Salt and road grime work their way onto the ski, rust the edges, corrode bindings, and dry out the bases.
- Check binding screws before each use—the most common ski repair is a stripped screw.
- When storing your skis for the season, clean off last year's wax and gunk, then rewax *without* scraping. This protects the edges and keeps moisture from penetrating the bases. Don't store skis in a ski bag, which will hold moisture.

to-ski rituals and the ideal answer to the question *What'll we do?* on long winter nights. Your boards will reward you with many years of face plants and whoop-de-whoops.

A FEW RULES OF THUMB

To get any leverage when tuning skis, you'll need to work out a vise system. If you're serious about ski care, a pair of sturdy ski vises is a worthwhile investment—they make the job efficient, safer, and a lot more enjoyable, so you're more likely to do it regularly. Suitable vises run about $50 from well-stocked outdoor shops, so you can't even use cost as an objection anymore.

Note: When waxing, scraping, or filing, always work from tip to tail.

SINGLE-CAMBER VERSUS DOUBLE-CAMBER

Most backcountry touring skis have double camber, which means they flex easily at the tip and tail, with a very stiff middle that only contacts the snow when all your weight is on that ski, that is, when kicking or climbing. To check camber: hold the skis base to base and press the waists together. If you can get the bases to meet in the middle with little effort, the camber is played—your skis are now objets d'art. If you have to squeeze hard, they're fine, so go skiing.

Telemark-oriented skis have a single-camber flex: the ski bends into a smooth, continuous arc with no defined wax pocket for carving smooth, powerful turns. You can easily press the skis together whether they're new or five seasons old. The chief concern with tele skis is bent tips; if you press the ski bottoms together and the shovels splay apart, you've tweaked a tip.

TRADITIONAL WOOD SKIS, A.K.A. HICKORY STICKS

With the advent of waxless skis, many frustrated folks tossed their "antique" but perfectly service-able waxable wooden touring boards in the barn or tacked them to cabin walls. Today these skis are available at your neighborhood yard sale for less than $10; a surprising number of them remain in like-new condition, albeit a touch dried out. A little preparation before storage would have preserved the skis' resiliency. Camberless wood skis are best used decoratively, but if you're lucky to find a pair with some life left, there's nothing quieter or naturally springier than swishing through the trees on a pair of wood skis, complete with Tonkin cane poles. Retro. Avant-garde. Delightfully cheap. Renewable!

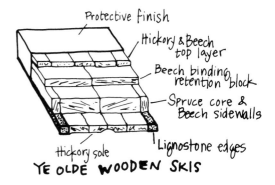

Protective finish
Hickory & Beech top layer
Beech binding retention block
Spruce core & Beech sidewalls
Lignostone edges
Hickory sole

YE OLDE WOODEN SKIS

Preserving the Camber of a Wood Ski

If left unprotected during storage, exposed wood will dry out, warp, or go flat.

- Prepare skis for storage by cleaning and pine-tarring the bases. Oil or varnish the tops.
- Tie or band the skis together at tips.
- Place a wooden block at the waist. The block should be large enough so there's tension when you tie the tails together.
- Rack skis on edge (typically in the barn rafters).

Wood skis require slightly more care than do their modern grandchildren, using old-time concoctions—principally pine tar—available at a hardware store, ski-touring center, or ski shop. Pine tar, or *grundvalla*, is wicked, gunky stuff, but its resinous nature both protects the ski and holds wax well.

After some hard use—and poor care—any ski's core layers will begin to stray. Delamination marks the beginning of the end of your relationship with the skis, and you can spot initial phases (usually at tips or tails) with regular inspection. Fix minor delams early, before they turn terminal.

If you're off in the boonies and the ski suffers a major, functional delamination, you can use splints, duct tape, or hose clamps to get you out of the woods.

Hose clamps and a metal scraper will go a long way toward scrunching a ski back together.

Predrilled ski-scraper splints. While many folks recommend this as a great field repair, we've yet to see the scraper splint in action or to talk with someone who has. Start the screw holes in the ski with the awl on your knife. Sandwich splints top and bottom and hobble home. This works on fiberglass or wood skis; it's less successful on skis with full metal layers.

Another glue-and-clamp session. At home again, you might salvage the season by first cleaning the separating layers to remove dirt, adhesives, and damaged material. Use matchsticks to block open various layers. Slice away splinters, then brush on some denatured alcohol; allow it to evaporate completely. Inject two-part epoxy into the split with a disposable syringe. Remove the matchsticks, then C-clamp the area on both sides of the ski using two metal scrapers (top and bottom) to even out the pressure between the clamps. Start looking for a new pair of skis.

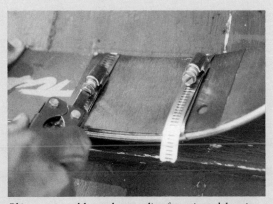

Ski scraper and hose clamp splint for serious delam in the field.

Preparing Wooden Ski Bases

1. Remove old wax and tar with scraper and/or hand torch with a flame-spreader attachment. After scraping, rub down the bases and edges with a rag soaked in turpentine or commercial wax solvent. (Best to do this job outside or in a well-ventilated shop.)

2. Hand-sand according to the condition of the base. Don't use a power sander, or you risk an undulating ride. Use 150-grit or finer sandpaper and a fist-sized flat sanding block. Wipe clean.

3. Paint the base with pine tar. Burn tar in with the torch, taking care not to singe the ski. The tip of the flame should barely brush the ski, and the pine tar should bubble lightly but not smoke. Wipe behind the torch flame with a soft cloth to smooth the finish. (Remember, this is all flammable stuff.)

4. Oil or varnish the top surface of the ski as needed.

Spare Tips

If you ski any distance into the backcountry with wood skis (especially those dried-out $10 yard-sale oldies), a spare tip is a good idea. Other field fixes include sapling-and-string splints, hose clamps, duct tape, and leather mittens.

WAXLESS SKIS

Ski snobs may scoff at waxless skis, but for transitional snow (at or around freezing) and irregular terrain, these zithery-sounding boards make an hour-long lunch-break tour possible. Given the variable snows prevailing around our coastal Maine abode (i.e., warm and wet), waxless skis have literally saved the sport for both of us.

Waxless skis employ a pattern of scales or ridges underfoot to provide purchase for the kick. Hence, waxless—but only in the middle. The rest of the base needs waxing just like any other ski, hot-waxed with a gliding base wax at least once per season. Many waxless fans prefer to use a wipe-on liquid, like Maxi-Glide, which doesn't interfere with the scales and keeps nasty ball-ups at bay on warm spring afternoons. It's a good product to carry with you.

Waxless skiers tend to be cavalier about their bases and are known to march across gravel roads, open rocky streams, and barbed-wire fences without a second thought. That's fine, if you don't mind the slow glide of fuzzy bases and a slippery, smashed grip area. Examine your scale pattern and trim any hangnails with a razor knife.

If the scales are really mushed, you can try to redefine the base by trimming the rounded scale edges square again. If smooth areas of the base are furry, hand-sand to prep for a therapeutic hot wax (see below). The waxless bases on Dave's long-time favorite Karhus were so mangled that he had the bases stone-ground smooth at a local ski-tuning shop, thus turning them into very effective waxable boards.

Sharpening metal-edged waxless skis is tricky because you cannot flat-file over the protruding scales of the grip pattern. Side-file the edges the best you can with the end of the file so you don't damage the base.

WAXABLE AND METAL-EDGED BACKCOUNTRY SKIS

Even the best sintered polyethylene (P-Tex) base will dry out over a summer with no storage preparation (cleaning and waxing without scraping). An unprotected base will lose its ability to hold kicker wax, which can be insanely annoying on any tour. You can discover whether the base has deteriorated by looking for the presence of a film or a furriness under the light. This means that your base has become extremely porous; any wax will fall right out of it, and water will penetrate.

Restore your base by hand-sanding—not scraping—with a sanding block. Use 150- to 180-grit paper or an emery cloth. Better yet, take your skis to a competent alpine ski technician who can stone-grind them.

A few winters back, we headed into Baxter State Park, Maine, for some ice climbing. Annie was psyched to use her new red Valentine skis, hot-waxed the night before, and expected a glorious cruise to the hut. Less than a mile from the trailhead the slapstick waxing comedy began: zero grip going uphill, with hand-rubbed wax coats coming off every few hundred yards. She felt totally persecuted for 15 miles of rolling terrain, loaded with hardware, at –10°F. Guess who reached the hut in the dark.

We didn't make the connection that the new skis had been drying in the shop for two seasons, victims of benign neglect. Only later did we treat the new boards to a proper base prep, after which they treated Annie far better on the trail. When you buy a new pair of skis, ask the shop to throw them on the grinder for a light touch-up.

SPRING CLEANING

Lay your skis on the bench and survey the mileage. Clean off old wax, inspect and lube bindings, attend to bases and edges, then apply a thick layer of binder or base wax before storing.

REMOVING WAX FROM FABRIC

Forgotten tins of ski wax have a nasty tendency to glue parka pockets shut during summer storage. Establish a wax bag—a zippered, packcloth pocket is ideal—and save yourself some grief. For a stuck-shut pocket, first heat the fabric with a hair dryer or by dipping it into just-boiled water. Peel apart the two layers of fabric. Next, freeze and crack off the wax. Then lay a scrap of clean cotton or a brown grocery bag directly over the spot. Iron the scrap, taking care not to overheat and melt the fabric underneath. This should draw out any shreds of base material but will probably leave a stain. You can try a degreaser, but don't go overboard trying to erase a little mileage. Remember Lady Macbeth?

Soft waxes and klister are best removed using a commercial solvent wax remover, turpentine, kerosene, or CitraSolv. When carrying klister-coated skis on your pack, make sure they're traveling base side out . . . trust us on this one.

The first run of the season is curtailed as Amy Fischer realizes that she neglected to spring-clean her skis.

Clean Off Old Wax

Scraping alone won't remove wax from pores in the base. Nasty wax solvents (paint thinner or commercial stuff) are the fastest way. A good alternative is CitraSolv (see appendix B, Low-Tox Cleaning Solutions, beginning on page 216), which takes slightly longer to act. Let the citrus solvent sit 15 minutes on the base before rubbing off, then rub the base down with a clean rag wetted with the solvent.

Don't be tempted to use a torch to melt off old wax. This is just a good way of ruining P-Tex bases unless you're highly skilled, which means you've ruined enough bases to know better.

Another method of removing old wax is to apply a generous layer of very soft wax (with a low melting point), then immediately scrape it off while the wax is still warm. Follow the hot-wax instructions below; you may need to repeat the process.

Hot-Wax Treatment

Use a ski iron or yard-sale iron (you'll never get to use it for anything else again) at the "wool" setting. Dribble a pattern of wax along the base, but don't let the wax get so hot that it smokes. Skim the iron over wax droplets to achieve a smooth film on the ski base. Don't hold the iron in one place too long, or you risk delaminating the base in that area. The skis shouldn't become too hot to touch. Store the skis without scraping them.

FLESH WOUNDS

Preparing bases and hot-waxing will take care of minor nicks and scrapes, but flesh wounds should be filled. A really deep gash exposing core material is best filled by a ski technician who has access to the actual base material and a plastic welder. For moderate lacerations and gouges, use a P-Tex candle, available at your favorite ski shop. After you've cut away any lingering hangnails, thoroughly clean the wound with alcohol.

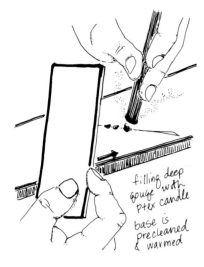

filling deep gouge with ptex candle

base is precleaned & warmed

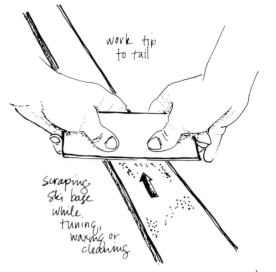

work tip to tail

scraping ski base while tuning, waxing or cleaning

Prewarm the damaged area with the heat from a blow dryer. Light the P-Tex stick and hold it horizontally—molten plastic dropped on skin produces a serious, painful burn. The trick is to keep the flame small so you don't get blobs of black carbon into the repair. You can twist the stick on a metal scraper to keep it clean while burning. To avoid dripping flaming blobs onto the ski, keep the stick almost on the surface and "flow" molten plastic into the gouge so the flaming tip helps preheat the repair area. Slightly overfill the repair area, then allow the plastic to harden until cooled to base temperature before scraping the base flat.

TUNING AND FILING

Check your bases for flatness. Backcountry ski bases are often higher than the edges, or the edges may "rail" higher than the base. A truly flat base means a more consistently responsive ski. Use a true bar (a machined cylinder—ask at an alpine ski shop) or scraper under a strong light to see where your skis are high or low—light will show under the gaps.

Scraping Bases

If your base is high, you can take it to a mechanic for an efficient, machine-ground treatment, or you can scrape it yourself. Use long, even, pulling strokes with a *sharp* metal scraper tipped away from you, being careful not to bend the scraper into the base. Constantly check your work under the light to make sure that you aren't overcorrecting.

A **sharp scraper** makes all the difference.

Secure it in a vise and use your file to square the business edges. If you don't have a vise, lay the file flat, pointing away from you, and draw the scraper toward you.

File scraper edges square in a vise.

Burrs

Smooth over burrs with a sharpening stone to maximize your fun quotient (you can and should do this in the field). Burrs will terrorize skin, gaiters, and the inseams of your fancy new Gore-Tex pants. Once home, you can work out the ding when you file bases and edges.

Filing

Allow skis to reach room temperature before working on them. If you bring a cold ski into a warm shop, the condensation will make metal filings stick to the ski (and to you) and generally make a mess. Use a mill bastard file long enough (12 inches) to allow a full grip with both hands. Files cut best at about a 45-degree angle to the ski lengthwise—you can feel the action and adjust accordingly. Apply pressure where the file contacts the base, not out at the end; pressing the ends bows the file, and you'll round off the edges you're supposed to be sharpening. Use even strokes, tip to tail, constantly brushing metal flakes off both base and file.

Tuning skis is an art form that has generated esoteric protocols and ongoing controversies that transcend the scope of this book. If you want more performance from your skis, you'll need to develop your filing, waxing, and general tuning

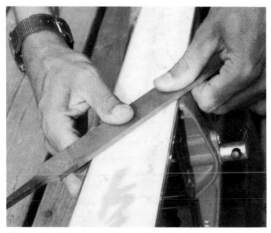

When flat-filing, press down where the file meets the base to make even, consistent contact.

Work carefully to maintain a 90-degree angle to the edge. Watch shiny area of new exposed metal to gauge the cut.

skills, including edge beveling. Appendix G, Materials Resources (beginning on page 236), lists references that discuss tuning and waxing, as do countless other skiing guides.

THESE MODERN SKIS ARE KINKY AND TWISTED

Metal-edge backcountry skis are very difficult to break but relatively easy to bend, especially when lift-served skiing in moguls. You can spot a bent ski by pressing the bases together. As you press, a bent ski will pull away from its mate (usually at the tip). A bent ski still functions, but it won't hold a turn like its designer intended. While it is possible to tweak a bend back into form, even experienced ski mechanics acknowledge that this is a hit-or-miss operation. Some suggest that bent skis might just be better for crud, since the tips won't dive!

SMASHED TAILS

A common malady, caused by stuffing your skis into a crusty snowbank at every rest. Unfortunately, smashed tails are exceptionally hard to repair permanently, since the nice flat surfaces necessary for effective gluing are now all mangled by granite or pavement. Even the Neanderthal ski technician's solution (bolting separated layers back together) won't work, because the protruding bolt heads catch on the other ski and will constantly wipe you out. Prevent tail delamination—lean your skis gently against a tree or hut.

Bindings

No matter what type of binding you prefer, regular inspection and maintenance will save you the terrific hassle of fumbling with screws and glues in subzero temperatures.

Bindings undergo a phenomenal amount of stress and torque, which is transferred to the skis by a few little screws holding them onto the skis' top skin. Stripped binding screws are the most likely repair, but these can usually be avoided with regular inspection of your bindings.

Carry several extra screws in your kit, as well as glue and filler for field fixes. Virtually all binding screws are installed with Pozi-Drive screws, which take a specific bit available at hardware or ski shops (a Phillips head bit does *not* fit). If a screw tends to work loose but the threads still snug tight, try a little epoxy in the hole. If you're setting screws in a wood-core ski, use two-part epoxy; for foam-core or composite skis, use an adhesive like Elmer's Carpenter's Glue. Don't epoxy screws into foam–composite core skis: if you ever have to remove a screw, the core comes out too—in big chunks—and you'll face major repairs.

BINDINGS IN THE (SNOW) FIELD
Galactic-certified powder hound David Goodman actually had a spare binding on hand last spring when his broke. Unfortunately, all the parts on the mountain did no good without a Pozi-Drive screwdriver (the Phillips head on a Swiss Army is too small). Even after that experience, Goodman will probably forget his Pozi-driver again—will he never learn?

To remove epoxy-set screws, heat your Pozi-

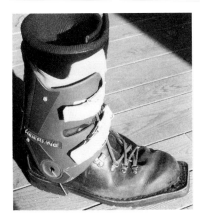

Soup-up tired tele boots by converting them to "Stein Comps." Scavenge the upper boot and the liner cuff from yard-sale alpine boots.

Drive bit, set it into the screw head long enough to heat the threads, then back it out slowly. In the field, use a butane lighter or hut woodstove to heat the bit. If the screws are stripped, pack a little steel wool or a matchstick into the hole. Goodman recommends using Superglue for setting screws in the field, since it works better than epoxy in really cold conditions (see appendix C, Kit Suggestions, page 219, for Goodman's favorite fix-its).

Binding Bindings
A squeaky binding can drive you and your tour mates to distraction. Regularly lubricating moving parts with TriFlow or silicone is a good idea. In the field, try a little lip goop or sunscreen.

If you suffer from snow sticking mercilessly to your bindings, smooth scratches and burrs with emery cloth or steel wool, then spritz liberally with silicone.

BASIC BINDING STYLES
Three-Pin
Traditional "rat trap" bindings are still favored for general touring. While older-style bindings had removable (read: *breakable*) toe bails and were notorious nuisances, today's three-pin styles have riveted bails that rarely detach themselves. Broken three-pin bindings can be creatively repaired in the field using baling wire or a spare old-style bail (robbed from yard-sale skis or from a dusty box at the ski shop). Since three-pin toepieces fit specifically right or left boots, on extended tours it's worth packing a spare pair.

Typical backcountry three-pin binding

Three-pin bindings are known to be hard on boots' pin holes, so take care when stepping in and make sure the pins engage properly. Twisting from the toe also causes substantial wear to the boots' midsoles, rendering them over time as floppy as huarache sandals. Cable bindings are one way to reduce this wear. Cables offer more torsional rigidity, don't rely on pins, and can usually be completely repaired in the field.

Cable

Whether you have front-throw cables or popular heel-latch versions (there's little functional difference), get to know these bindings well and inspect them regularly. Watch for frayed, stretched, or kinked cables, loose screws, cracked metal fittings, sprung springs. Our friend Ben managed to tour the better part of 40 miles with a broken cable binding, thanks to ingenuity, a bungee cord, and some nylon line. On a long trip, bring spare cables plus the correct wrench and replacement nuts.

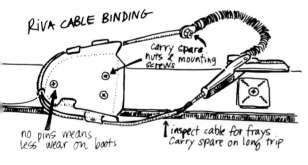

RIVA CABLE BINDING

carry spare nuts & mounting screws

no pins means less wear on boots

inspect cable for frays. Carry spare on long trip

System Bindings

If you use a boot-binding system like New Nordic Norm Back Country (NNN-BC), be sure to pack a spare toepiece if you're going on a remote tour, since neither boot nor binding will be interchangeable with other types. There's not much

you can wreck or fiddle with, since the torsion bar is molded directly into the boot and the binding's mechanics are housed in plastic. You can purchase flexor plugs of varying density to adjust the action. Otherwise, just pay attention to the mounting screws as with any other binding.

SKI SAFETY STRAPS

One of the least appealing aspects of retro-simple backcountry gear is the need for *safety* leashes at downhill areas. Always connect ski leashes to the boot, not your ankle. You can make a leash with a hook and some parachute cord girth-hitched around the binding. Clip this to a ring strung through the boot laces at the toe. If you wear supergaiters, sew a loop to the toebox fabric. In the backcountry, stash these leashes in your wax kit so they won't snag on brush. Incidentally, a 50-pound-test fishing leader is a superlight leash alternative or spare.

Poles

All ski poles employ the same parts: grip, strap, shaft, basket, tip. Losing a basket or tearing the straps is common; more serious is a bent, splintered, or broken shaft. Poles are natural spools for storing duct tape—wind a few dozen turns right under the grips for quick fixes.

Just one long descent without a basket will encourage anyone to carry a spare. (After once plunging, lunging, and wrenching desperately down a gully sans basket, Annie racked her brain for a substitute and smugly sacrificed the lid of her favorite camp mug. Pure genius.)

Insulated mug lid sacrificed for a ski pole basket.

While lightweight fiberglass poles are springy and resilient for woods touring, they are torsion-

A QUIVER OF POLE SPLINTS

Anything will do in a pinch, but common cures for pole fractures include:

- Aluminum tent stake, secured with duct tape or hose clamps.
- Aluminum flashing or soda can, wrapped and taped.

- Green tree branch plugged inside the shaft or used as a splint.
- Ramer's Pole Patch (two steel sleeves that snap around a fracture).
- An aluminum cigar tube (Dave's favorite "saved-my-trip" repair story from the last few years).

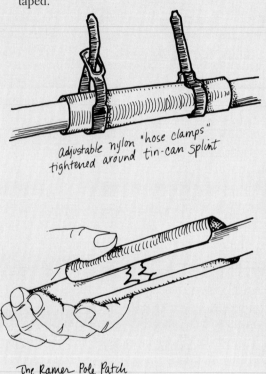

adjustable nylon "hose clamps" tightened around tin-can splint

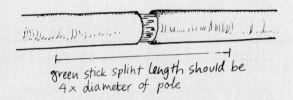

green stick splint length should be 4x diameter of pole

The Ramer Pole Patch

This ski pole broke on the first day of a week-long wilderness trip. A plug whittled out of Sierra pine and a sleeve fashioned from Dave's cigar tube (plus duct tape, of course) saved the trip.

ally weak and often splinter along their length. If this happens, you can try to repair the split with fiberglass strapping tape (which isn't very weatherproof) or by splinting with a green branch, tape, or clamps.

El cheapo (nontempered) aluminum poles are fine for light touring, but they tend to bend very easily and won't endure much abuse on the steeps. Be prepared to splint this type of pole. Alpine or collapsible probe poles are made with tempered

aluminum and will break rather than bend, so they're much easier to repair.

ADJUSTABLE POLES

Adjustable poles have quickly become de rigueur in the backcountry, but their many parts invite quirky behavior. Identify the trouble-prone moving parts and pick up some spares—Dave went through three tips one ski holiday, though the manufacturer assured him that these were "old-

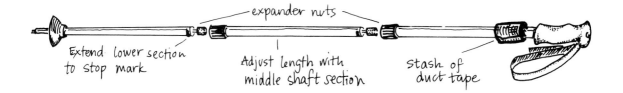

Extend lower section
to stop mark

expander nuts

Adjust length with
middle shaft section

stash of
duct tape

THE AMAZING
SHRINKING SKI POLE
Usually means the
expander nut has
become unscrewed.

style" tips. Maybe so, since those poles have now survived countless trips with the same two tips; nonetheless, Dave always packs a spare pole tip in his wax kit.

It's common to bend or break the lower section, for various reasons. One is that you must never adjust any section beyond the *stop* or *maximum* line at a joint. Don't use the pole as a lever to pull yourself up or for strange tasks. Telemarkers who take time to shorten their poles before descending will break fewer of them.

If yours is a three-section pole, pull the lower, more tapered section to its maximum length and make fine adjustments with the middle section. Shortening the tapered end leaves too much play inside the barrel.

Collapsing Collapsibles

If your pole shrinks during a crucial plant, you probably unthreaded the expander when you adjusted the pole length. Take a few minutes to understand how the expander inside your adjustable pole works. Grasp the joint collar with one hand and loosen the barrel—one or two turns is sufficient. Pull the lower section past the stop mark to expose the threads and expander plug. You can see that there's a fine line between a secure fit and unpredictability.

If tightening the joint collar in cold weather seems unrealistically difficult, check to see that the plug is threaded properly and that there's no grit inside. *Do not* lubricate the pole; just clean it with a damp cloth if necessary. A wrap of duct tape at the bottom of each section will give you better grip to torque them tighter in the field. "Clacking" of older adjustable poles can be alleviated by clamping with a band cut from a bicycle inner tube.

Skins

Whether your climbing skins are made of mohair, nylon, or a blend, you should care for them all the same way.

Always fold skins adhesive to adhesive to keep glue from gumming up the business side—and leaves, pack-pocket lint, and accumulated dog hair from gumming up the adhesive. Skins should be hung to dry after use, but never too close to a woodstove. In the field, drape them across poles or skis during a sunny lunch break. Many people stash skins in their gaiters during the day to keep them warm, dry, and sticky. For best adhesion, be sure to dry off your skis before applying the skins. Store your skins in a cool, dry place (especially during the summer). Even 80°F heat can cook the glue and change its constituents, possibly damaging the skins.

Skin adhesive is toothy stuff and with proper care will last several seasons. Occasionally someone will complain of skin glue coming off on skis. Usually this is because the ski base has dried out or the base wax is very dirty—skin adhesives will cling readily to dirt or fuzzy bases. Your best bet for removing stuck adhesive is to use a solvent,

Fold skins to preserve the adhesive and keep clean. Fold tail to middle, then fold tip to middle—adhesive to adhesive—then roll.

since heat or scraping will drive dirt deeper into the ski base.

CUSTOM FIT

Many people are unaware that skins may be trimmed to fit better in both length and width. Cut the skins just before ski tails flare upward, since this is where they tend to work loose first. Use a round cut—sharp corners will catch and peel.

Another solution is to fit tail clips to your skins; this also requires trimming the length. You can allow extra length at the tip for future adjustment. Tail clips eliminate the need to reglue tails as frequently, and they provide a snug, custom fit. (See appendix G, Materials Resources, beginning on page 236, for parts.)

THE PLUSH SIDE

There's a common assumption that a spritz of silicone on your skins will help increase their gliding potential. However, silicone coating causes the plush fibers to wick moisture to the adhesive side of a skin, and glue will not stick to silicone. Improve your glide instead with a bar of plain paraffin wax—just rub on skins, in light strokes, tip to tail, as needed in the field.

During an outing, skins pick up dirt, wax, pitch, and pine needles, matting down the pile and inhibiting performance. Once they are dry, you can beat or brush them to remove detritus, but at season's end you may want to clean them. Lay dry skins out on your deck or bench (or on the skis), spritz with citrus cleaner (containing *no*

Customizing skins with tail clips reduces reliance on adhesives.

mineral spirits, which might dissolve glues on the opposite side), and let stand for 15 minutes or so. Use a stiff nylon brush to clean, then rinse with water. Allow the skins to dry thoroughly. This session won't inhibit adhesion. If you have a tough spot of pitch, spot-clean with a little turpentine, but use sparingly.

REMOVING ADHESIVE

See also appendix A, Adhesives, beginning on page 212

The easiest way to remove tenacious skin glue is with a heat-gun paint stripper. Lacking that, Paul Hebert of Ascension Enterprises recommends this technique: Lay a brown paper grocery bag on the area to be reglued, then iron through the bag using the "wool" setting. Peel the bag off the skin while still warm. This will remove old glue quite effectively, but you may need to repeat the process.

Solvents are another option, but they are not recommended over the iron-and-paper-bag technique, since solvents will dry out and fatigue the skin materials. Hebert recommends Kwik Citra-Clean, a solvent used in ski shops that contains citrus oils and mineral spirits. Ask your favorite ski mechanic to sell you some.

Remove old adhesive by ironing over a brown paper bag.

HERBERT'S CARDINAL RULES FOR SKIN CARE

1. Don't reglue a larger area than necessary — removing adhesive dries out your skins.
2. Always work in a well-ventilated area.
3. Minimize the amount of glue used. More is not better!

REGLUING SKINS

Ask three skiers which skin adhesive they prefer, and you'll get six different answers. For home gluing, you're limited to solvent-based adhesives. While newer, water-based glues are certainly the trend and worth every effort to incorporate wherever possible, they just don't make it for skins—you're skiing on water, after all. Water-based glues also freeze into ineffectiveness faster than solvent-based types. Coll-Tex is a popular solvent brand, but if you're in cold country (below-zero temps), forget

TRIED-AND-TRUE

Paul Hebert offers his tried-and-true skin-gluing method:

1. Always work in a well-ventilated area, away from any heat source.
2. Be stingy with the glue—too much and it's a real mess.
3. Three thin coats 20 minutes apart gives best adhesion.
4. Apply masking tape to the plush side; you're bound to get glue on them no matter what your finesse quotient.
5. Use a staple gun to secure the skins taut on a deck or long workbench.
6. Run a thin bead of glue down the center of the skin.
7. Using an old credit card (or one with a high balance) as a squeegee, spread the glue from side to side. Lift the card at the end of each stroke, just inside the edge of the skin. Next, hold the card at an angle and skim straight down the center, trying not to let glue goop over the edges. Add more glue as necessary, but remember—thin is good.
8. Repeat the process on the second skin.
9. Apply two more coats to each, 20 minutes apart, and allow to dry overnight (preferably longer) before folding or using.

it, or plan to ski with your ski skins next to your own skin to keep them supple. Ascension Enterprises' Gold Label glue works well at lower temperatures.

If you wish to use nonsolvent adhesive on your skins, Ramer Products will reglue your skins using a unique "hot-melt" laminating process with an inert adhesive that stays sticky down to –50°F. The caveat: If your skins have seen silicone, the lamination won't succeed. Ramer also offers a wide range of parts—tips and tail hooks, etc.—as does Ascension Enterprises. (See appendix G, Materials Resources, beginning on page 236.)

Snowshoes
WOODEN SNOWSHOES

Allegorical symbols of winter wanderers, wooden snowshoes evoke more romantic images than almost any other type of gear (which is why you see them so often above the fireplace or in urbane magazine ads). The snowshoe is more than an icon, as the recent renaissance would indicate. In fact, says Bill Osgood, intrepid New England tramper and author of *The Snowshoe Book*, his first pair of shoes have seen four generations of tots and will undoubtedly be called into service by his great-grandchildren.

Wooden snowshoes require modest but regular care to remain functional. If you're looking at a secondhand pair for real use and not for decoration, you can easily tell if they're dried out by poking the wood with a knife point—if the point

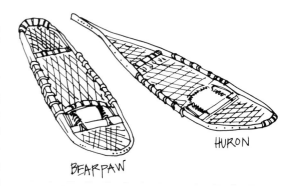

BEARPAW

HURON

enters easily, they're pretty far gone. Porous, splintery wood and brittle lacings won't last long underfoot. However, some splintering at the apex of the tip is not unusual.

If the wood's in good shape but the lacing is weary, consider renovating the shoes with a kit from Tubbs, one of the last holdouts of wooden snowshoe makers (see appendix G, Materials Resources, beginning on page 236). Established in 1846, Tubbs offers repair kits and service for every imaginable style of shoe. The weaving of snowshoe laces is akin to advanced cat's cradle, and Tubbs supplies a terrific how-to booklet with its repair kits.

For those interested in the elegant art and intricacy of indigenous snowshoe building, seek out a copy of Henri Vaillancourt's fine treatise, *Making the Attikamek Snowshoe*.

An annual coat of varnish on the frame and the rawhide webbing will maintain waterproofness and resiliency. If the webbing is not protected, soggy rawhide thongs will stretch and weaken. Properly maintained, however, rawhide remains the most durable, longest-lasting lacing material, as well as the only renewable one. Neoprene laces (neoprene-coated synthetic fabric) require less care but may fray and deteriorate over time. Pass a lighter back and forth along any fray to melt back stray fibers.

A break in the frame is a permanent structural failure, but you can splint the structure in the field with hose clamps, string, and a stout stick. The laces may snap or cut along the frame, and splic-

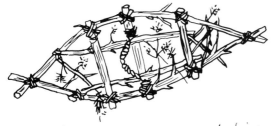

in a pinch you can use lashing skills to tie spruce boughs into functional snowshoes

ing materials are limited only by your imagination: parachute cord, snips of woolen scarf, slices of belts, cattail reeds, and, of course, twisted duct tape.

If your laces are of rawhide, once home you can soak the shoe in water to soften them enough to splice. The process is somewhat like darning mittens. Use soaked and softened rawhide of similar density. With a clove hitch around the frame, fasten one end of the rawhide to a structurally intact section of webbing. Follow the lacing pattern, working into the damaged area and beyond.

You can protect the vulnerable toe bend and laces with a wrapping of soft, soaked rawhide. Clove-hitch one end, then wrap snugly to the opposite side. Finish by tucking the lace under itself and pulling snug.

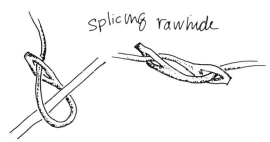

"WESTERN" ALUMINUM SNOWSHOES

Modern snowshoes are virtually carefree. Crafted with tempered aluminum frames, integrated crampons, nylon bindings, and Hypalon or neoprene solid decking, these are quintessentially high-tech units. All employ modern materials to a design that's been around for two millennia.

Some versions attach decking with laces, using supple vinyl to lash a stiff synthetic deck to the frame; others simply stretch and rivet Hypalon decking around the tubes. Both styles are prone to abrasion on the outside edge of the frames; the riveted type will withstand more wear and tear before you're faced with repair. Periodically check rivets, however.

Laces commonly cut along this outer edge.

You can protect laces by wrapping duct tape snugly around a sensitive area of lashing (similar to toe winding on a wooden shoe) or by stitching a patch of neoprene or webbing into place.

In the field, splice tattered laces with a length of nylon cord or twisted duct tape. These laces are tensioned and secured with metal clamps called "hog rings" or "cage clips," rather than knotted. You can purchase an inexpensive kit to replace hog rings—a special pincer is required—but the

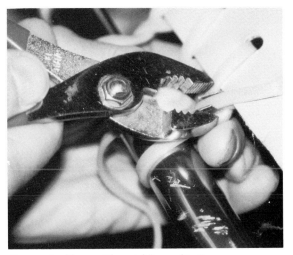

Secure vinyl laces with metal "cage clips."

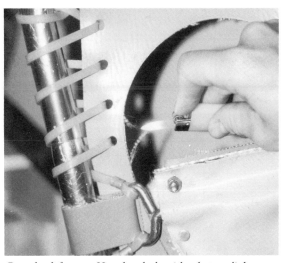

Burn back frays on Hypalon decks with a butane lighter.

lacings are best obtained directly from the snow-shoe manufacturer.

Hypalon decks are prone to puncturing from crampons, ski poles, and sharp sticks. These can be patched at home with Aquaseal. Watch for abrasion spots and melt back any fraying fibers with the flame of a lighter. Don't use a stove or torch—you may do more harm than good.

SNOWSHOE BINDINGS
Traditional

Wooden snowshoes often employ an H-shaped leather binding, complete with metal buckles. These must be well oiled for smooth operation in the cold (wipe the buckles with silicone too). Leather snowshoe bindings may not be as chemically stable as nylon, but the fit is excellent—like a moccasin. Another popular style is the speedy A binding, which is simple and effective. You may

For snowshoe bindings, fewer parts mean fewer bits to break. Watch those plastic buckles like a hawk!

want to silicone the laces to prevent them from icing up.

High-Tech Crampon Bindings

Aluminum snowshoes generally use nylon-web bindings with nylon hardware. Many parts of these bindings are likely to crack in the cold weather, so bring spares or be prepared to cannibalize parts off your pack.

Make sure crampons are secure and operating smoothly; lubricate the binding's pivot points

toestrap

Algonquin, Ojibway, Cree & Attikamek peoples employed this simply elegant snowshoe harness; winter travelers would be wise to master this craft.

Traditional leather "H" binding

Bent snowshoe crampons are easily straightened with pliers.

underfoot with light oil or silicone. Snowshoe crampons are prone to balling up with snow. You can alleviate this problem with silicone or wax—silicone is equally effective in preventing laces from icing up.

Snowshoe crampons made of hardened aluminum rarely bend; the teeth also remain sharper longer than nonhardened versions. If your lightweight crampons are bent, wait until the snowshoe is warm before hammering out any kinks, or you may shear the metal. You can often bring crampons back into shape simply by bending them in a vise or with pliers.

Collapsible Avalanche Shovels

The most common shovel injury is a fractured blade caused by prying wet, compressed snow. The most effective shoveling method is to patiently cut snow into blocks.

Another area of weakness is the joint between blade and shaft. Check to see that it isn't wobbly. Loose rivets may be replaced with pop rivets.

Be careful not to pry when cutting snow

Take your shovel apart occasionally and clean the shaft of grit. A little silicone spritzed on pop-pins will keep them from icing up. You should also rub silicone on the blade to prevent snow from balling up.

Sleds and Pulks

If you're towing a wooden pulk or sled, treat it the same as you would wooden skis. Weatherproof it each season with oil or varnish, watching for loose joinery or hardware. Treat the runners with pine tar and base wax.

Molded plastic or fiberglass sleds should be treated like their waterborne kayak cousins. Store out of the sun, away from heat. Pay attention to the hardware, which is prone to jiggling itself loose. Loc-Tite on screw threads is a good idea. Inspect contacts where traces join the sled. If a tubular metal trace snaps, repair it as you might repair a busted ski pole (see page 146).

Feel free to wax a plastic sled; a gouged bottom can be filled with P-Tex (for quality plastic models) or even epoxy and gelcoat on fiberglass versions (see chapter 17, Hull Materials).

Molded plastic kids' sleds are popular for backcountry hikers because of their economy. Too often, though, they're tossed off the trail, discarded because of a crack in the bottom—they're cheaper to replace than repair, right? Well, you can have a sidewalk sale with these salvaged castoffs. In the field, use duct tape. At home, drill a small hole in each end of the crack to prevent it from spreading. Don't bother removing the duct tape. Next, pop-rivet a patch of similar material (semirigid plastic if possible, a scrap of vinyl house siding; or a chunk cut from a 5-gallon sheet-rock-mud bucket). Overlap the crack by at least an inch or so.

Fix your cracked cargo sled with a pop-riveted patch made from a scrap of vinyl siding or carved from a plastic sheet-rock-mud bucket. Rivet heads go outside the sled.

PART 4

Paddling

Consider the Alternatives

One glance at Audrey Sutherland tells you she's a woman with a mission. "Go light, go solo, go now" is her mantra; her vehicle, a small inflatable kayak. At seventy-plus, Audrey has logged more than 15,000 miles in her "rubber ducky" during the last 30 years, touring coasts from Samoa to Scotland, Alaska, and Hawaii, where she makes her home.

Audrey's infectious energy sparks from crinkled blue eyes and radiates through her shock of sun-bleached hair. While many people describe this world paddler as "tough," our family sees her as resourceful, practical, and beautifully balanced. Audrey's self-reliance is legendary, her fears unknown. What is most intriguing about Audrey is the way ordinary objects become essen-

Audrey Sutherland is quick to spot alternative uses for everyday objects.

tials in her traveling kit. She may go out of her way to find a low-cost alternative to a high-tech piece of gear, but she'll gladly pay the price of a fine wine.

Here are a few care and repair tips and alternatives as prescribed by Audrey:

Favorite repair ingredient? "Dental floss—like the gut Eskimos used for sewing. Carry a needle with a large enough eye to thread it through. I've used it in place of wire, rope, duct tape, whipping line, eyeglass hinge screws."

Best maintenance tip? "A dental Water Pik with hot water at Force 10." Audrey uses it to get gunky peanut butter and old glue out of her Swiss Army knife and to blast lint out of the corners of shirt pockets. The pressure also blows carbon from camp stove jets or sand from the screw threads in kayak hatch covers.

Unusual repair ingredient? "Condoms. Make a slingshot for survival; waterproof your watch or exposed film; carry water (reinforced by using inside a sock); make a spear gun for fishing; or use a fluorescent orange one for a crab trap float. Tie several together end-to-end as a long, superstrong rubber band."

Frugal tip: "Repair your water bag bladder by substituting a boxed wine bladder. Twice as strong, it uses the same cap/spout and can be used as a pillow, kayak seat, crab trap float, shower bag. Priced right, too."

CHAPTER 15

Boats

The first gear-related gift Dave ever gave Annie was a roto-molded plastic white-water kayak—a petite, glitzy, girl-colored craft complete with requisite matching accessories. There was one catch, however (besides Annie): she hated whitewater kayaking.

She gave the sport a fair shot, dog-paddling after him through swirls and drops, swimming a few rapids and practicing her roll at the lake. She mewed like a kitty stranded on midstream boulders while he fished disparate parts of her gear from the froth. Nice try but no go: something about taking on yet another helmet sport just didn't feel right. A few months later some lucky river rat got a great deal on a (very) slightly used purple torpedo.

To his credit, Dave cashed in his own white-water gear, and we bought two plastic sea kayaks instead. A sleek Kevlar flatwater canoe soon followed. Turns out Annie absolutely loved white-water tandem boating. After a few close calls running rapids in the fragile Kevlar cruiser, we picked up an agile yet bombproof ABS whitewater tandem canoe. Or was that after we sold one of the sea kayak singles to score a gorgeous 21-foot fiberglass double? Well, it was definitely before we got into solo canoeing, and our amorphous little fleet added up to a full half-dozen.

Get the picture? This rapid descent into multiple boat ownership is a typical progression for those bitten by the paddling bug. It's also an expensive learning curve when it comes to picking out the right boat materials. Here's hoping our own experience can save you some time and money finding the right boat (see sidebar, page 157).

Demystifying and qualifying the gamut of materials used to build twentieth-century canoes and kayaks could certainly justify a book or two in itself. For the average boater, however, a rudimentary understanding of hull materials provides the foundation for most any repair situation that might arise.

Regardless of design, purpose, or style, canoe and kayak construction falls into one of the following categories: ABS/Royalex, aluminum, fiberglass or Kevlar, polyethylene, wood and canvas, or skin over frame.

Whether you're a wild creek boater, a quiet-water tourist, or a surf fanatic, you may well trash your hull before you ever reach water. We've seen a roto-molded sea kayak that launched from an auto roof rack at 70 mph, skirted four lanes of Atlanta rush-hour traffic, cartwheeled over the median strip, then T-boned the cab of a city garbage truck. Damage total: one wrinkled kayak nose, two scuffed decals, three broken truck windows, and one extremely lucky—and unscathed—truck driver. Other, more tragic tales of roof-rack terror abound:

One friend, speeding north through a subzero breeze for Christmas with a holiday-red poly kayak on the roof, was shocked when the boat shattered upon impact with the pavement.

After a surreal, nearly desperate crossing ahead of a looming thunderstorm, Annie and her friend (continued page 159)

FIRST BOAT: WHAT YOU NEED TO KNOW BEFORE YOU BUY

Maybe you dimly recall some long-ago canoe trip at summer camp; perhaps you've read about exotic sea-kayak adventures. Whatever your memories, you're simply aching to buy that first canoe or kayak. Trouble is, the shorter your experience, the longer your chances for picking exactly the wrong starter boat. Too many people who buy their first canoe or kayak do little more than buy into a dream.

To awaken you to paddling reality, we say don't buy anything until after you've been on the water (or in it). Start by finding yourself a qualified salesperson at a specialty paddling shop, the kind of place run by paddlers for paddlers. This person will reveal him- or herself as truly savvy by first asking you a bunch of questions about your paddling experience and goals, then suggesting you take a one-day guided trip or a basic canoe or kayak class. If the salesperson just starts spouting off about his or her own favorite boat being exactly right for you, keep shopping.

Novices may want to consider renting before buying. Some shops allow rental credits toward an eventual purchase. Likewise, a paddling club will help you stroke your way up the steepest part of the initial learning curve. Just don't be offended if your new paddling friends wisely decline to lend you a boat to learn in.

Key Questions:

- **Who will be paddling?** That is, are you buying a boat for you, for your family, or for use with a specific partner? Decide who's going to use and enjoy the boat—don't expect a spouse or kid to have the same feelings about it that you do. Don't get soaked. If you're not certain, forgo the boat purchase and invest in a guided paddling trip for the whole family so you can guage everybody's interest before taking the plunge.
- **Where do you want to go?** This all depends on where you live and the type of water you typically plan to travel. If you're into backwater birdwatching, a small open canoe or open-cockpit touring kayak will serve. Swift rivers demand tough, nimble canoes or whitewater kayaks. A well-handled canoe is adaptable to surprisingly large waters, but big windy lakes and choppy ocean bays spell *k-a-y-a-k* to the novice. Pay careful attention to this decision; too many people end up with a generic recreational canoe because they're unwilling or unable to decide about how they'll actually use the boat ... until a season or two later, when they're back shopping for a more specialized design.
- **What's your style?** If you're a persnickety purist married to a bumbler, that's almost certainly a mandate for two solo sea kayaks. If you seek specialization in automobiles, kitchen appliances, or bicycles, chances are you won't be content for long with a general-purpose design. The top-selling boats are 16- or 17-foot family recreational canoes, basically the minvans of small boats. Specialization complicates the choice; avoid the temptation to choose a highly targeted craft until you're sure that's what you want. Expect a steep (i.e., wet) learning curve with some special-purpose boats, but the payoff is performance.

Read up. Educate yourself. Collect brochures and handouts about available designs. Boat catalogues are often thoughtfully written and packed with useful information. Even though canoes and kayaks are about as simple as boats can be, homework helps you translate the sales spiel and strain significance from the bilge.

Just *do* it. Read and test all you can, but beware of "analysis paralysis," wherein uncertainty overwhelms the urge to act. There is absolutely no substitue for simply climbing aboard a boat—any boat—and swinging your paddle.

HULL MATERIALS AT A GLANCE

	ABS	Polyethylene	Fiberglass	Kevlar	Aluminum	Wood and Canvas	Birchbark
Intrinsic properties: positive vs negative	+Tremendous impact resistance, sturdy, slips over rocks, resilient. – Floppy, hard to mold efficient shapes, heavy, low abrasion resistance, chemically sensitive.	+Great impact resistance, sturdy, inexpensive. – Floppy, heavy, can shatter in very cold, poor abrasion resistance, easily UV damaged, poor bonding surface.	+Inexpensive, stiff, efficient, abrasion resistant, moderate weight. – Limited impact resistance, stiffened areas difficult to fix.	+Superstrong for weight, very light, rigid. – Expensive, hard to make smooth repair, skin-coat prone to UV damage.	+Zero maintenance, stiff, immune to general abuse. – Loud, cold, grabby, hard to restore smooth shape once bent.	+Organic, renewable, warm, resilient. – Expensive, moderately heavy, high-maintenance.	+Beautiful, organic, renewable. – Obselete, resource short-lived.
Deform under its own weight	Yes	Yes	Minor	No	No	Yes	No
Special maintenance or storage requirements	Wood trim requires regular oiling, also preparation for cold storage. Rack on gunwales out of sun.	Must be racked on rails or decks, supported at bulkheads. Hanging also suitable. Keep out of sun.	Keep out of sun to prevent gelcoat from fading.	Store out of sun to prevent darkening of Kevlar, fading of gelcoat.	Racked on rails, un-level, to prevent water from pooling and producing cracks.	Requires regular varnish, fabric filling to prevent mildew. Rack on gunwales indoors.	Regular application of spruce gum.
UV protection	303 Protectant	303 Protectant	303 Protectant to buffed hull. Wax has no UV inhibitors.	303 Protectant to buffed hull. Wax has no UV inhibitors.	N/A	Varnish and canvas filler paint.	Like, totally organic, man.
Abrasion resistance	Low	Low	Medium	Medium	High	Low to Medium	Medium
Impact resistance	High	High	Low to Medium	Low to Medium	High	Medium	Low to Medium
Most common repair	Abrasions and dents filled, also cold cracks from improper storage, skid plates added.	Leaky fittings, leaking or shifting bulkheads. Abraded holes from pebbles between seats and hull.	Gelcoat chips, impact damage to stems, stress fractures (spiderweb cracks) in laminate.	Gelcoat chips, resin cracks that separate laminated layers, also stem damage.	Dents	Torn fabric, gouged rails and cracked ribs. Wood rot from outdoor storage and lack of maintenance.	Stem abrasion in pine tar and spruce gum
Ease of repair	Easy	Very difficult	Moderate to Difficult	Moderate to Difficult	Moderate	Easy to Difficult	Difficult
Best bonding agent for repair and outfitting	Epoxy putty, epoxy resin for repairs and skid plates. Vynabond for vinyl, 3M Urethane structural adhesive, contact cement for outfitting.	Urethane adhesive caulk, urethane structural adhesives for both. Contact cement not recommended.	Polyester resin, epoxy putty for repair, urethane caulk or structural adhesive for outfitting. Vynabond or contact cement not recommended. Can be restored to its original shape.	Polyester or epoxy resin, epoxy putty for repair; urethane caulk or structural adhesive for outfitting. Vynabond or contact cement not recommended. Difficult to access commercial vinylester resin.	Metal-proved epoxy, urethane caulk or adhesive for repair.	Yellow wood glue, ambroid glue, epoxy, varnish, canvas filler paint, copper nails.	Spruce root lashing epoxy.

(continued from page 156)

Mary reached the boat landing in a stinging downpour, leaped out, and literally threw their light glass double onto the waiting trailer—and punched a hole broadside as the boat kissed the end of a crossbar.

An island friend—and a mountain of a man— helped us portage our loaded boats with his big truck. Geoff effortlessly hoisted the bow while Dave wrestled with the stern. Geoff's powerful heft was enough to break the fraying bow grab loop; the sharp bowstem splintered on contact with the unforgiving island granite.

An uneventful Canadian odyssey culminated in a raucous packing-up session as crew members tossed packs and boats unceremoniously onto roof racks. We both listened in horror to the cracking canoe as an overzealous, beer-lubed lout cranked his stern line just a little tighter.

These transport tales of terror aside, any paddler should know what sort of performance to expect from his or her boat material, how to deal with catastrophe in the field, and maybe how to prevent it in the first place. The accompanying chart helps to illustrate the properties of various materials; you'll find more in-depth coverage in the corresponding discussions.

Once you've mastered the hull-material characteristics, other structural and rigging idiosyncrasies become specific to the type of craft: leaking bulkheads, broken cockpit coaming, or worn rudder assembly on kayaks; cracked rails, torn seats, or blown D-rings on canoes. Replacing rigging and hardware teeters at the brink of outfitting— altogether a different bailiwick than maintenance and repair.

However, the wide world of outfitting still plays an important role in the safety and performance of your paddling paraphernalia. For instance, if D-rings are incorrectly applied they can cause serious hull damage. Trying to walk the line, always ask yourself this question: could this job prevent a catastrophic failure in the future?

CHAPTER 16

Rules of the Resin

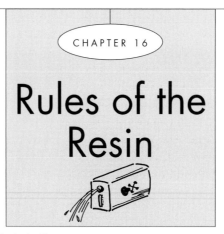

This particular portage at Navaite Rapids not only cost 2 ½ days of severe and incessant labor, but also cost something in damage to the canoes. The one in which I had been journeying was split in a manner which caused us serious uneasiness as to how long, even after being patched, it would last.

Theodore Roosevelt, *Through the Brazilian Wilderness*

Warnings about the Warnings

See also appendix A, Adhesives

Many experts interviewed regarding fiberglass or Kevlar repair discouraged home users from ever getting involved with the stuff. "By the time you've botched five or six jobs, invested a fair amount on toxic materials, and shortened your life span by breathing them all, you might be able to produce a viable glass patch," maintains one boatbuilder. Others simply point to the skull-and-crossbones warning labels. Enough said.

Unfortunately, many folks don't live anywhere near an experienced glass technician or boat-builder, and anyone heading out on an expedition should be prepared to patch a hole—you might be 100 miles from anywhere and the boat your only ticket back. Although the process is not all that difficult for an amateur, controlling the working environment is. The home user's best options for glass and Kevlar repairs are prepackaged kits from canoe or kayak manufacturers, because they come with exact mixing quantities, the proper patch materials, and step-by-step instructions.

While they may seem expensive, the resins and fillers delivered from the manufacturer are developed specifically for use on your particular hull, and there's less room for error than if you cobbled together materials from the meager selection at your local auto parts shop or hardware store. Finally, kits provide you with small, easy-to-use-up quantities of what's often highly caustic stuff with a specified shelf life, so you don't have to deal with long-term storage and disposal hassles.

If you find the kits limiting and your glass-repair enthusiasm survives the learning curve, select a specialized book on working with fiberglass and thermoset resins from the hundreds available. Better yet, take a course at your local community college or vo-tech school. Set up your shop accordingly and practice the art safely.

For most weekend warriors, boat repair involves filling gouges in gelcoat or substrate layers with suitable putty and applying skid plates to the bow and stern of a whitewater canoe. Once you've mastered these procedures, you'll probably feel confident and competent enough to tackle a structural repair.

The First Resins

Pine tar and latex rubber are indigenous organic ancestors of the present-day distillates we recognize as polyester, vinylester, and other synthetic hybrid resins. Abby, our woodcarver friend, never fails to stop and gather spruce gum whenever she spots it along a trail (where trees are typically scarred). She uses it as fill in her sculptures, but we've heard many stories in which gum smeared into a punctured fiberglass hull successfully sealed a leak beyond the duration of a wilderness journey.

Early wood-and-canvas canoe owners employed a techy alternative to pine tar: white lead. While this canvas filler had fewer fumes than today's resins, the dust was just as nasty. Modern wood-and-canvas craft are built with either oil- or water-based fillers rather than a synthetic resin.

Thermoset Resins: How They Work and What to Expect

When liquid resin is mixed with a catalyst, the reaction produces heat. The polymerized material cures (and shrinks) as it cools to a permanent hard finish. Curing begins in relatively short order (often in less than 15 minutes), leaving you with an urgently limited working time to effect your repair. Therefore, it is essential that you be orderly and organized when working with these substances. *If the worst thing you can do is to be in a hurry, the second-worst thing you can do is to take your time.*

A good cure depends both on the resin-catalyst mix and the ambient temperature and humidity. The mix you can control somewhat, but not the weather. A typical resin-to-catalyst ratio might be less than 2 percent, but even this recommendation is based on an ideal temperature range between 50° and 70°F.

The best conditions for a consistent cure are low humidity and moderate temperatures, and it's smart to wait for cooperative weather. Dampness may inhibit the mix from curing at all, while a hot, dry day is likely to produce a brittle concoction that sets up long before you're finished with the patch—neither of which will help you fix your busted boat on some remote riverbank.

Patching with cloth and resin in the field is very tricky because the conditions are usually not conducive to a proper cure. Since a fiberglass or Kevlar patch is essentially a permanent repair, it's better to limp out with a makeshift patch of duct tape or spruce gum and do a proper job at home. Glass patching on a wet, cold trip will likely produce a mess that will require a great effort to undo later.

An exception here is the newly introduced air-activated field patch, available at specialty paddling shops. This patch is sealed in a foil pouch; once exposed to air, it cures quickly with a tenacious hold. Proper surface prep, as always, improves the quality and longevity of the repair.

Some situations demand a structural patch, however, and if you ever find yourself having to make one on a sandbar somewhere, you'll be glad you practiced at home on an old hull or even an apple crate to get the feel of handling the basic mechanics of fabric-and-resin patches (see pages 179–81).

Resin Types
GELCOAT
Gelcoat forms the in-mold, pigmented coating for fiberglass and some Kevlar boats. Essentially cosmetic, gelcoat is heavy and commonly cracks or chips upon impact. Gelcoat's polyester base limits its ability to bond to other poly or vinyl resins; gelcoat does not adhere to epoxy. Gelcoat does, however, protect the underlying cloth layers from premature UV damage.

VINYLESTER
Vinylester is the resin likely to be used in a Kevlar layup, primarily because of its higher elongation (flexibility) when compared with polyester. However, its expense and limited shelf life make vinylester a rare commodity at the consumer level.

POLYESTER
Polyester resin is more readily available and is found in most kits. A polyester repair is best for long-term

fixes on glass or Kevlar laminate boats because it closely replicates the original hull. However, polyester does not bond especially well to wood and will separate with repeated impact. Expect horrified gasps if you mention that you've decided to glass over your grandfather's wood-and-canvas canoe.

EPOXY

Epoxy is easy to mix and work with in small quantities, so it's particularly handy to use at home or in the field for filling small punctures or deep gashes. Epoxy works as a two-part system. Epoxy mixes vary, but you can find a type that will bond to ABS, aluminum, wood, or just about anything. You can paint over epoxy, but be aware that polyester—including gelcoat—won't bond to it.

Epoxy is a popular solution for filling nasty dings in a sharp-entry bow or stern because it is very strong, has the least shrinkage of any resin, and can be combined with a variety of fillers. Its added strength makes surfaces tough to sand once cured; experienced users recommend smoothing the material with a Surform blade during the "green" phase, after the mix has set but before it has fully cured to a rock-hard finish.

Safe Sets

No matter what material you plan to use—gelcoat, polyester, vinylester, or epoxy—don't dismiss the importance of the following safety precautions. Most repair materials are just plain nasty, stinky, toxic goops. Use them sparingly and intelligently.

- Read all materials instructions and warnings carefully before attempting a repair. Any enlisted helpers should also read the instructions and warnings.
- Carefully prepare by laying out all your materials and by cutting and test-fitting patches before mixing the resin. Recite to yourself or write a quick outline of the steps involved—a systematic approach is more likely to yield the desired results.

Always wear an approved respirator when spray-painting or working with toxic resins.

- Work in a clean, airy (but not windy) location well away from any flame source and out of direct sunlight. A garage or well-ventilated shop is ideal.
- If working inside a building, use an ordinary household fan to ventilate the fumes; place the fan at your feet facing out an open door to blow the heavy gases outside.
- Lock kids and pets in the attic until you've finished the job.
- Wear safety glasses, gloves, and coveralls to protect eyes and skin.
- Gloves do two things: they keep the nasty stuff off your skin, and they keep your own skin oils from contaminating the repair.
- Use a respirator to prevent inhalation of fumes. Make sure the respirator is OSHA rated to filter out the toxic gases you'll be inhaling. This and eye protection are most important.
- Mix the resin and the catalyst in a clean, disposable container. Any leftover mixed material cannot be saved; allow it to harden completely in a cool outdoor setting before disposal.
- Tilt the container away from you when pouring or stirring so you don't catch splashes.
- For a really thorough mix and an even cure, count to 100 while stirring.
- Acetone is the typical prep and cleanup material—don't be lax when handling this volatile, extremely caustic substance. Acetone is quickly absorbed into the skin and attacks the liver. Always use it sparingly and wear gloves. Substitute denatured alcohol whenever possible.

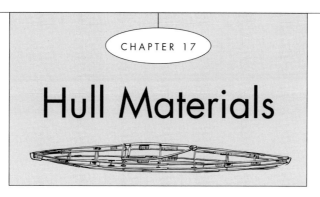

Hull Materials

An Indian at Greenville
told me that the winter
bark, that is, bark taken off before the sap flows in May,
was harder and much better than summer bark.

Henry David Thoreau, *The Maine Woods*

Of Canoes and Geologic Time

The bark canoe was plenty sophisticated by the time Europeans started thrashing around in the New World. Of the craft's evolution there is but little trace because of the compostable nature of early native prototypes. Birchbark boats of yore modestly disintegrated into duff, each generation's innovation preserved as collective knowledge.

Which is no bad thing. In fact, the idea of defunct, inert, modern plastic canoes stacking up across North America is starting to keep Annie up at night. She dreams that some remote Saskatchewan towns are bidding for the economic privilege of becoming the hemisphere's first canoe repository.

Those resilient yet temporary sheets of paper birch have been eclipsed by twentieth-century materials whose half-life has yet to be realized. Under "ideal conditions" a plastic hull will last forever, chirp the manufacturers. Maybe, but how many people *really* store their boat out of the sun or unscrew wooden rails for the winter? And do we *want* the shrunken corpses of infinite Discos to last infinitely?

Martin Brown, Maine Guide and renowned raconteur, offers true field experience when it comes to assessing the longevity of modern canoe materials. "Forever, maybe, for the average guy," grunts Martin, "but used commercially, a Royalex canoe is viable for about five years." He explains: "Like old people, who are brittle . . . as long as they don't fall on the ice they'll keep on trucking." Martin also suggests that sandwich construction has become flimsier—not stiffer—over the years. He contends that early Royalex boats, such as the venerable Blue Hole, are outliving more recent models; this may be due more to manufacturers' penny-pinching than to engineering.

Steve Scarborough, a designer and principal at Dagger Canoe Company who has a long history of building wooden paddles, takes another view. "We punish these newer boats more than ever, as our skills have evolved along with the designs. ABS-sandwich boats are made with premium plastic—and canoes and kayaks represent some of the toughest tests for any material."

Despite specialized refinements from clever designers, Royalex springs eternal, even after it has become too floppy to paddle. With this realization comes a new kind of respect for linear polyethylene and—*gasp*—aluminum canoes, both rendered from recyclable materials. These hulls represent the best choice available today for environmentally savvy canoeists (wood-and-canvas construction included, due to nasty fillers and paints).

Aluminum for aluminum's sake—it already exists in surplus, thanks to the military. And canoes are a great and peaceable use for hawk droppings.

BETULA PAPYRIFERA
(Canoe Birch)

Are the means
primitive or sophisticated—
⠀⠀⠀slaughter?
⠀⠀⠀husbandry?
to slay a living thing,
its seed the spoils
for sons to come?

Thawing wind swirls fog and
ruffles tendrils on the stiff hide
rolled up raw and seeping
⠀⠀⠀sharp astringent smell.

First we'll peel to ruddy inside
then gore and wrap and lace
around steambent ribs
with dusky damp split roots.

After big rains, we'll follow the ice
and fill this vessel with
spring harvest of
fiddleheads and lily beds,

gather spruce blood when we find it
to seal against the seasons
until the brittle skin
grows into forest floor.

⠀⠀⠀⠀Then we'll hunt one more.

⠀⠀⠀⠀⠀⠀⠀⠀A.G.

Roto-molded linear polyethylene, albeit not renewable, is thoroughly recyclable and can be sourced from a witches' brew of secondhand plastic. Credit Paul Farrow, a former environmental-cleanup executive, for his ingenuity in this regard. His Massachusetts manufacturing company, Walden Paddlers, is the first to source its compact kayaks from 100 percent postconsumer and indus-

trial waste. Ironically, some of Walden's raw material originates in Dagger Canoe's Tennessee plant.

Scarborough laughed when Annie tried to argue that wooden canoes are better because they are "sustainable." "What's sustainable about cutting old-growth cedar?" he counters. Plastic sources are not limited to petroleum. "Source resins can be vegetable. During a glut, we'll get epoxy from oil," explains Scarborough. "During a shortage, we'll make plastics from soy."

In the midst of these developments, Annie—who has always lived in cold places where paper birch grow—dreams of building a bark canoe. She greedily gathers curls of chalky skin from the snow as if they were seashells, marveling at the elastic possibility of each sheet as she kindles her woodstove with them. Her favorite fantasy is that her birchbark boat will dissolve into the ground like a beaver lodge, dust to dust.

ABS or Royalex

Writing about maintenance and repair brings guilty moments—every glance at the fading hulls racked, hung, and stacked around our barn and riverfront is a reminder that our boats sure could use some TLC. So we felt a lot better after spotting the ten-year-old Royalex Tripper of Zip Kellogg (a canoe celebrity) in a parking lot. The thing had led a rough life: dings, dents, and gouges nearly obscured its worn-through skid plates; the wood rails were splintery and gray; mildew blackened the cane seats. But the boat was still solid, ready to paddle, and obviously had some stories to tell.

Many, probably most, paddlers could never devote enough time on the water to accumulate that kind of wear. Even so, with some simple preventive maintenance through the years your Royalex canoe will likely outlive you.

This class of canoe may be labeled ABS (acrylonitrile butadiene styrene)—the plastic that forms

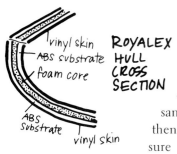

vinyl skin
ABS substrate
foam core

ROYALEX HULL CROSS SECTION

ABS Substrate

vinyl skin

the strong substrate layer in a Royalex laminate. ABS laminate is made from various plastic sheets sandwiched together, then heated under pressure to fuse the layers, crosslink the vinyl outer skin, activate agents to produce a foam core that stiffens the hull, and provide shock absorption and inherent flotation.

ROYALEX AND ITS EVIL ENEMIES

Three things have claimed more Royalex boats than all the world's rapids and rocks combined: sun, careless adhesive use, and improper winter storage. We know this from experience. The stout Mad River Freedom canoe that lives on the riverbank in our backyard has endured each of these tortures, serving as a sort of guinea pig for this book. Every malady listed here has been carefully documented. Yes, we *know* we are treating this boat unspeakably, yet we haven't the heart to get rid of it. All the neighborhood kids have learned to paddle in it; we use it to gather garden poles and washed-up treasures; it goes fishing and poling and beaver-dam-bashing; the dogs would be devastated without their daily canoe adventure. In short, it's a semisacrificial boat that has been loved (i.e., *used*) more than all our others combined.

Evil Royalex Enemy No. 1: The Sun

Although it's tempting to store something as carefree as a Royalex canoe outside, nothing could be worse over the long term. UV radiation will eventually fade and weaken the vinyl outer skin. Protected storage is crucial. Rack the canoe indoors or at least under a shed roof. Regular applications of 303 Protectant will also help maintain the color and resilient qualities of your ABS hull. If you must store your boat outdoors, see that any scratches exposing ABS layers are filled or painted to protect against UV damage.

Even though the average canoe spends 90 percent of its life upside down on a rack, the interior of a well-used canoe should also be treated. However, don't apply protectant to the interior just before a whitewater run, when you need purchase along the floor! A single application to the interior just before winter storage should be sufficient. Dorcas Miller solves the problem of a slippery canoe floor by strategically placing self-adhesive shower or stair treads. Glued-down foam pads are also popular.

D-ring

Evil Royalex Enemy No. 2: Careless Adhesive Use

adhesives can easily damage rather than enhance.

ABS Hull

Solvents such as acetone and those in contact cements can seriously damage Royalex laminates. Our long-suffering Freedom has four dimpled areas on the bottom that attest to where Dave hastily installed kneepads and the solvents in the glue softened the foam core. If using acetone to etch a surface for adhesion, apply it sparingly and don't rub too hard. Allow it to evaporate completely before attempting bonding. Use denatured alcohol whenever possible. Never touch a pre-

Note rippled hull, due to impatient glue job. Trapped fumes will distort ABS.

pared surface with your hands—even momentary contact practically guarantees the bond to fail in that spot.

In the same vein, use special care when outfitting your ABS boat with vinyl D-rings or minicell foam. Contact cement or Vynabond users: gluing surfaces should be almost dry to the touch—not tacky or shiny. If you join surfaces before the solvents have completely evaporated, the solvents can migrate through the hull sandwich and create a soft spot, likely to fail. Mad River Canoe recommends 3M-3552 urethane structural adhesive for outfitting purposes.

Evil Royalex Enemy No. 3: Below-Zero Temps

Royalex has a high shrink coefficient and will expand and contract significantly between a hot August day and a winter night when temperatures dip below zero. Many ABS canoes feature wood gunwales, which contract at a radically different rate; this difference can create pressures great enough to crack the laminate. These "cold cracks" may be up to 5 inches long, and must be repaired by removing rails entirely and patching the interior with Kevlar structural patches. At least our poor Freedom doesn't have cold cracks in the hull; the wood rails are too punky to split the laminate.

When preparing your ABS boat for hibernation, loosen the screws that secure the gunwales by back-

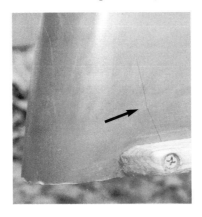

This hairline "cold crack" in a Royalex hull could easily have been prevented by loosening gunwale screws before winter storage.

ing them out several turns. Longer deck screws should be completely removed to open outwales and separate the decks from the hull. Come spring, dab a bit of penetrating oil into each hole, then replace and tighten the screws.

SCRATCHES

When the outer vinyl skin is scratched deeply enough to expose the ABS layer, you should mask the substrate as soon as possible to prevent certain UV deterioration. Use a vinyl spray paint (available from the boat manufacturer or your local auto parts store) to touch up surface scratches and abrasions. Remember to clean and prep the area first.

DENTS

Whamming a midstream rock demonstrates Royalex's charm: you slide off and keep going. Later inspection may reveal a dent, easily dealt with—just leave the dent exposed to the sun's warming rays and the depression will often spring back to its molded memory with no help at all. A hair dryer or heat gun will also do the trick. If using a heat gun or paint stripper, hold it several inches away and use a circular motion to prevent overheating, which can cause delamination. Never let the vinyl skin get too hot to touch.

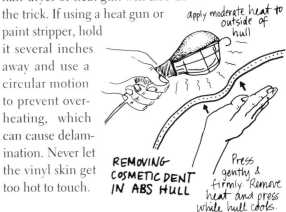

GOUGES

Full-steam, head-on contact with a boulder may bash a permanent divot in a bow or stern stem if your boat has no skid plates, a.k.a. grunch pads—Kevlar reinforcements cemented on the hull to prevent this very occurrence. Epoxy putty can restore the shape, and grunch pads can prevent further damage.

Deep gouges should be filled with a waterproof resin. Ask at your local outfitter for a two-part urethane adhesive with structural integrity for Royalex hulls; the hardware-store alternative is waterproof epoxy putty like PC-7 or some other quick-setting epoxy.

With most boats, the worst damage is often perpetrated during transport, as when a new tripping canoe arrived just in time for our big adventure—with two forklift scars gouged nearly through the bottom. Our initial disappointment abated when the manufacturer sent us a tube of Sea Goin' five-minute epoxy putty. The stuff is clean and easy to use in the field because it will cure even when immersed. By all means carry this in your repair kit.

On an older Royalex canoe that's been stored outdoors, molding faults or heat-damaged areas may raise blisters along the hull, indicating delamination of the sandwich layers. This is something to be aware of, but you don't really need to worry

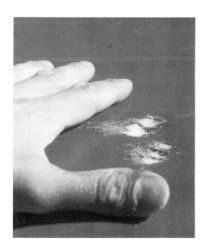

This abrasion damage to an ABS canoe occurred during shipping.

about it. However, trauma from impact or freezing and thawing may cause a blister to break or crack, at which time you may decide to fill the resultant hole as recommended.

CREASES

Creases that result from almost-but-not-quite folding your ABS boat around a midstream rock should be repaired with a Kevlar structural patch. A crease weakens the hull and may eventually become the hinge point for catastrophic failure.

TEARS

Cold cracks or serious bites out of an ABS hull require structural evaluation and repair not really suited to the field. Mad River recommends its Kevlar patch kit with epoxy, applied to the interior as outlined here.

SKID PLATES: A POUND OF PREVENTION

Alan Kesselheim, a modern voyageur with many epic canoe adventures behind him, agrees that grunch pads are good additions to a boat, especially for long trips. However, added weight and change in hull performance complicate the decision of when to add them. "I now delay adding skid plates until there's a reason—deep gouges, abrasions, etc.," says Kesselheim. "Often it's years before I add them."

If you're ready for skid plates, take our advice: buy a kit. The nice precut Kevlar patches and perfectly formulated resins infinitely outclass any homegrown concoction. Dave tried fiberglass cloth and polyester resin grunch pads on a family "heirloom" and was distinctly underwhelmed with the results: the poly resin was way too brittle for the flexy hull, and his crude cloth patches didn't integrate as well as Kevlar would have done. Kits are modestly priced and yield neat, professional results. Order one from your canoe's manufacturer for the best match.

The quintessential quickie patch: Cut away any damaged material so there's a bevel or V. Sand and clean to prep. Slightly overfill with quick-set epoxy—use a minicell squeegee to even out the fill. Next, lay a piece of waxed paper over the repair and squeegee over the paper to feather fill and give a smooth finish that requires little sanding. Once set—but before completely hard—peel paper, then sand down to hull shape; paint as desired.

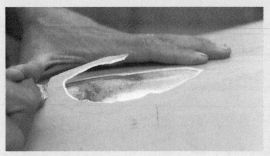

Beveled edges provide the best adhesion.

A small wedge of minicell foam serves as an excellent squeegee for smoothing out fill cement.

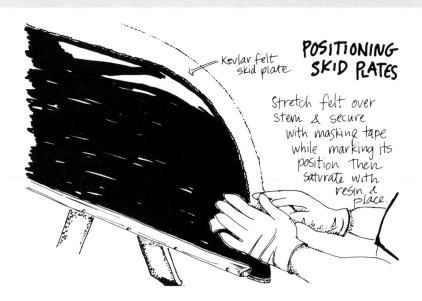

Kevlar felt skid plate

POSITIONING SKID PLATES

Stretch felt over stem & secure with masking tape while marking its position. Then saturate with resin & place.

A Few General Tips for Applying Skid Plates:

- Read chapter 16, Rules of the Resin.
- Position the pad 6 inches from the peak of the stem. Tape the top of the patch securely and slightly stretch along the stem.
- Outline the precut pad with a pencil.
- Prep just inside the outline—the adhesive will

ABS STRUCTURAL PATCH

1. Read chapter 16, Rules of the Resin .
2. Position the boat so it will not rock and so the surface to be patched is horizontal and easily accessed.
3. Remove the gunwale if necessary.
4. A hair dryer or other moderate heat source (even full, warm sun can suffice) will make the Royalex pliable enough to bend. Realign the edges of the torn Royalex material, joining the laceration as if preparing to suture.
5. Use a sharp utility knife to slice away a beveled V from both sides of the tear (use a deeper V on the interior).
6. Prep the exposed areas by sanding and then cleaning with denatured alcohol or a *small* amount of acetone. Be sure to prep a surface slightly bigger than the largest patch.
7. Back the outside V with a slice of duct tape.
8. Cut two or more layers of Kevlar to cover the tear. The first piece should just cover the tear; cut the second about 1 inch larger all the way around. Fraying an edge strand or two will make the cloth easier to feather.
9. Mix the resin components thoroughly— count 100 strokes.
10. Build the patch on a scrap of cardboard—

it's easier to control the flexing fabric that way. Paint epoxy directly onto the cardboard. Lay the largest cloth into the wet epoxy, then spread more goop directly onto the cloth so it's thoroughly saturated. Lay the second (smaller) patch on the first, then spread on more goop. Repeat with the smallest patch.
11. Now fill the interior crack with adhesive.
12. Pick up the entire patch—still wet—and position it over the crack, with the largest cloth to the outside. Paint the entire patch with a thin layer of epoxy, building a topcoat with feathered edges for sanding.
13. Apply waxed paper and smooth the patch with a corrugator, rolling pin, or foam squeegee.
14. If you've removed the rails, clamp them into place over the patched, paper-covered area to make an impression in the adhesive—otherwise you'll have hard work sanding it down later. Remove the clamps after a few minutes.
15. Allow to cure fully for 24 hours before filling the exterior V with putty.
16. Remove the waxed paper from the interior patch, sand, then spray with vinyl paint.

shrink the felt somewhat, and this allows for feathering.

- Pour the mixed resin onto a cardboard slab, then lay the patch onto it. This allows the goop to penetrate up through the felt until it becomes transparent.
- Use a corrugator to laterally squeegee out excess resin and work into dry spots.
- After applying the pad, squeegee out the resin from side to side, working from top to bottom. Run an acetone-soaked rag along the edge of the pad to clean the hull.

Aluminum

Boat snobs may disdain aluminum canoes, but after compiling care requirements for other hull materials, "tin boats" look better all the time. Indeed, Dave's Dad found a 16-foot Grumman washed up on a beach thirty years ago, and that boat is still clipping along after more than a generation of outdoor storage with a sum total of exactly zero maintenance.

Wherever there's a classic canoe route, you can be pretty sure it has been successfully negotiated in strong, stiff, aluminum boats. Occasionally you'll also see where some gnarly, twisting rapid has reduced one to silver shrapnel—any other craft would have been pummeled into matchsticks.

STORAGE

Racking an aluminum canoe for the winter offers one of the few opportunities for preventive maintenance. Rack the boat slightly off-level, both lengthwise and laterally. This allows any water that might pool inside the gunwales to drain. (If water collects, freezes, and expands, cracks could result.) As with other hull types, do not cover or let any fabrics or lines contact the boat, which can result in pitting of the hull.

EPOXY TO THE RESCUE

Many aluminum hull repairs rely on epoxy fill putty (see chapter 16, Rules of the Resin). Make sure the epoxy you use is formulated to work on metal, like the popular PC-7 fill cement. Surface preparation is essential, and the repair area must be perfectly dry before applying adhesive.

RIVETS

Most aluminum boats are held together by hundreds of riveted fasteners; though strong, they are prone to leaking after successive impacts. A ring of black oxidation around a rivet head means the fitting is loose.

Setting Rivets

Set or tighten rivets by holding an "anvil" (steel bar, axe head, what have you) against one side of the rivet while you whack the head—really hard—with a hammer.

A loose, leaky, or broken rivet can be patched in the field with a piece of duct tape or filled with epoxy. If the rivet was holding a thwart or seat in place, you'll need to pop out what remains of the old fastener (use your camping axe as a hammer and the awl on your knife as a center punch) and

replace it with a bolt or baling wire from your fix-all kit.

The Fixall.

At home, under controlled conditions, rivets should be removed with care so as not to enlarge the original hole—this makes installation of a new rivet easier. As when removing a broken snap, drill the depth of the rivet head, then use pliers to pull off the head. Use a hammer and punch to pop the remaining half out the other side.

Be sure to use aluminum rivets on aluminum boats. Any other metal will cause galvanic corrosion, marked by powdery white fuzz. If circumstances do force you to place a steel, copper, or brass rivet into aluminum, use a rubber gasket to insulate the metals.

Typical hardware-store pop rivets work fine for repairs, though they usually leak without further caulking. Just be sure to place the head end *outside* the canoe.

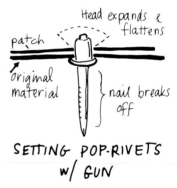

SETTING POP-RIVETS w/ GUN

SCRATCHES

Aluminum's tendency to grab and stick to rocks causes burrs and pocks along the hull surface. These minor scratches and dings are best viewed as mileage markers, but you might wish to grind down any sharp-edged gouges with emery cloth or a power sander.

DENTS

Small dings that do not affect hull performance are also better left alone, since constant hammering or working the metal stretches and somewhat weakens it. However, a fist-sized dent below the waterline should be "convinced" back into shape with a wood or rubber mallet. In the field, a stone in the toe of your Bean boot should do the trick. Another, infinitely tested riverside option is to beach the canoe in sand or grass and jump on the bump.

Hammering Out a Dent

Use a wood block as an anvil. Hammer the dent from its perimeter and work toward the center. Extremely stretched metal is likely to rupture—drill or punch a hole at the apex of the dent before pounding to circumvent a likely tear. Patch the hole with duct tape, spruce gum, or epoxy fill cement.

Start at outside of dent and hammer toward center.

drill hole

wooden block as anvil

Coaxing Out an Inaccessible Dent

A divot in the curved bow or stern may be gently pulled out by drilling one or more small holes directly into the dent. Drive a self-tapping screw a few turns into each hole, then pry each screw outward with a claw hammer braced by a wooden block. Sand and fill screw holes with epoxy.

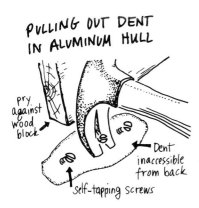

PULLING OUT DENT IN ALUMINUM HULL

pry against wood block

Dent inaccessible from back

self-tapping screws

CREASES, CRACKS, AND TEARS

A large dent with a crease in the metal should be treated as a crack, since the crease will eventually become a hinge point for the hull. Cracks must ultimately be repaired with a structural patch, usually a tape or fiberglass patch in the field or a pop-riveted patch at home in the shop. You might also consider taking a severe repair job to a welding shop that works on aluminum.

drill holes in end of cracks

Stop cracks in aluminum or polyethylene hulls

FIELD PATCHING

Depending on the terrain and the circumstances, most folks will fill cracks in an aluminum hull to stop a leak rather than perform a full-fledged structural patch in poor conditions. Spruce gum, chewing gum, duct tape, and epoxy putty are all viable plug options.

Temporary Glass Patch

Though many bush pilots carry a full aluminum patch kit and rivet gun for aircraft repairs, paddlers are not likely to haul all that gear into the outback. In the field, your best chance of restoring integrity to a cracked aluminum hull is with a fiberglass-and-epoxy patch.

Hammer the damaged area into shape as much as possible, working torn metal with a stone (the stone also works to roughen and prep the surface). Back the crack with tape (on the outer hull surface) and follow the instructions for fiberglass patching (pages 179–81), but substitute aluminum-approved epoxy for the polyester resin.

Remember, this is a field patch, to be removed for the long-term repair once home. Therefore, don't bond the patch closer than an inch to a structural element such as a gunwale or keel; you'll need that extra inch for fixing a permanent patch later. A glass patch can certainly hold a metal boat together for a season or so, but differences in the flex and expansion patterns of the two materials will eventually cause the patch to loosen.

Riveted Patch

A riveted patch—covering the entire mess with a proper metal patch—is the only truly permanent solution for a torn hull.

1. Try to use the same thickness and alloy as your boat—contact the manufacturer for specifics.
2. Hammer the damaged area back into contour, drilling holes in crack ends as shown.
3. If the tear is jagged, trim it with a file or saw to make a clean edge.
4. Center the patch and hammer it to replicate the curvature of the hull.

cut line

For large tears in aluminum, cut away damaged area.

5. Mark the patch position on the hull.
6. Drill rivet-sized holes in each corner of the patch. Position the patch on the hull and mark the placement of the holes.
7. Drill corresponding holes into the hull, then bolt the patch into position.
8. Mark the placement of interior rivets about 1 inch apart and drill holes through the patch and hull.
9. Remove the patch and use a stone and file to clean off burrs and soften edges. Lightly sand the patch face with an emery cloth.
10. Apply urethane caulk to the face of the patch—unless you don't mind if it leaks!
11. Fasten the patch to the hull with corner bolts.

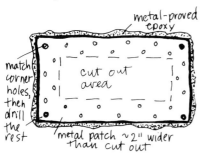

metal-proved epoxy

match corner holes, then drill the rest

cut out area

metal patch ~2" wider than cut out

12. Rivet through all the holes, remove the corner bolts, and rivet the corners.

Skin-over-Frame, a.k.a. Folding Boats

On a film shoot a few years ago, Dave discovered that an outboard-motor propeller makes a pretty effective kayak Cuisinart. Halfway through a shoot the camera boat backed into the host's Klepper folding kayak. Fortunately, nobody was hurt, but the Klepper was so severely gashed that it would no longer float: with no spare kayak for the host, the whole shoot was in danger of sinking.

Dave sat disconsolate on an idyllic Bahamas beach, desperately digging through his meager repair kit, hoping against hope that he had the right bits to stitch and patch the boat back together.

A couple hours later the Klepper's own repair kit had disgorged an 8-inch rubberized hull patch and the glues he needed. He'd managed to sew up a foot-long gash in the fabric deck with dental floss and a broken-off awl needle. But the punctured air sponson was proving harder to fix; duct tape patches wouldn't hold air pressure, nor would electrical tape stick to the sponson's slick vinyl air bladder. Without an airtight sponson to fill out the hull shape, the TV star's kayak looked like a deformed, beached whale.

Finally, the solution dawned. He pawed deep into his personal gear bag, pulled out his sleeping pad, and . . . yes! There was a PVC patch kit conveniently stashed in a flap of the air mattress's stuff sack. Fixing the slash required every square inch of patch material in the kit, but that sponson was still airtight when he returned the wounded boat to the Klepper dealer two weeks later.

SKIN DISEASE

As Dave discovered in the Bahamas, most damage to folding boats is to the skin rather than to the frame.

Sunlight fatigues the deck, while abrasions, lacerations, and punctures from a world studded with pointy objects nibble both inside and outside the hull. Add a dose of mildew from improper storage, and your fabric skin may no longer be seaworthy.

"The skin is the most important [read: *expensive*] part of any folding boat," cautions Larry Edwards, exacting proprietor of Baidarka Boats in Sitka, Alaska. A former aeronautical engineer, Edwards is the only North American dealer who knows intimately every part of every folding kayak ever built, and he is a goldmine of useful nuggets regarding all boats foldable. He's seen twenty-five-year-old skins in perfect condition, though he notes that original natural latex hulls are less durable than today's Hypalon hybrids.

Cleaning

Most modern skin-over-frame hulls are made of super-durable Hypalon laminate—a combination of urethane-coated nylons reinforced with areas of rubber or urethane.

Whether or not you break down your folding boat after each use, it is very important to rinse sand and salt from the inside with fresh water as often as possible. Otherwise grit deposits in the joints of the frame—and worse, between the frame and skin—will cause certain abrasion damage from the inside out. A garden hose is ideal for blasting out the cooties, but during trips, dousing with the bailer or sponge is usually sufficient. Examine the skin for cuts and worn spots as you rinse.

Cleaning the fabric is best done when the skin is stretched. A nondetergent soap and a soft brush will remove most grime from the hull. Diluted vinegar or super-diluted CitraSolv (gently scrubbed and quickly rinsed; see appendix B, page 216) should take care of tenacious cling-ons. Commercial degreasers may be too harsh and damage the fabric—and what's a little stain but a good story? Rinse again and allow to dry completely before making any repairs or disassembling the boat.

Before applying any fabric treatments, determine whether any areas might require a urethane adhesive patch (see below). Water-based 303 Protectant applied in moderation to the entire deck will help shield against UV deterioration. Larry Edwards warns that although Hypalon is tough enough for use on whitewater rafts, flat factory roofs, and earthmover conveyor belts, it is *highly* sensitive to some chemicals. *Never* use ArmorAll petroleum-based protectant on Hypalon skins, or it will deteriorate before your crying eyes. Edwards recommends only Klepper Hull Polish, a liquid wax for use on rubber hull bottoms.

PATCHING

In the field, use good old duct tape for non-airtight patches. Urethane adhesive patches are the general modus operandi for filling gouges in Hypalon or for small, thumb-sized patches in nylon decking. Aquaseal is a suitable filler-adhesive for such repairs, since it cures in fairly short order (see sidebar, page 9). For permanent repairs, Edwards recommends liquid Hypalon products like Gaco-Flex or SpanTex covercoat (available where you

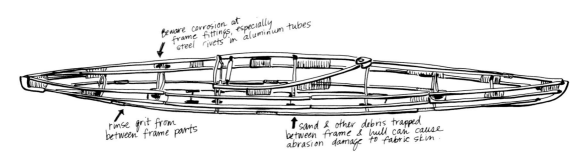

Beware corrosion at frame fittings, especially steel rivets in aluminum tubes

rinse grit from between frame parts

sand & other debris trapped between frame & hull can cause abrasion damage to fabric skin.

buy exterior paint), which vulcanizes, or chemically cross-links, to the Hypalon hull material in a couple of weeks.

Larger fabric patches—say, to deck or sprayskirt—may be applied with urethane adhesive. Hypalon patch kits usually bond to the hull with contact cement—ask a whitewater outfitter for a raft patch. The only truly permanent deck repair is a sewn patch, which requires a section of decking material from your manufacturer, both a straight and a curved sewing awl, heavy-duty nylon thread, and a good seam sealer to caulk the stitch holes.

STORAGE

It's quite all right to leave your folding boat together all the time—stored indoors, out of the sun, that is—but you should test the assembly periodically and watch for corrosion between the frame parts.

Mark Eckhart, at the North American Klepper Service Center, sees long-term storage as the most important area of maintenance, and he offers these suggestions for preserving a fabric hull:

- Never pack away your boat when it is wet.
- Clean and thoroughly dry the skin and keep in a cool, dry location out of direct sunlight.
- A light sprinkle of talcum powder inside and outside the hull is a good idea.
- Optimally, the skin should have as few folds as possible—storing it folded in half under a bed, on a carpet, is recommended. The folds should be changed every six months, no matter where you stash it. Avoid folding along narrow sections of rubber (like a keel strip), which risks stressing the adhesive bond.

FRAME CARE
Wood Frame

Wooden skeletons should be carefully rinsed of sand and checked for worn finish, which is where water penetrates and rot can begin if left unattended. Sand the part with fine (220-grit) sandpa-

per, then use a tack cloth to clean any dust before coating the frame sections with spar varnish (best), Varathane, or Thompson's Water Seal as needed, taking care to apply only very thin, successive coats. Thick coats will not dry properly and will cause the framing to stick together most unbecomingly. If you need to sand down to bare wood to eliminate peeling, blistered varnish—a common problem with coamings or floorboards—then cut the spar varnish 50-50 with thinner and apply two coats.

In the field, be prepared for breakage: Keep a serrated saw blade, an assortment of brass wood screws and rivets, wire, and cord in your kit. Small packets of epoxy may also be useful for bonding wooden sections. Duct tape is likely sufficient for most field repairs.

Count the parts, again and again. Memorize them so you know if anything is missing. If a part is AWOL, your boat might not work.

Aluminum Frame

Aluminum-tube frames require somewhat less maintenance than wood frames, but they are vulnerable to sand and corrosion binding up section joints. Regular cleaning with fresh water will help, but periodic lubrication will preserve the anodizing and inhibit corrosion. Try dry graphite lubricant, a

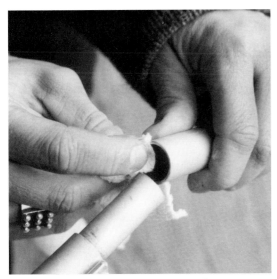

Regularly lubricate the joints of tubular aluminum frames. This prevents corrosion and forces you to inspect each section carefully.

dab of gel silicone lubricant, or a spritz of TriFlow brand spray lube. (Take care to keep silicone off the fabric, in case you need to patch it with adhesive at some later date.) As with tent poles, stiff joints can develop teensy hairline cracks. For an unusually tight joint, first check to see that it is not kinked or cracked and that it is still round.

Doug Simpson, at Feathercraft, recommends bringing hose clamps and a "pocket chain saw" (an abrasive cable with rings) or a hacksaw replacement blade on long trips: "As long as the skin is intact, you can improvise. . . . One day in a big surf, a friend bailed out of his boat, which filled with water—the bars were bent a full 90 degrees! By cutting bent sections, bracing and cannibalizing tubes, and splinting with duct tape, he managed to paddle home a weird-looking boat!" (see sidebar, page 146).

Outfitting

The bad news: your folding kayak has extremely sensitive skin and does not take kindly to barnacles, gravel, granite, or even being dragged across sand. The good news: you can add keel strips as preventive maintenance if you're hard on gear or as a patch for abraded contact points. Available from your kayak's manufacturer or from Baidarka Boats, these strips are best adhered with Barge cement or McNett Seal Cement so they can be peeled off later. If you're keen to add D-rings or anything permanent, Edwards favors Bostik contact cement.

Fiberglass and Kevlar

Most paddlers rely exclusively on duct tape to repair fiberglass canoes in the field. With enough duct tape and ingenuity you can usually repair anything. . . . Furnace tape on a canoe is a paddler's gray badge of courage.

Cliff Jacobson, *Canoeing Wild Rivers*

Fiberglass and its space-age cousin Kevlar are man-made fibers that, when filled with a hardening resin, can be molded into sleek, efficient, rugged shapes. Both materials serve the same function in a laminated boat and are cared for in essentially the same manner. The fabrics look similar but are fundamentally different.

FIBERGLASS

The building blocks of fiberglass include alumina, magnesium, and silica, which are melted together with other inorganic ingredients, spun into yarn, and woven into cloth. Resins and other "sizing" treatments are applied during the weaving process to prevent fiber breakage; adhesion between resin and filaments is critical to the strength of the resultant fabric.

There are many types and weights of fiberglass cloth, with varying compositions, including E glass and S glass, both of which are commonly built into small boats. Heavier-weight fiberglass, used for reinforcement, comes in coarsely woven sheets called *roving* or *mat*, a feltlike material that is to fiberglass what pressboard is to plywood: heavier, cheaper, not as strong. Fiberglass cloth weighs from 4 to 20 ounces per square yard (its strength correlates accordingly). The typical repair weight is 7.5 ounces.

Canoe and kayak manufacturers—and consumers—continually strive for the best compromise of resins, cloth weights, and number of layers to achieve a light, durable, affordable mix. Once you're ready to make a repair, carefully examine the damaged area to identify both the weave and the weight of the fiberglass layers you'll need, or contact the manufacturer.

KEVLAR

Kevlar has been around since the early 1970s, when DuPont won the first heat of the race to develop a "superfiber." This man-made Aramid fiber's highly oriented molecules (they line up in formation) provide great tensile strength, thermal stability, and low density. In fact, Kevlar fabric is so rugged that the real limiting factor in a Kevlar hull is the resin used to bind each layer—upon impact, the resin will crack before fibers tear. Similarly, Kevlar's resilient fibers can spring back after extreme stretching, while resin cannot. Vinylester is a popular match for Kevlar layups because of its high elongation properties (flexibility).

The distinctive golden color of Kevlar darkens as it ages. Any light source will cause some discoloration, and in a superlight layup with a clear skin coat the "suntan" is most obvious. Of course, excessive exposure to UV is a limiting factor, but the darkening is generally nothing to worry about. Some manufacturers sacrifice a little weight for a very thin, nearly clear gelcoat layer that provides sun protection and more even coloration.

Kevlar fabric can be difficult to work with. Tough to cut, the stuff is even tougher to sand—it frizzes and fuzzes like cotton candy. For this reason, most people patch Kevlar hulls with fiberglass. If you're planning to lay a Kevlar structural patch on your bashed-up Kevlar hull, first cut away

A laminate is only as strong as weakest link.

although kevlar fabric may rebound after impact, less flexible bonding resins will crack after high elongation, causing delamination.

the damaged area as best you can. Next, apply a thin coat of activated resin over the working area and allow it to harden overnight. When you're ready to patch, sand the resin-primed areas (no fuzz) and prep accordingly.

CHEWED-UP STEM

As with most materials (and personalities), the strength of a fiberglass or Kevlar layup also represent its greatest weakness. For instance, the deep, squared-off bow stem of our 18-foot cruiser makes a nice slice through the water but is too sharp for

Take the time to mask the hull around the repair area.

its own good when we scrunch into things. The stem looks quite a bit worse for wear, its accumulated chips and dings corrected and recorrected with epoxy and gelcoat of many colors.

For nose jobs, epoxy is probably your best bet, since you need to restore the structure with a strong fill. Epoxy sticks just fine to cured hulls of any layup, and you can paint the hardened material. However, polyester-based resins and gelcoat do *not* adhere well to epoxy. Use a marine-grade epoxy like the WEST System kit (which includes fillers of different densities); Marine-Tex epoxy putty is another favorite. We have added gelcoat pigment to an epoxy mix with fair to good results, but the color match has been approximate at best.

If you wish to make a gelcoat patch on a glass boat with severe divot damage to the stem, you can chop up fiberglass and use it as thickener in a polyester resin fill. Apply as a putty and allow it to cure fully before sanding and adding gelcoat.

STEM REINFORCEMENT

See also ABS or Royalex: Skid Plates, beginning on page 167

Fiberglass and Kevlar designs are generally suitable for low-impact, performance paddlers, but they are not the best choices for cavalier whitewater warriors. For this reason, skid plates are not very popular with Kevlar or fiberglass hulls; another layer adds weight and hydrodynamic drag but not substantially greater impact resistance. But if you're a hammerhead who likes to motor in shallow rocky streams, the added bow and stern protection (the stern gets equal abuse) is probably a good idea.

You can purchase preformed graphite skid plates for some designs from your boat's manufacturer. A stiff, super-thin graphite layer does not appreciably change your boat's needlenose shape and adds a fair degree of protection. A cheaper but less rugged alternative is to paint the stems with a few thin coats of clear epoxy.

Wet-sand cured gelcoat by hand using fine-grit paper wrapped around a foam block.

ABRASION

Most fabric layups are molded with a thin gelcoat outer finish. Normal wear includes scratches in the gelcoat that appear white. With repeated abrasion, such as from beach landings, even the tough gelcoat can be worn through, exposing the Kevlar or fiberglass weave. With luck, you'll spot the abrasion before it gets to the fibers; if not, the simplest solution is to apply a thin layer of clear epoxy or polyester resin to the prepped surface. A gelcoat patch may also be appropriate (see pages 182–83).

Abrasion Prevention

Brad Finn, of Indian Island Kayak Company in Maine, applies colored duct tape to the bow and stern of his glass sea kayaks for lightweight but effective abrasion protection from Maine's rocky beaches. For a more permanent abrasion guard, Brad has often painted worn areas on his hulls with Marine-Tex; he swears by this technique but warns that the application should be very thin and the surface well prepped.

PUNCTURES, CREASES, NASTY BITES

Whenever your fiberglass or Kevlar layup is bashed hard enough to crack through the gelcoat and into the resin—marked by fine cracks on the inside of the laminate and a soft spot that flexes under hand pressure—you must repair the area with a structural patch. More obvious wounds warrant the same treatment.

The real beauty of glass becomes apparent upon repair. A patch can completely restore the strength and rigidity of the original hull material, and the process is fairly straightforward. Still, it's not a bad idea to practice laying up a glass patch on cardboard scrap before you attack your boat. It's possible to make a patch too strong (using too many layers of cloth or excessive resin), which can cause eventual fractures at patch joints. Carefully assess the damage and try to match the number of fabric layers in surrounding areas when planning a repair.

Patching in the Field

The basic patching technique is the same for most fiberglass or Kevlar patches. On shorter trips, duct tape and epoxy putty patches are favored as quick fixes (duct tape sealed a thumb-sized, below-waterline crunch in our fiberglass double kayak for two seasons), but for long expeditions, when the structural integrity of your craft is crucial, you must be prepared to make a resin-and-cloth repair. This means carrying (in addition to duct tape): a few feet of repair cloth, rough sandpaper, an adequate supply of resin and a catalyst, a mixing container, alcohol swabs, and an applicator brush.

In the boonies, conditions are rarely conducive to a good cure. Expect your patch to look funkily rudimentary unless you have a lot of time to prep the surface and enough food to last while you wait for the perfect ambient temperature. To compensate for damp, coolish conditions you may have to add more catalyst (perhaps twice as much as recommended) and work fast. If using epoxy, remember that once cured, it is difficult to sand or remove.

While your emergency patch should be perfectly functional, once you are home, you'll prob-

ably want to remove the patch and start over. Polyester is easy to sand, and removing the quick patch is quite straightforward: just sand away the resin at the joints—wear a mask!—and pop the patch out. The patch is likely to be very brittle because of its catalyst overdose.

"Fast Patch" Prepackaged Glass Patches

Perhaps you've heard of Syntho-Glass, a prepackaged fiberglass patch that is water-activated and also cures under water. While this sounds like a paddler's dream come true, the product is not really designed for flat-patching applications (as on the hull of a canoe or kayak); rather, Syntho-Glass was developed to be wadded and stuffed into hardware fittings on large vessels. Syntho-Glass does stick to itself and thus may be used to wrap a broken paddle shaft or stuffed into small cracks in a coaming, but its usefulness to paddlers is rather limited.

However, new on the market is the E-Z UV Cure Patch, which may indeed turn out to be a paddler's dream come true. The patch consists of an 8- by 8-inch fiberglass mat and cloth sandwich impregnated with a unique UV-activated resin. To use it, you simply tear open the pouch, place it on a fiberglass, Kevlar, aluminum, or Royalex hull, and wait for the sun to cure the patch—in

---

COLD CURE

To aid curing in cool weather, you might try external heat. First tape plastic wrap smoothly over the repair to protect it and retain heat, then apply warm (not hot) pebbles in a plastic bag; or use a small, clear plastic "tent" taped over a repair to provide a greenhouse effect to trap sunlight or heat from a campfire. I have used a Ziploc bag in this way for paddle blade and joint repairs in cool sunlight quite a few times.

Randel Washburne, *The Coastal Kayaker's Manual*

as little as 30 minutes. Luke Hallman, at Headwaters, the only source for this tripper's dream (see appendix G, beginning on page 236), says the patch will even bond to wet surfaces. Resin left inside the foil pouch hardens, so packing out is no trouble at all. Wow!

Cloth-and-Resin Patch

When repairing a canoe, the main structural patch goes on the hull *interior*; a cosmetic patch seals the exterior. This allows you to restore the hull's integrity with minimal alteration to its shape or drag.

STANDARD FIBERGLASS

See also chapter 16, Rules of the Resin

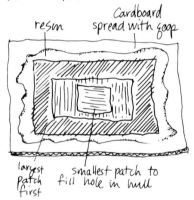

Build a glass patch on cardboard--easier to control flexing fabric & saturate fibers.

Cardboard spread with goop

resin

largest patch first

smallest patch to fill hole in hull

PATCH, SHOPSIDE

1. Wear a protective mask and gloves.
2. Use paint stripper to remove interior paint from the repair area, following manufacturer's instructions. After removing most of the paint, another coat of stripper may be applied and hand-sanded with coarse (60-grit) paper to remove residual paint from within the weave of the cloth.

3. Remove all damaged material from the hull laminate. Wrecked glass appears white, fuzzy, frayed. Use a razor knife or power grinder. Bevel or feather the edges as much as possible.
4. Prep the repair area by sanding for the largest patch.
5. Apply backing to the hull exterior to retain a smooth profile. Use duct tape, cardboard, or wood over a layer of waxed paper so the temporary backing won't stick to the repair area.
6. Cut patches. The number of layers depends on the size of the damage and whether it's below the waterline (larger areas and those under water require more layers). If you're working in a curved spot, bias- or diagonally cut fabric will lay easier. Or try narrow strips, as if making a papier-mâché piñata. For really tight curves (inside the stem or cockpit coaming), cut up chunks of cloth or use nonwoven mat, which is easier to shape (but not as strong as) strips of cloth.
7. The first layer equals the damaged area plus 1 inch. Each successive layer should extend 1 inch farther all the way around than the previous one.
8. Fray several strands of weave from each patch perimeter. This makes feathering, or blending, easier.
9. Just prior to mixing the resin, prep the sanded area with denatured alcohol, taking care not to touch the surface with your fingers.
10. Mix the resin according to the manufacturer's instructions.
11. Paint the hull area to be patched with a thin coat of resin.
12. Place the smallest patch. (Schools of thought vary: you can either presaturate the patch on a cardboard work surface or place the patch and saturate it in position.)
13. Both fiberglass and Kevlar become transparent when saturated. If a whitish dry spot appears, it's usually due to an air bubble between the

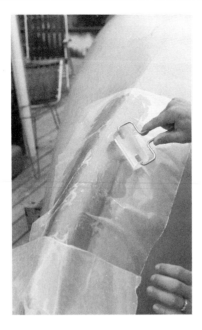

Use a roller or corrugator for a consistent bond and feathered edges.

cloth and the previous layer. Use a corrugator or squeegee to work out the bubble and properly saturate the cloth.

14. Continue to add saturated layers of cloth, working from the center of the material and forcing air to the outer edge. Roll out excess resin this way as well.

15. Wipe any drips or runs off the hull with a rag soaked in denatured alcohol.

16. Place a sheet of waxed paper over entire patch area. Use the corrugator or squeegee to create a smooth, feathered surface.

17. Clean brushes and the corrugator immediately.

18. Set the remaining activated resin outdoors to cure before disposal.

19. Once the resin has cured, sand any rough edges or high spots, then apply a gelcoat (cosmetic) patch to the exterior for resistance to abrasions and moisture (see pages 182–83).

Exterior Fiberglass Patch

Unfortunately for sea kayakers, Murphy's Law kicks in: the most likely area of damage at the very bow or stern is going to be in a totally inac-

cessible spot. Not to worry—you just repair the hull exterior. If you're unluckier still, the damage will occur just within reach of the cockpit, requiring that you perform the surgery with your head and torso inside a fume-filled hull. In that case, build the entire patch on a slab of cardboard first (see sidebar, page 169), in order to limit the time you are trapped in a toxic airlock. Wear a respirator mask.

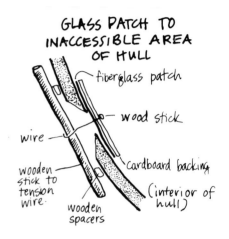

GLASS PATCH TO INACCESSIBLE AREA OF HULL

- fiberglass patch
- wood stick
- wire
- wooden stick to tension wire
- wooden spacers
- cardboard backing
- (interior of hull)

Follow the instructions for patching glass, above, but with these variations:

1. Cut away the damaged area of fiberglass.

2. Make a serious effort to sand the edges inside the hole—awkward but important. Feather the exterior edges and sand as well.

3. Clean with alcohol.

4. Cut a scrap of cardboard about 2 inches larger than the damaged area.

5. Thread the center of the cardboard with thin wire around a backing stick as shown, then back through.

6. Cut a patch the size of the cardboard; cut a second patch about ½ inch smaller. Fray edge strands on both.

7. Mix the resin. Lay the first (larger) patch on the cardboard and saturate with resin. Add the second layer and saturate.

8. Paint the inside hull edges with resin.
9. Gently work the cardboard into the hole, bending but not folding, and work the bridging stick across the center.
10. Once the cardboard is inside, tug the wires to create tension. This forms the backing for an exterior patch, and the stick allows you to pull the form taut.
11. Wrap wire against a second, exterior stick or lath, then block it as shown to maintain tension during cure.
12. Paint resin around the exterior edges for additional sealing.
13. After the patch has dried, snip the wires flush and perform a cosmetic gelcoat patch.

The Key to a Successful Fiberglass Patch

Spend a lot of time preparing the hull, preparing yourself, and preparing your work area. This methodical approach will naturally limit the amount of time you are in contact with toxic resins and will ensure a cleaner, superior repair.

Gelcoat

See also chapter 16, Rules of the Resin; and pages 175–81

Fiberglass and other laminated boats generally sport a gelcoated—not painted—exterior surface. Gelcoat forms the first layer in a mold, and its polyester resin base bonds with the resin in the layup for a finish more durable than enamel. Besides polyester and cosmetic pigments, other added promoters and inhibitors determine the flow characteristics, flexibility, and UV-resistance of the gelcoat.

More is not better with gelcoat. It is heavy, and a too-thick layer will crack with normal flexing of the hull. Cracks usually result from impact, abrasion, or overtightened hardware, however, and show up white. Most boaters accept these as mileage scars and ignore them.

Gelcoat is somewhat porous. Water and coatings (like wax or surfacing agents used in manufacture) can permeate and cause deterioration over time. On an older hull, latent imperfections (air bubbles) in the layup may manifest themselves as pockmarks on the surface.

Despite its UV inhibitors, gelcoat fades quickly; constant exposure will lighten a hull by several shades and leaves a chalky finish. For this reason, many people prefer a *white* hull, which will not show age or wear and tear as markedly.

Minor gelcoat faults can be treated with elbow grease, rubbing compound, or sandpaper. Rubbing compound from a canoe manufacturer, auto parts store, or marine shop will go a long way toward restoring the overall color. Shallow cuts in the gelcoat are probably best left alone, since damage from overzealous cleaning can be worse than the original wound. Wet-sanding will expose the underlying color and smooth hull surface. If you own several glass boats, consider investing in a power buffer, available for under $60.

SCRATCH AND FADE REMOVAL

Tips for those who can't countenance a faded, scratched bottom:

- Wet-sand by hand, beginning with 320-grit wet/dry sandpaper wrapped around a foam sanding block. Use a lot of water. This both lubricates the surface and makes your sandpaper last longer.
- Sand with successively finer grits to remove the scratch. Spend longer with each grade of paper; that is, if you spend five minutes sanding with 320-grit, spend eight minutes with 400-grit, fifteen minutes with 600-grit. This obsessive sanding ensures that you'll remove heavier scratches caused by the previous sanding, but it is practiced only by those with many long winter nights to fill.
- After sanding, polish with rubbing compound using a sheepskin, chamois cloth, or PakTowl.

Dave prefers to use the same orbital buffer that polishes his old Porsche. Power buffers should only be used at low speed settings—you don't want to heat the gelcoat unnecessarily.

- Many people like to wax their fiberglass boats for maximum performance, but wax offers little UV protection; 303 Protectant works to sunscreen a gelcoat hull.

GELCOAT PATCHING

After making a structural repair to your favorite cruiser, you should apply a moisture-proof seal to the cracked outer hull. Remember that gelcoat's polyester base won't bond well to cured epoxy; if you want to restore the gelcoat finish to a large patched area, use polyester resin for your repair. Again, the easiest way to achieve a structure close to that of the original hull is to use a kit from the manufacturer. This also gives you the best odds of approximating the original finish and color. Even then, matching gelcoat exactly is virtually impossible. The older, original coating will have faded, and no two mixes are ever the same. Don't turn into an axe murderer trying to achieve an identical color match!

Gelcoat is available in two forms. The *putty* form is easy to work with and suited for filling chips, but it cures brittle. *Liquid gelcoat* is more versatile, goes on thin, and is easier to feather into the original gelcoat for a less visible patch.

Gelcoat shrinks as it cures, so when using putty, overfill. When filling a scratch with liquid gelcoat, several thin layers, with at least an hour between applications, may be needed to overfill the gouge. Liquid gelcoat may be thickened after catalyzation. Use talcum powder or even powdered wood putty (from the hardware store) to make a paste or putty. Be forewarned: once you thicken liquid gelcoat, it will shrink more as it cures.

Caution: Gelcoat's catalyst is MEKP (methyl-ethyl-ketone peroxide). Don't even *think* about making a gelcoat repair without gloves or eye protection. Always mix the smallest amount possible—just a teaspoon is all that's required for an average chip or gouge. (See chapter 16, Rules of the Resin.)

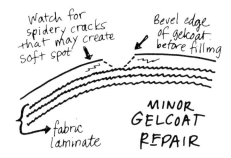

The gelcoat on this kayak bow stem has chipped off to expose underlying fiberglass cloth. Epoxy putty offers the most durable repair here.

Surface Preparation

1. For the best color match, the hull should first be buffed or sanded as recommended above; this exposes the original, unfaded gelcoat.

2. Cut, sand, or grind away the damaged, flaking material, grinding deeper than the actual area and beveling edges slightly for the best adhesion.

3. If you're making a cosmetic patch over a cured structural patch where you have backed the laminated patch on the exterior of the hull, be sure your patch has been made with poly resin, not epoxy. Epoxy resin must be painted with

enamel, epoxy, or urethane paint; gelcoat will not adhere to an epoxy patch.

4. Clean the patch area with denatured alcohol; wear gloves to prevent contamination of the repair.

Home Color Match

If mixing your own gelcoat, it's worth the extra time to test for a good color match.

1. Purchase appropriate tubes of coloring agents— the three primary colors may be enough.
2. Mix the color into clear gelcoat on a scrap of plastic (a clear coffee can lid) until you think you have a match.
3. Draw off a teaspoon of gelcoat and add a minuscule drop of catalyst (which will affect the color).
4. Spoon the test on a scrap of waxed paper and allow it to dry. Compare it with your original and make any necessary adjustments.

Filling Chips and Gouges

Chips that expose the underlying fabric should be filled to prevent water from penetrating the laminate. Gelcoat putty offers the simplest fix. Fill the void with material obtained from the hull manufacturer (for the best material and color match) or with putty from an auto parts store. Cover it with waxed paper, squeegee to feather the edges, and allow it to cure about eight hours. Wet-sand, then use rubbing compound to finish.

You may also fill chips with liquid gelcoat applied in layers, as discussed on page 182.

OLD SCREW AND HARDWARE HOLES

Holes should be filled with putty, but not gelcoat putty. For small holes that you wish to fill and cover with a cosmetic gelcoat patch, use a polyester-based fairing putty (like Bondo) to fill the gap. Bondo is not recommended for repairing large areas because of its great stiffness, although its structural properties make it suitable for filling small holes.

1. Prep the area as instructed. Carefully remove any traces of sealant that may have been used to caulk the fitting.
2. Isolate the repair from the rest of the hull with masking tape.
3. Back the interior of the hole with masking tape.
4. Use a razor knife to make one or two tiny slits in the tape. This prevents air bubbles from forming inside (which will weaken the repair).
5. Slightly overfill the hole (to allow for shrinkage). Let dry. Remove tape immediately as putty sets up.
6. Once dry, sand flush to the hull, taking care not to oversand the original gelcoat. Carefully create a shallow dish in the repair to allow for a liquid gelcoat patch.

SERIOUS GELCOAT CRACKS

Make sure there is no damage to the laminate (see pages 179–81). Remove the surrounding gelcoat down to the laminate layer, creating a V-shaped channel with the laminate at the bottom. Use the edge of a file if you don't have a grinder. Be sure to follow the crack to its terminus, or your repair is likely to fail.

Super-Thin Liquid Method

You can never be too rich or too thin. The closer the laminate fabric to the outer hull, the better. At a canoe symposium we watched fiberglass wizard Sandy Martin create a perfect, invisible gelcoat patch—quite a feat for a patch at least 6 inches square.

After prepping and masking the exterior area opposite a cured structural patch, Sandy got out his secret weapon: an $8 Preval sprayer from an auto parts store. He catalyzed the liquid gelcoat, then thinned the mix to a paintlike consistency with acetone to allow it to pass through the sprayer valve.

Sandy used short, controlled side-to-side strokes, gradually building the gelcoat surface. Short spritzes decrease the likelihood of drips—if you suffer drips, wipe off the sprayer head and shorten the length of each spray, as when painting. Once the area has cured, wet-sand and finish with rubbing compound.

handheld sprayer for sealants, gelcoat

Polyethylene

Polyethylene is the plastic material used in single-wall, roto-molded kayak hulls and multilayer roto-molded canoes. Most people buy a polyethylene boat for two reasons: low price and low maintenance. However, just because your boat can withstand being hammered on a rocky coast does *not* mean that it is carefree.

If you own a polyethylene boat, how you store, transport, and protect the craft from unnecessary UV exposure can mean the difference between a 6-year hull and a 10-year hull. A basic understanding of polyethylene's properties will help you accept your plastic boat's idiosyncrasies and care requirements.

POLYETHYLENE PRIMER

Your polyethylene kayak or canoe differs from Tupperware in several respects. First, it is manufactured from a high-density polyethylene designed for abrasion- and impact-resistance. The basic building block (polyethylene monomer chains) may have either a linear or a cross-linked molecular structure—different schools argue for one or the other.

Cross-linked polyethylene, while more structurally durable and impact-resistant, cannot be recycled or remolded, which makes patching vir-

tually impossible. *Linear polyethylene* can be remolded, and therefore it can be patched. Various additives to either mix provide other desirable qualities: lubricants for better molding, plasticizers for increased flexibility, stabilizers for UV-protection.

It should be said that plastics technology is improving all the time, and even five years marks huge advances in the trade. So a kayak from 1992 is very different from a vintage 1988 model, and a 2000 model is another animal still.

A typical *single-layer polyethylene* kayak hull is molded in a rotating form: Plastic resin or powder is poured inside the mold, which slides into a giant oven and spins like a high-speed rotisserie. The plastic melts and coats the inside of the form.

A *multilayer polyethylene* canoe hull follows a similar procedure, except that three layers are "dumped" and melted into the form—an outer skin, a foam core for stiffening and flotation, and an inner skin.

Once all these ingredients are cooked and spun around in a vacuum, the resultant hull is allowed to cool before it's removed from the mold, outfitted, marketed, and sold as a carefree water toy. However—and this is important—as with an infant, timing is everything. Some hulls are popped from their mold-womb too soon, or spanked too hard, and this inner-child stuff is recorded in the polyethylene memory bank. If your kayak seems tweaked to the left, blame it on a right-brain memory (and get yourself a rudder).

Flippancy aside, the memory of your plastic hull is an important key to performance. Heat and improper storage can seriously distort a hull, but often that initial memory can be regained with time by hanging the boat from a grab loop and letting gravity have its way.

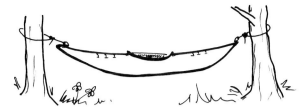

STORAGE AND TRANSPORT

Because plastic boats are not nearly as stiff as fiberglass, they are fabricated with thicker, heavier walls that can deform by their own weight. Consider your boat's original design when you rack or carry it. Try to keep the weight off its rounded bottom as much as possible. Store upside down on a rack with supports located under bulkheads (which provide structural integrity). If it is stored outside, watch for any snow or ice buildup. Keeping the boat out of the hot sun is very important, lest your new boat develop a Dali-esque droop.

Likewise when cartopping: carry the kayak on the rails (on edge), or locate rack bars and contoured cradles directly beneath bulkheads whenever possible. When one of our vehicles prohibited proper rack crossbar spacing, we made a wood "bulkhead" for transport use to protect the hull from rippling. If you don't have kayak saddles on your roof rack, carry the boat deckside down to eliminate the possibility of denting the bottom.

Hull rippling, or *oil-canning*, makes for inefficient paddling and unnecessarily stresses the hull; if ignored, it can result in permanent deformity. If your hull is waving at you, take this as a sign. Correct by placing the boat bottom up to face the sun for even, gentle reheating. Then press out the

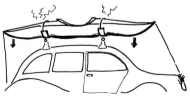

an all-too-common sight: over-zealous tying down bottom "oil-cans" as a result on poly hulls

dents and cool the hull that way to reawaken the memory of a smooth-skinned inner child.

Hogged

Paddling around Down East yacht harbors quickly teaches one the meaning of the term *hogged* as applied to the hull of a well-used wooden craft whose keel lost her line a grandfather ago. A hogged polyethylene kayak can usually be traced directly to unmindful roof-rack practices. Hogged boats should be hung to correct the bend as shown. Hang the hull, then add a few inches of hot (*not* boiling) tap water to soften the plastic and "convince" the wayward hull back to its rocker shape.

SUN PROTECTION

Store your polyethylene beast deckside down, out of the sun. UV is its worst enemy, so take precautions. As your boat ages (after 6 to 10 years a poly hull has reached maturity), it becomes ever more susceptible to impact damage, just like your grandma's hip. Regular rubdowns with 303 Protectant are vital to sustain its flexibility and resiliency.

BENDS AND BUCKLES

Any acquired wrinkles (for example, from broaching on a boulder in a tricky reversing falls) may be corrected with an afternoon's sunbath. If you're living in a foggy, cool region, you may have to resort to a hair dryer or heat lamp placed several feet away so the skin doesn't blister. Allow plenty of time for your plastic hull to relax from its traumatic experience.

SCARS AND STRIPES

Smooth out your furry, battle-scarred plastic hull with a Surform planing tool, which allows you to remove peeling ridges without compromising the hull surface. A sharp metal ski scraper works great too. Save the curls and peels for melting into patch areas later. Review any deep gouges for structural damage and needed patching.

CRACKS AND WORSE

When you notice fine cracks in the hull—usually around areas where flex is greatest (beneath the seat or along unsupported sections of the hull)—it's time to retire your boat to planter duty or the kids' sandbox. The plastic has deteriorated to the point that the craft is no longer safe.

It's important to realize the effects cold weather will have on an aged plastic hull—frozen, brittle boats have been known to crack and even shatter upon sharp impact (from falling off a roof rack or during a long drag across frozen territory). Older poly hulls probably should not be invited on arduous journeys.

PATCHING WOUNDED POLYETHYLENE

Actual punctures rarely occur without drama—a high-velocity meeting with rocks during a surf landing or an unintended ejection from a roof rack. A puncture may appear as a deep, leaky dent or as an obvious hole. As you examine the dent, crack, or puncture, look for fragmented hairline cracks that radiate from the point of impact, as on a broken windshield. These indicate that the plastic hull has become brittle from exposure and is a candidate for early retirement.

New boats (a season or two old) that suffer cracks should be referred to the manufacturer for possible warranty coverage. The manufacturer will ask you for the boat's serial number, which reveals the type and vintage of the original hull resin. The manufacturer may choose to replace the boat or supply you with a section of your exact hull material with instructions for patching.

Polyethylene Adhesives

Manufacturers struggle a lot with the problem of developing an adhesive that bonds to polyethylene yet remains elastic enough to withstand constant flexing. Caulking bulkheads is challenge enough, but sealing a leak or drilled fastener hole? For some time the most popular bet was clear silicone

Dents and dishes often result from improper storage or roof-racking. This ripple came out after heating the hull with a hair dryer—just don't heat the material hotter than you can touch.

Poly hulls are tough, but they aren't immune to punctures if they're dropped, in this case off a wall rack and onto unfortunately placed circular saw.

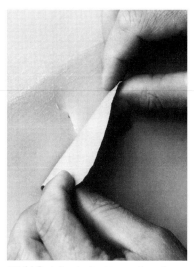

Field-fix is basic duct tape after cleaning with alcohol. A permanent patch will likely require plastic welding.

caulk, which produced a temporarily viable bond. Now manufacturers and outfitters commonly offer Sikaflex or Lexel polyurethane caulks for sealing jobs. Another popular adhesive recommended by those in the trade is 3M-5200 urethane.

Note: While there are some successes with welded patches and fillers, bonding requires heating the hull, which changes the structure of the plastic, thereby weakening it. Your repair will stop leaks, but it won't restore the boat to its original integrity. You also run the risk of overheating your hull and *really* ruining the boat.

Hot Flashes

If manufacturers can't get a good bond, how can you? Sources say you can make P-Tex (sintered polyethylene ski base repair material) or resin filler stick by first flashing the surface of the hull with a torch or heat gun. This draws out and evaporates residual oils and plasticizers that inhibit adhesion. Stroke the blue tip of a torch flame across the area to be repaired as if using a paintbrush. Don't melt (bubble) or blacken the surface.

If you're going to try to fill the hull with plastic, whether P-Tex, matched plastic from the boat's manufacturer, or low-density plastic (used in plastic welding), first flash the hull, then roughen the surface with a Surform plane, rasp, or piece of Dragonskin abrasive sanding sheet. Clean the surface with alcohol, then attempt to fill.

As with ski bases, the damaged area should be prewarmed to accept molten plastic fill. Do this with a hair dryer or heat gun held several inches from the hull. The idea of preheating the hull over a fire or camp stove *seems* viable, but these dirty heat sources would probably inhibit a bond.

Old Town Canoe Company offers a two-part polyurethane resin-adhesive for repairing its line of multilayer polyethylene Discovery canoes. According to tech rep Scott Phillips, this material works for filling gouges and sealing cracks once the hull has been flashed.

FIELD FIXES FOR LEAKY POLYETHYLENE

Manufacturers often recommend this field fix, which combines an adhesive "primer" with the fabric structure of duct tape.

1. Warm the hull if possible.
2. Prep the damaged area by sanding, then purify with alcohol.
3. Apply a very thin coat of marine contact cement (Sea Bond or HydroGrip) to an area slightly larger than the duct tape patch will be.
4. Allow the glue to dry almost completely, about 5 minutes (it should be only slightly tacky). While the glue dries, cut the duct tape to size, rounding the corners.
5. Apply the duct tape patch. If possible, warm the patch area slightly to fix the bond. Burnish.

Mojo Rogers at Dagger suggests that a thin slice of absorbent minicell foam secured with duct tape is a sufficient patch for most field situations. (Even a simple duct tape job requires thorough preparation as suggested above.)

FIELD PATCH FOR CRACKED POLYETHYLENE HULL

adhesive & duct tape combination

Pop-Rivet Patch

Occasionally a pop-rivet patch, though somewhat ungainly, makes an effective, permanent repair. A crack in the hull should be bored or drilled at each end to limit the fracture. Then prepare the area for a patch. (See also pages 171–72.)

1. Use a band of vinyl siding, a slice of your child's sled, or (best) a section of hull material obtained from the manufacturer.
2. Cut the patch larger than the hole and try to trim the edges with a knife, file, or rasp to feather the profile so the patch won't catch on rocks.

3. Drill holes in the crack termini as suggested above.
4. Flash the hull and allow the repair area to cool.
5. Apply contact cement to both the boat and the patch before positioning.
6. Position the patch on the hull, then drill rivet holes.
7. Rivet the patch, using washers to prevent the rivets from pulling through.

Welded Patches

Plastic welding is not a recommended home repair unless you own a plastic welder and have had plenty of chances to practice this arcane art on a trashed hull. For an interesting discussion of the craft, consult the winter 1992 *Sea Kayaker* feature by Rick Williams, a Seattle engineer who's repaired boats in this way for several years. A scattering of backyard welders around the country will also weld your kayak—with no guarantees. You'll need to do a little investigative work. Start with your favorite outfitter. Surprisingly, your local RV dealer may be a good source for plastic-welding repairs; RVs feature numerous polyethylene holding tanks, and dealers often have skilled welders on their staffs.

Inflatables

Annie, long a hard-hull aficionada, recently discovered the joys of paddling an inflatable canoe. She was paddling around the coast of the Big Island of Hawaii with adventurer Audrey Sutherland. These two genuine wild women backpacked their boats to a remote stretch of coastline, pumped them up, launched through the surf, and cove-hopped their way down one of the world's most spectacular coastlines. They landed by swimming in through the surf, towing the canoes behind them on tethers.

The inflatable canoes worked great, and the stout PVC hulls withstood the sharp lava rocks and coral heads that sliced the women to ribbons as they were pummeled by surf in the landing zones. Hard-shell boats would have been crunched to bits.

Whether you're looking at a canoe, kayak, or raft, an inflatable boat is deceptively simple. You'll find two main materials choices: fabrics coated with plastomers like polyvinylchloride (PVC) or urethane; or synthetic rubber compounds like chlorosulfonated polyethylene (Hypalon) or neoprene. Internal baffles create separate air chambers for flotation redundancy, while most rafts have crosswise inflatable thwarts to stiffen the structure. Then there's all that superlight free stuff—the air.

We say "deceptively simple" because today's inflatable boats give away less than you might think in hull shape, stiffness, and performance to their hard-shell relatives. And whether you're rowing a hot-rod whitewater cataraft, coordinating a six-person crew in an agile self-bailing paddle raft, or soloing rapids in a super-forgiving IK (inflatable kayak), care and repair of the crafts is basically similar.

PVC hulls are the lightest type and generally provide the stiffest, most high-performance shapes. This material, along with urethane, typically features welded, rather than glued, construction. Check the seams on welded hulls; a correct weld will be almost twice as thick as the combined original material.

Hypalon hulls are superresistant to abrasion and stand up to the abuse of constant whitewater duty on long trips with constant UV exposure. Joints are stitched and glued or simply glued. Hypalon is heavier and more expensive but has such a reputation for toughness that it remains the material of choice for whitewater outfitters.

Repairs to these resilient creatures are usually fairly straightforward. The hulls themselves are extraordinarily stout, withstanding impacts and abrasion in horrific river wrecks that would pretzel hard-shell craft. More common is replacing D-rings, grab handles, or footholds ripped out by rapids-happy rafters. Inflation valves may be cracked, gouged, or broken. Tubular-aluminum

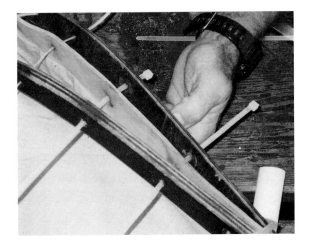

This inflatable kayak has a wood stem. When the retaining screws turned up missing, we improvised . . . with nylon tie-wraps!

oar frames are generally so overbuilt that even the most heinous flip won't faze them.

INFLATABLE HULL REPAIRS

All you need here is to be prepared. Pack a few strips of your boat's hull material, a half-pint of the proper adhesive, a can of solvent for surface cleaning, a couple sheets of sandpaper to rough up the surface before gluing, a sewing awl for odd jobs, and a waterproof case to keep it all dry. Now you're ready for whatever the river throws your way.

Crack whitewater raft suppliers like Oregon's Cascade Outfitters offer repair kits for PVC and Hypalon inflatables complete with repair patches measuring 6 inches by 4 feet that can be color-matched to your particular craft. You'll want some midweight material (420-denier Hypalon or 18-ounce PVC) for tube repairs, and heavy-duty stuff (840-denier Hypalon, or 42-ounce PVC) for floor fixes. Glue needs for Hypalon: Look for something like Shore Adhesive and a toluol solvent/cleaner. Among PVC adhesives the best bet is good old Vynabond—the same glue that fixes vinyl float bags and air mattresses—with MEK (methy ethyl ketone) solvent.

A temporary patch called RamPatch makes a compelling option for go-light raft trippers. This is a temporary rubber-and-plastic patch that folds up, gets punched through a puncture, then flattened and clamped in place inside the tube. Ram-Patch effects a short-term fix to get you home, where you can fix the blown tube right, with the parts listed above.

As for the technique of patching an inflatable, well, if you've ever patched a bicycle inner tube, you already know the drill. (These same gluing/patching techniques work for applying D-rings, grab handles, and footholds.) Remember the basic patching techniques: rounded patch edges, thorough surface prep, etc. (see page 8).

1. Mark the outline of the patch so you can prepare a surface area of correct size; remember, you want a patch that's considerably larger than the hole. The extra glue area ensures an airtight repair.

2. Rough up the area around the puncture to give the adhesive a better bonding surface. Use sandpaper or a roller rasp (a neat rafter's tool that has a rasp on one end and a curved burnishing surface on the other).

3. Clean the sanded area with the appropriate solvent. Wipe down the back side of the patch material with solvent. Do not touch cleaned areas with your greasy fingers.

4. Apply adhesive to both the sanded area and the patch in thin, even layers—more is not better.

Let the glues dry according to the manufacturers' instructions; most are contact cements that require a certain drying time before applying the patch.

5. Once the glue is ready, apply the patch. If patch is over a curved area of tube or floor, drape the area over something similar in shape (a log, bailing bucket, or handy boulder) to improve the adhesion and shape retention of the patch. Make sure that you get it lined up right the first time—you won't get a chance to reposition the patch. (This is why you marked it all out first, right?)

6. Burnish the patch with the roller rasp or another hard, smooth object for best adhesion. Pay particular attention to curves and edges.

INFLATABLE VALVE REPLACEMENT

One often overlooked element of an inflatable repair kit is a replacement valve. Or two. Or three. You might as well be up a creek without a paddle as halfway through a wilderness trip without a new valve.

Valve replacement isn't difficult—you just need the right part and the right tools to make the switch. Obtain proper valves from your craft's manufacturer or a good whitewater supply shop. While you're at it, make sure to procure any specialized tools needed for the job, though many valves can be replaced with nothing more exotic than the Phillips screwdriver on your pocket knife.

Some replacement valves press-fit snugly into hard rubber fittings. Others twist into place, and still others are held into recessed boots with a bunch of little screws.

Wood-and-Canvas

Artful, renewable wood-and-canvas hulls, like rawhide-laced wooden snowshoes, are often overlooked as viable craft today. Yet these boats can be resurrected, restored, rejuvenated, and revitalized to their original form more completely than any other type of canoe. Your grandfather's perfectly good duck boat was probably racked in favor of a maintenance-free aluminum skiff and quickly forgotten.

Fortunately, the art of building and restoring these canoes has not died and may even be entering a renaissance as enlightened folks seek non-petroleum-based alternatives. Today's wood-and-canvas construction is lighter than you remember, and every bit as practical as a glass hull—if you have a barn and like to putter around in it. Wood-and-canvas hulls really must be stored out of the sun and weather. If you can't store your historic craft indoors, at least rig a waterproof tarp to shed rain and snow (make sure the tarp doesn't touch the hull itself).

If you plan to work on a wood-and-canvas boat of any vintage, order a copy of *The Wood and Canvas Canoe*, by Jerry Stelmok and Rollin Thurlow. This book is the best available guide to anything you'll ever need or wish to learn about wood-and-canvas hulls, including where to get materials. The book, plans, kits, supplies, and advice are all available from the Northwoods Canoe Company (see appendix G, beginning on page 236).

Many people think they must paint their canvas hull each year, but this adds unnecessary weight to the boat. Multiple paint layers are more likely to crack and chip upon impact, too. Simply touching up dings and scratches is a better practice; Stelmok and Thurlow recommend filling deep gouges with two-part plastic auto body compound (Bondo), applied with a putty knife.

For field repairs, a scrap of canvas with ambroid glue—a liquid waterproof cement—constitutes the traditional kit. Ambroid glue is fast-drying and requires no mixing, so it is ideal for field use. This is also available from Northwoods Canoe.

(See also chapter 18, Canoe Inspection, for tips on how to keep gunwales and other wood trim in shape.)

Canoe Inspection

See also chapter 17, Hull Materials

Our Indian said that he used black spruce roots to sew canoes with, obtaining it from high lands or mountains. The St. Francis Indian thought that white spruce roots might be the best.

Henry David Thoreau,
The Maine Woods

Once you've taken the time to study the options and then addressed the nature of your canoe's hull material to determine the appropriate care, your energy and attention must next be applied to the furniture—rails, seats, and thwarts—and finally the rigging and hardware. The myriad materials involved in creating your canoe's furniture require countless specific repair approaches, whether for sanding an aluminum gunwale or replacing a cane seat.

Gunwales
ALUMINUM AND VINYL RAILS
Occasional sanding of any burrs in the bare metal is about all you can find to mess with on an aluminum-railed canoe. Vinyl gunwales are really vinyl-coated aluminum. Apply 303 Protectant to the vinyl when you treat the hull.

Other than that, these types of gunwales are essentially maintenance-free. If you wrap the canoe and bend the rails, however, you must replace the entire section, because they cannot be effectively spliced. You can temporarily work the kinked section back into form, but the bend marks

a structural weak place and invites material failure.

If a damaged canoe gets dumped again, the kinked rail acts as a "stress riser" and concentrates tearing forces into the hull itself. We've seen boats literally torn in half by this. Of course, this may have had something to do with the fact that our Maine Guide friend's boat (we agreed not to name him because he holds similar grime on us) was completely wrapped around a boulder, and then six beefy college men were enlisted to haul on a rescue rope attached to a single thwart . . . at least both sections floated free so he could retrieve them.

WOOD RAILS
Wood is usually preferred over vinyl for several reasons: ash or spruce gunwales are aesthetically pleasing, highly resilient, surprisingly impact-resistant, and easy to repair (you can glue cracks or splice in small sections if necessary). However, regular maintenance is important to prevent the wood from rotting, splintering, and cracking; shrinking dried-out wood can even cause cracks in the hull. A wrinkle in any laminate beneath the gunwales indicates that the wood has shrunk, pressuring and deforming the layup. Oiling should restore the wood's expansion ability and correct the problem.

Gray Wood
Ash trim in particular goes gray naturally as it ages and weathers, but this does not necessarily mean that it has deteriorated. You can test your wood

rails for integrity with the point of a knife: if the point enters the grain only with effort, the wood is sound; but if you can bury the point easily, then you may need to consider new rails or at least a substantial overhaul.

Splicing Wood Rails

Gunwale sections can be spliced successfully to restore your gunwales to their full strength. Obtain a compatible section of ash from your local lumbermill or the canoe manufacturer (who will also provide four pages of single-spaced instructions for the procedure). This is a more involved process than it appears on the surface—you basically must take the entire canoe apart. While you can certainly splice in a section of hardwood from your local lumberyard, a rail from the factory should be milled precisely to match your original. Consult your local outfitter, a wood-and-canvas guide, or your favorite canoe manufacturer for more detailed advice.

This is not a rail repair! Splicing gunwale sections will determine ultimate torsional strength of your canoe.

Furniture: Seats and Thwarts

In the event of a wilderness mishap, you may need to replace or back up a broken, bent, or cracked thwart. This easy repair is essential since thwarts maintain much of a canoe's structural integrity.

Pipe insulation and duct tape make your portage yoke slightly less painful.

Use a section of green sapling or a beautifully weathered beaver-chewed stick of approximately the same diameter as the original thwart. Lash it in place, or reuse the original fasteners if they're still available. This provides an effective ingenuity test and may leave your boat with a great story to tell.

SEATS

Hanging seats bear your weight, plus terrific torquing and twisting as you pry or draw. Regular inspection of the hardware is important. Tighten the bolts as needed, but also watch for cracked wooden supports. Seats are usually coated with spar varnish and need annual touchups to prevent mildew.

SLIDERS

Adjustable sliding bow seats flex more than regular hanging versions and should also be inspected regularly. Clean away any sand, salt, or grit, but don't lubricate the sliding rails or you'll slip back and forth constantly. If the slider moves too easily, consider drilling holes at regular intervals along the track for a stopper pin. Don't drill the hole larger than one quarter the diameter of the track.

OILING PROCEDURE FOR WOOD RAILS

Regular applications of penetrating oil (at least once a year) will minimize the likelihood of rotting, drying, or cracking upon impact, as well as cold cracks developing in the hull. Watco Oil, our longtime favorite wood-rail treatment, was discontinued a few years ago (thanks to an alarmist 60 *Minutes* product-safety exposé), and has now reappeared. Deks Olje brand is a recommended alternative. Both contain fungicides and soak deep into the wood, offering a flexible, abrasion-resistant finish. Varnish is not compatible with the constant give and bend of canoe rails and soon cracks off.

1. Treat small, splintering cracks or gouges to a fill session with a water-based yellow wood glue or epoxy. Clamp until cured.
2. Mask off the hull with masking tape to protect it from sandpaper scratching and oil buildup. **Note:** Don't leave masking tape on the hull for more than a few days: removing the residue will be a bear.
3. On Royalex canoes with top-mounted decks, remove the decks to gain access to the entire length of the gunwales.
4. Prep the rails by sanding with medium sandpaper (150- to 220-grit, depending upon the condition of wood). If you use too fine a grit, you'll polish the grain hard rather than opening it to accept oil. Steel wool is not recommended because the iron residue tends to block oil,

resulting in a gummy, nonpenetrating finish.

5. Turn the canoe upside down and sand the underside of the rails just as thoroughly as the tops (this is usually the most weathered area due to being stored upside down on racks).
6. If you wish to apply stain to darken or restore the finish, apply it before the oil and allow it to dry. Stain does *not* protect the wood as oil does, so continue with the treatment.
7. Use a brush or rag to apply a generous coat of oil; make sure to work the oil into screw holes, which are likely entries for rot and mildew.
8. Allow the oil to sit for 10 minutes or so, then wipe off any excess.
9. Repeat this process several times, with 12 to 24 hours between coats. With each application, less oil will be absorbed, until very little penetrates at all. This means that your wood is saturated and protected.
10. When you've fully saturated the rails, allow them to dry completely, then wet-sand with 400-grit sandpaper, using oil as the lubricating agent. Change the paper frequently, and keep both rail and sandpaper wetted with oil. This gives a smooth, satiny topcoat.
11. Follow this procedure for any other nonvarnished wood surface on your canoe.

(For tips on maintaining varnished seats and thwarts, see also page 192.)

THE PAIN OF CANE

Elegant cane seats can quickly degenerate into sagging "pain pockets" if you neglect their seasonal varnish requirements. The cane becomes brittle with exposure and either pulls from its seating or fractures with the slightest pressure from a bony derriere. Unseated cane can be worked back into the groove that holds it onto the frame and encouraged to stay there with epoxy. Don't bother trying to reweave a broken section—replace the webbing once you've punched through part of the cane.

In the field, stretch a scrap of pack cloth from your repair kit over the frame and secure it with needle and thread. Interwoven parachute cord can give stout support for a foam pad seat too.

Fortunately, most modern cane seats are constructed of prewoven panels; replacement seat

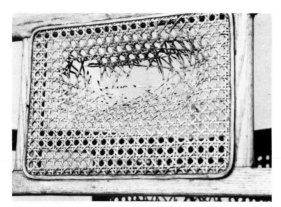

Forget it. It's best to replace the webbing once it reaches this point.

Nylon web seat is a good alternative to cane for those who store canoes outside.

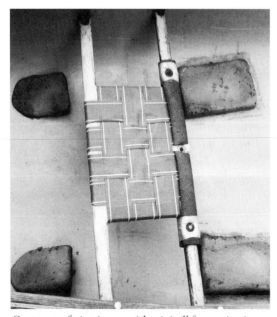

Custom outfitting is easy with minicell foam, pipe insulation, and duct tape. Lawn-chair webbing is a comfortable and economical alternative to new cane seats.

panels are readily available at most outfitters or from manufacturers.

We do not recommend attempting to reweave a classic cane seat, though there are many books available to illustrate the arduous task. Here is one instance where the repair does not really save costs, especially since the materials are renewable and degradable. Because caning is a traditional, skilled profession, one might heartily support its practitioners. Wood-and-canvas guru Rollin Thurlow recommends contacting the Perkins Company for thorough caning instructions, supplies, and advice (see appendix G, beginning on page 236).

For those who store their canoes outside, unscrew the cane seat panels and bring them indoors for the winter. One nice alternative to cane seats is a woven webbing seat—you can make your own on a deposed cane frame using prosaic chaise-lounge repair webbing from the hardware store. Alternatively, purchase the seat panel as you would a cane version. A webbed seat is comfortable, flexible, and more durable than cane, and it has a handsome appearance.

RIGGING

Since canoe painters (bow and stern lines) are generally used as tie-downs on auto roof racks, you should inspect them regularly for friction burns and cuts from metal eyes, bumpers, and exhaust pipes. Likewise, check grab loop knots for frays.

Flotation lashing should be made with cord no stronger than 500-pound breaking strength—otherwise your canoe may get permanently hung up midstream if the lacing snags on something.

OTHER OUTFITTING: LASH POINTS, D-RINGS, SADDLES

As mentioned earlier, the line between outfitting and maintenance gets blurry, but remember, the wrong outfitting adhesive may lead to serious repairs (imagine if your thigh strap pulled out during a crucial draw. . .). Check all D-rings and other glued accessories, and be aware of the hazards of contact cement on ABS hulls (see page 166). For rigging ABS boats, most outfitters are beginning to recommend two-part urethane adhesive, which traps less solvent in the bond.

For terrific service, knowledgeable advice, and all the outfitting accessories you could possibly imagine for any small boat, consult a specialty whitewater shop (see appendix G, beginning on page 236).

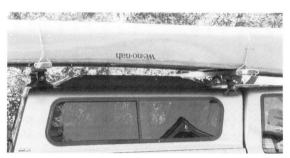

If you like your canoe, space the crossbars as far apart as possible to support the canoe's length.

Not a roof rack!

Use a trucker's hitch for solid tie-downs (see appendix E, beginning on page 227).

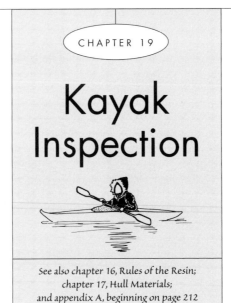

CHAPTER 19

Kayak Inspection

See also chapter 16, Rules of the Resin; chapter 17, Hull Materials; and appendix A, beginning on page 212

If you want a boat for the living room, keep it in the living room.

John Abbenhouse,
Northwest Kayaks

John puts it exactly right. Kayaks are designed to negotiate rugged seascapes, absorb constant wave action, and withstand pounding surf landings and drags along rocky shores. That's a lot to ask of a slim little craft, and to expect your boat to come through these trials unscathed is unrealistic if not downright unreasonable.

Kayaks are built with a lot more parts than canoes, so they naturally require more maintenance and repair awareness. On long trips with big crossings, the key to healthy performance is to check all elements for secure fit, trying to circum-vent or plug any leaks before they cut into your fun (and safety) factor.

In his book *Sea Kayaking*, the inveterate British sea-kayak guru Derek Hutchin-son tells of discovering, well out to sea, that his back hatch was filled with water. During the sandy beach launch his boat had scraped along a broken bottle and acquired several small punctures. In this situation, he and his partners were able to perform a rescue on his boat because he had his minimum repair kit (duct tape) handy in the cockpit.

Bulkheads

Bulkheads serve two purposes. Structurally, they stiffen a hull and act as deck supports; as interior walls they seal off a section of the boat to create flotation chambers and watertight storage compartments. The best bulkheads are molded or glassed into place, but the standard for many years has been a block of minicell foam wedged and caulked into place. Periodically check the foam for mildew and give it a spritz with vinegar to kill any cooties.

Hose off! Your boat, that is. Del Smith leaves no trace of salt on her craft after a day on the bay.

196

Carefully monitor the condition of rudder cables for smooth, safe operation.

Spritz a little silicone lubricant wherever rudder cables bend or pass through fittings.

Cable   swage

Rudder Assembly

Losing control of your rudder in a following sea is more adventure than most paddlers bargain for. That's just what happened to Annie on a long crossing when a cable popped and the chop prohibited any attempt to fix the dang thing while she was afloat. Thankfully, the day was fair, but the tension and effort to hold her course took their toll. After landing, she was more useless than usual for the rest of the day.

Now she is completely paranoid and futzes with the rudder assembly before each outing. A foot-controlled rudder system, though simple, is like any machine—*expect* its moving parts to break and you'll get along fine.

Check all mounting hardware, especially if the rudder is hanging off the stern by a pin. On a long trip, carry extra bolts, spare rudder cables and plenty of cable swages, plus Vise-Grips for prying the old stuff apart and squeezing the new stuff back together. You'll also need something to cut the cables with, or make sure they're the right length before setting out.

Although you probably cannot visually examine an internal rudder cable, the most likely points of damage are where it connects with the rudder or passes with a bend through the hull. Corrosion

concentrates in spots like this, especially if the cable is connecting dissimilar metals. Salt water combined with two different metals makes a passable battery, otherwise known as galvanic corrosion. Even though the least corrosion-prone pairing is stainless steel and aluminum, rust never sleeps. Watch for frays or corrosion in the cable and lubricate lightly with TriFlow.

Some rudders rely on nylon cord for blade retractors or to control the action—easy to fix but also quick to wear out in sun and salt. Clean these lines as you would rigging: check knots, then trim and melt the frays. Dave was surprised to see that one otherwise solid system relied on a cheesy little plastic loop to secure the retractor and immediately replaced it with a stainless fixture.

Annie discovered that rudder inspection isn't just a start-of-the-season ritual; mechanical contraptions hanging off kayak sterns require constant vigilance. She was launching off a shell beach on a solo trip. After securing herself into the sprayskirt suspenders, paddle jacket, and PFD (a sweaty, ten-minute operation), she found that the rudder was jammed with shell fragments and sand. With no one around to flip the blade down for her, she had to haul ashore and start over.

RECAULKING FOAM BULKHEADS

Foam bulkheads need periodic caulking to remain watertight and to stay put in their designated place. Working inside a kayak is awkward and claustrophobic—allow plenty of time so you can take plenty of breathers, and wear gloves and a respirator mask. Use urethane adhesive, not silicone. *Warning to family members:* people who are working wriggled up inside a kayak are apt to come out cranky and demanding.

1. Remove old caulk from each side of the bulkhead with a sharp scraper or knife. If you're lucky, the stuff will just peel off with finger pressure.
2. Mark the placement of the bulkhead very clearly.
3. Push the bulkhead back about ½ inch (not too much, and be deliberate, especially if there are rudder cables running through the foam).
4. Clean grime and slime away from around the bulkhead. You'll probably need a scratchy pad and some vinegar. Don't use CitraSolv, which contains oils that may inhibit the adhesive.

Make sure you can still see the bulkhead marker.

5. Use 150-grit sandpaper to prepare the gluing surface. Clean with denatured alcohol; wear gloves so you don't contaminate the bonding area. Also clean the edge of the foam block with alcohol. Allow surfaces to dry completely.
6. Push the bulkhead back to its original position.
7. Begin caulking an inner bead, forcing the nozzle *underneath* the edge of the block—don't just push the gun, because you may break the nozzle. Apply an outer bead immediately to the joint.
8. Dip a gloved finger into a cup of cold water and tool along the bead of caulk to give a smooth, even texture. (The water keeps caulk from sticking to the glove.)
9. Allow the adhesive to cure completely according to the manufacturer's instructions. If you flex the hull before the glue has dried, you risk ruining the bond, and you'll have to stick your head inside the hull again.

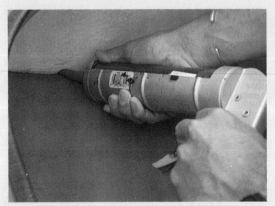

Carefully insert the caulk nozzle between the foam and the hull to direct a bead of sealant well underneath the bulkhead.

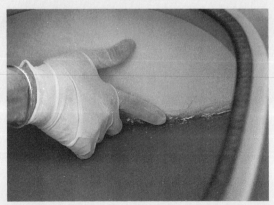

"Tool" caulk with a gloved finger dipped in cold water.

Hatches

Hatches vary by design, but their job is the same: to provide access to a sealed chamber for stowing gear and to keep water out of the chamber if the boat swamps. Most hatches have rims, or coamings, to be treated as you would a cockpit coaming. The covers may be made of neoprene, molded glass or plastic, or some combination of materials, secured either by straps or by a self-locking closure. A few hatches are screw-on types, and the threads must be kept clean.

Always remove hatch covers before storage, especially neoprene covers, which rot quickly in the sun (see Sprayskirts, page 200, for care).

Some of the best, most watertight hatches ever made are rubber with a self-locking band, as on Valley Canoes. The trouble with these is that they work almost too well. If left on for extended periods during storage, condensation inside the chamber can cause a vacuum or vapor lock, making the covers almost impossible to remove. This situation can also occur on a summer day when warm air is trapped inside the warm hatch. Once the boat is immersed in cold water, the warm air contracts, creating vacuumlike stress on the deck, which may actually crack. One remedy for this problem is to drill a tiny hole through the bulkhead to allow air exchange. (Where it's appropriate to drill this hole is debatable: if the hole is drilled at the base, water will travel from your cockpit; if it's drilled at the top, it will be the first place to leak in a capsize. The middle seems a good compromise.)

Cockpit Coaming

On polyethylene kayaks, the coaming is typically rimmed with automobile trim—vinyl-clad aluminum braid—that buffers the sharp-edged plastic. If this trim does not fit snugly, use pliers and crimp it every few inches to bend the wire core into shape.

Sometimes poly coamings don't provide much gripping surface for sprayskirts. If your skirt persists in popping off, use a rasp or piece of Dragonskin to rough up the underside of the rim slightly.

Molded fiberglass coamings are known to fail. Every time you enter and exit the cockpit you place great stress on the rim—even more if an attached seat is not sufficiently blocked (see Hanging Seats, next section). If the rim fails while you're on the water, you'll lose structural integrity as well as a watertight seal. Check the coaming before launching.

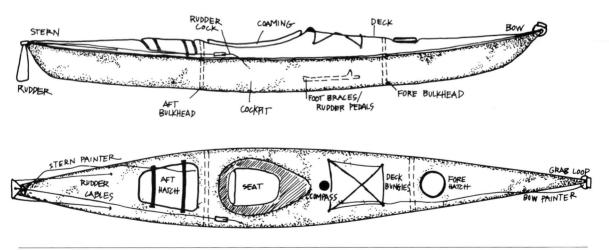

Normally you can fix a broken rim with duct tape to get you home and weather the season, but on a long journey you must be prepared to make a more substantial fiberglass repair. An emergency rim reseating is probably best accomplished with quick-setting epoxy putty—bear in mind that this is a permanent fix. A poly resin repair is best made by adding filler (mat or other milled fibers) to the catalyzed mix to make putty the consistency of peanut butter.

Hanging Seats

An unsupported seat is the source of much fiberglass boat angst. Examine yours carefully to see that its mounting hardware and surrounding layup are not becoming unnecessarily fatigued from the constant flexing of the boat. Even under normal use, seat-mounting screws work loose and wear an elliptical hole that must be repaired. Grit trapped beneath the seat will gradually sand and grind its way through the hull.

Avoid these problems by ensuring that your hanging seat is supported with a block of minicell foam from beneath, caulked into place as recommended for bulkheads. This foam acts as a shock absorber each time you step into the boat, and it keeps debris from lodging in a vulnerable area.

Regularly tighten bolts, and on long trips carry a few bolts of the next-larger size to fill enlarged holes. Once home, drill a new hole and plug the old one with putty or a patch as needed.

Footbraces

Due to the curved nature of a kayak hull, footbraces may abrade through the layup if not protected by a track. The track is mounted with screws at or near the waterline, and they will eventually corrode, even if they're stainless. Prevent galvanic corrosion and leaks by spacing with rubber gaskets rather than aluminum, and watch the fittings—if a

corroded metal part breaks off, it will be a bear to dismantle. Because the footbrace mounting hole is something you may at some point wish to fill and reposition, don't apply any lubricant containing silicone to the hardware, which will inhibit later adhesion of the fill. Plastic or rubber spacers will deteriorate and shrink, so gently tighten these fittings and replace washers as necessary.

Regularly remove footbraces and clean sand and salt out of the mounting tracks. If you have plastic footbraces and tracks, make sure they're clean and give them a coat of 303 Protectant as flexibility insurance. For aluminum, watch for reactive corrosion. If you spot any white, powdery buildup, sand with emery cloth (not steel wool), then clean with soap and water. Rub down the metal with a little TriFlow lubricant and allow it to dry. This will improve the action and help prevent corrosion.

Watch for galvanic corrosion on boat hardware, caused by contact between dissimilar metals (usually steel and aluminum).

Sprayskirts

A sprayskirt's job is to provide a watertight seal around the cockpit rim. The elastic should fit snugly around the coaming.

There are two basic types of sprayskirts: coated

nylon fabric and neoprene. No matter which type you opt for, the sprayskirt gets blasted by sun and salt and must be treated like the delicate and critical garment it is. Regular rinsing with fresh water is essential.

Suspenders on a nylon skirt are not a fashion statement—they serve to tension the fabric so water won't puddle up and leak through the seams. Seamsealing may be necessary. Treat the coated nylon as you would a tent or shell garment to maintain water repellency. (See page 36.)

Neoprene sprayskirts are by far the most effective water barrier. Unfortunately, neoprene is also one of the materials most quickly damaged by UV, so try to minimize the amount of exposure time. (Don't use your skirt as a travel or storage cover—invest in a nylon fabric cockpit cover.)

A neoprene skirt will first fade and break down wherever it's stretched over the cockpit rim. The neoprene itself doesn't give much structural strength—the nylon fabric facing does. One really good way to add durability to your sprayskirt before the fabric tears—and it will—is to use McNett's Iron Mend, an iron-on nylon patch designed specifically for neoprene repairs. (See pages 37–39.)

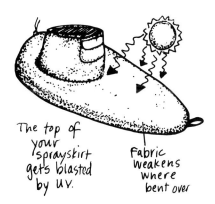

The top of your sprayskirt gets blasted by UV.

Fabric weakens where bent over

Neoprene patching is a little tricky because even the most flexible urethane adhesive becomes rigid over time and won't stretch with the fabric. If you are patching a large surface area (more than a few inches), then stretch the skirt over the cockpit before attempting to repair it with an adhesive patch.

Hardware

If you're trying to track down a persistent, minor leak, check all the deck hardware meticulously. With constant hull flexing, bolts regularly work loose or enlarge their holes. Tighten any bolted fittings until snug, but don't overtighten and pinch the hull material. Use plastic or rubber washers with stainless bolts—not aluminum.

If a bolt hole is leaking (likely), create a seal around the bolt with a rubber washer or a dollop of urethane adhesive caulk. *Do not* use silicone caulk, which will migrate into the laminate, rendering future adhesive repairs unreliable.

Watch around fittings to see that they're not too tight and causing hairline cracks to radiate out from the hole. If a too-loose bolt has caused the hole to become elliptical, reseat the bolt an inch away if possible, then fill or patch the old hole.

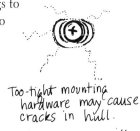

Too-tight mounting hardware may cause cracks in hull.

Too-loose screws will vibrate & create an enlarged, elliptical hole.

Although cheaper, lighter, and less reflective than stainless, nylon or plastic deck fasteners are UV-sensitive and will not last as long. Expect these fittings to break, especially if they become faded or mottled in appearance, which means they've turned brittle. Preventive maintenance: 303 Protectant and covered storage.

Seams

If you've exhausted all possibilities for pinpointing a leak in your fiberglass boat, consider the seam joining the hull to the deck. Typically, seams are bound with a ribbon of glass cloth and are stronger than any point of the hull. Often the exterior seam will be covered with vinyl tape rather than gelcoat, and any damage or irregularities may be difficult to spot. You may have a better chance of spotting a soft spot by getting inside the hull with a flashlight. Otherwise, inch along the seam with your fingers, feeling for any give or ridges that may have delaminated.

A typical spot for a seam to separate is at the vulnerable bow stem of a low-volume kayak. After a few rocky landings, chips in the gelcoat open this area to water. Repair with epoxy putty or a fiberglass patch from the inside if you can (see pages 179–81).

Deck Rigging

Deck lines soak up salt and sun just like all your other gear. When you rinse your boat, make sure you brush and rinse the deck lines too. Every now and then, scooch the lines so that sharp bends are not always wearing in the same spot.

If you find that elastic rigging has stretched out, the rubber core is probably fatigued and the internal strands have become brittle. You can buy a little more time by tightening at the knot, but expect to replace the cord before long. The nylon sheath may be frayed at the ends or where it bends through eyelets; simply melt back any threads with a lighter. Don't attempt to burn the rubber core!

PAINTERS

Bow and stern lines, or painters, should also be reviewed for strength, since you may rely on these for haul-offs on rocky coasts, and for cartop tie-downs.

GRAB LOOPS

Our friend Mary's bow grab loop is so flimsy-looking that Annie just about loses sleep over it. Maybe a worn grab loop doesn't seem like a big deal, but if the thing snaps when you're hefting a loaded boat over ledges, you'll be faced with a full-fledged hull repair. Also check the holes or hardware drilled for the loop for signs of fatigue or cracking. Sharp edges that might abrade the loop can be sanded or filed smooth.

Storage Tips

- If you use a rack, support the kayak directly beneath the bulkheads. If your rack consists of typical two-by-four wood construction, consider covering the crossbars with scrap pieces of 2½-inch PVC plastic pipe. The pipe spreads out the contact pressure on the hull to minimize denting, makes it easier to slide boats on and off the

---

TRIMMING BUNGEE

Ed Stebbins, at Northwest Kayaks, offers the following method for trimming deck bungees:
1. Mark the cut with a wrap of masking tape.
2. Cleanly cut the cord in the middle of the tape with very sharp diagonal cutters.
3. Peel off tape.
4. Pull the sheath to extend around the end of the core.
5. Use a torch or small flame to seal the sheath.
6. Dip the last inch of the cord in vinyl tool dip (from the hardware store).

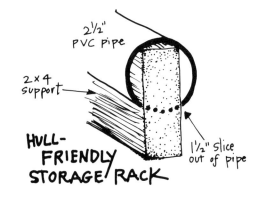

2½" PVC pipe

2×4 support

1½" slice out of pipe

HULL-FRIENDLY STORAGE RACK

TO FIND AN ELUSIVE LEAK

1. Dry off the entire boat, especially caulked bulkheads.
2. Suspend the kayak with loops from rafters, trees, etc., so that you can easily adjust the level from either bow or stern.
3. Pour a gallon of water into the cockpit.
4. Raise one end of the hull just slightly—an inch is plenty.
5. Observe the bulkhead from the opposite side as well as from the exterior hull.
6. Watching carefully, turn the hull from rail to rail, varying the level of the kayak to move the water around.
7. Repeat the procedure with water in other compartments.
8. Mark any leaks and repair as needed.

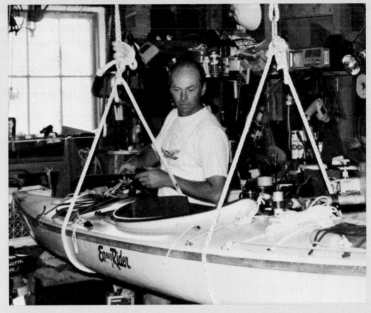

Brad Finn, kayak guide and sauna tender, maintains his boats by hanging them in adjustable slings.

support bars, and holds less water against the boat and rack as well. Use a power jigsaw to slice a 1½-inch strip out of the pipe lengthwise, then slip the pieces over your bars.

- Hanging from grab loops is okay, but it tends to increase the hull rocker over time.
- Hot tip for storing plastic kayaks: stand them on end, bow on ground. This is how manufacturers warehouse their boats, and so should you—if you have the headroom.
- On the side: rack the boat on edge, where sharper hull curves support the weight of a plastic hull with negligible deformation.
- Store with hatch covers off. This prevents your kayak from becoming a giant petri dish for mildew inside the hull.

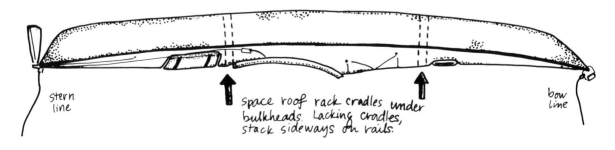

stern line

space roof rack cradles under bulkheads. Lacking cradles, stack sideways on rails.

bow line

CHAPTER 20

Paddles and PFDs

*Frichette shook his head
and spread his thick fingers
apart on his knees.
"There is no future for me if I
cannot paddle a canoe up the
big rivers any more."*

Willa Cather, *Shadows on the Rock*

Wood Paddles

Nothing beats the natural spring of a fine wood paddle, which will remain resilient for years with just seasonal varnish touch-ups. Varnish protects the wood in two ways: it protects wood from drying from the inside out, and from rotting from the outside in. But even the superhard finish of a fine marine varnish cannot withstand constant abrasion from rocky shorelines and zillions of strokes; worn spots on blade and shaft expose wood to the increasing effects of sun, salt, and water.

Unchecked moisture penetrates the grain and will soften or delaminate blades and cause further blistering of varnish (making a bigger repair job

later). Regular, thin coatings of marine varnish or polyurethane are essential and easily applied. Pre- and post-season coats keep the gray at bay.

Copper tips on our dinghy oars made Dave realize the benefit of a protective blade sheath. Those metal tips are heavy, though! He uses epoxy resin to clearcoat the edges of our wood paddle blades, which waylays the inevitable furring or splitting of the end grain.

RESURRECTING A TIRED WOODEN PADDLE

1. Allow the paddle to dry completely in the sun.
2. Sand dulled, gray, and furry end grain to a fine, tapered finish. Start with medium (150-grit) and finish with fine (320-grit) sandpaper.
3. Also sand any areas where varnish has blistered, peeled, or abraded or any stained spots. If the paddle is nearly varnish-less, remove all finish and replace with marine-grade oil (see sidebar, page 193).
4. Check T-grips for security. If they are at all loose, chip away glue or heat with a hair dryer to soften. Remove the grip, sand well. If you have no plans to shorten the paddle, you may as well epoxy the grip back on (make sure you retain the proper orientation of grip and blade!); if you want the option, use yellow wood glue and varnish the joint well.
5. Coat the blade tip with a protective epoxy shield.

Sand the end grain to a fine, tapered finish.

6. Correct any gouges or splits with epoxy as well.

7. Allow the epoxy to fully cure overnight.

8. Apply several thin coats of varnish (or oil) to the sanded area, finally working the topcoat over the entire paddle.

9. Varnish is not normally applied to a canoe paddle grip because it can cause friction blisters; the oil from your hands lubricates bare wood to develop a fine sheen. Sand any splinters with fine sandpaper. If you wish, apply a little tung or linseed oil to the unfinished wood.

SPLIT BLADE

During a low-flowage session of "fightwater" with Dave, Annie's favorite laminated bent-shaft paddle developed a 2-inch crack from bashing one of a hundred hidden rocks (*not* Dave's skull). This was easily repaired with epoxy and some careful clamping.

SPLIT PADDLE BLADE

Repair split with clear epoxy

Sandwich between wood blocks & clamp evenly.

When we were paddling upriver with the repaired paddle, the blade cracked again. Duct tape made a fine field repair and was still holding a hundred miles later. Back at home, Dave peeled off the duct tape, cleaned up the adhesive residue with solvent, re-epoxied the crack, then covered the entire blade with a thin layer of epoxied fiberglass cloth followed by several layers of polyurethane sealer. The paddle still looks new four years later.

BROKEN SHAFT

Nine times out of ten you'll crack the blade before damaging a shaft. Field repair of a broken paddle shaft is usually accomplished by reaching for the spare paddle you wisely brought along. Lacking that, you're probably looking at an improvised fix with a section of bow line lashed around a sapling splint. If you're wilderness tripping, chances are you'll have a repair kit with hose clamps or duct tape for a techier, sleeker splint.

up the creek without your paddle?

improvise!

On a shallow river you could forget your broken paddle entirely and switch to poling. Find yourself a straight spruce stick that's about 10 feet long and no bigger around than a baseball bat at the base. Peel the bark and whittle off the branch stubs so that the pole passes smoothly through your hands. You'll soon discover how native peoples and old-time canoe guides could make such great progress upstream!

Composite Paddles

Exotic composites of carbon fiber, epoxy, and various structural forms have brought us 12-ounce paddles so tough you could almost chop kindling with them. Even so, the best way to protect your composite paddle from damage is never to loan it; you alone should experience the satisfaction and chagrin of chipping, cracking, or otherwise wrecking your pricey technopaddle.

Catastrophic paddle breakage usually happens during transport—by stepping on the blade in camp or in an unexplained, unapologized-for airline baggage trauma. Take your paddles as carry-on luggage if possible and use a paddle bag, even for portaging. Always secure paddles to the boat when

FIELD-TESTED TIPS FOR FINDING THE RIGHT PADDLE

- **General materials advice.** Choose a composite paddle if you're new to the sport, hard on gear, or plan on hard-core whitewater. Aesthetes, traditionalists, and maintenance-ophiles will prefer the organic "bounce" of wood propulsion.

- **Design choices for canoeists.** For all-around tripping use, go for a fairly flexible shaft and midsize blade to ease the strain of long paddling days. Avoid cheapie models with metal shafts and plastic blades—you deserve better. The classic tripper's tool is a graceful ash "beavertail" type. For flatwater cranking, a 15-degree bent shaft is the only rational choice, offering 10 to 15 percent greater efficiency. Choose wood or high-tech composites based on your materials preference and checkbook thickness. Whitewater types want stiff shafts and large blades for "turn-right-*now*!" responsiveness. Composite sticks rule here, though reinforced wood paddles boast vocal adherents on even the steepest creeks.

- **Design choices for kayakers.** Touring types generally want a longer paddle with narrower blades. A long shaft offers greater leverage at lower stroke rates, while a smaller blade is akin to lower gears on a bicycle—you'll end up going farther with less wear and tear on the transmission (your arms, back, and torso muscles). Whitewater fans opt for shorter lengths and larger blades. Shorter paddles suit higher paddling cadence and quick reaction strokes; the larger blades support last-ditch braces and desperate rolls in aerated froth.

- **Canoe paddle sizing.** No more "blade on ground, grip at yer chin" extra-long paddles; those went out with horse-collar life jackets. Put your canoe on the floor, climb aboard, and assume a kneeling position. Extend your arm at a 90-degree angle to the floor and grasp the paddle upside down, with the grip on the floor; your hand should be right where the shaft flares out into the blade. Experiment an inch or two either way to fine-tune your preference. To vary your output on a long day's tour, consider having a bent shaft a few inches shorter for flatwater cranking, and alternate between the two lengths when you feel tired. (Size your flatwater paddle the same way, but sitting in the seat.)

- **Kayak paddle sizing.** For whitewater, the choice is simple: average-size folks start at an overall length of 200 centimeters overall length. Smaller folks go down to 196 or 197; high-ape-index types go up to 203 to 205. Touring paddle length depends somewhat on the beam of your boat; wider kayaks require longer shafts, and vice versa. Don't go so short that you end up rocking the boat from side to side; conversely, excessive paddle length is just swinging useless weight and increasing your risk of tendonitis. Start out at about 220 centimeters and work up or down from there depending on the boat beam and your personal preference.

beached or stash them safely upright among tree limbs, out of the way of wind and tromping feet.

Paddle parks can be rigged with a utility holder from the hardware store or with deck bungees. Carabiners aren't just for rock-jocks; use an oversized biner clipped to deck lines or D-ring as a temporary paddle park.

While carbon-and-fiberglass blades are incredibly strong, use your noggin and don't pry with excessive torque. Digging a few clams in loose sand is one thing; levering stones is quite another.

The most likely wear your composite paddle will exhibit is along blade edges and tips—points of contact with rocks, ledges, or hard-packed sand.

Digging clams on a sandy beach is OK, but don't try levering a boulder.

Carefully inspect the blade for furry or frayed exposed fibers. A stray fray can catch on rocks and cause a splinter that tears along the blade's length. Prevent chips and shears by coating the last half-inch of blade with a thin layer of epoxy. This will add negligible weight to your paddle and is worthwhile if you're hard on gear.

You can correct any cracks, gouges, or chips in your paddle blade by treating it as you would any fiberglass boat (see pages 179–81 and 181–83). The maintenance is also similar, including buffing and waxing or coating with 303 Protectant, as recommended for hull care.

TAKE-APARTS

Two-piece kayak paddles are favored for their versatility— you can adjust the feather, adapt into two canoe paddles, or break down the shaft for

more manageable transport and storage. The joint is usually as simple as a molded ferrule with a spring-loaded button that snaps into correlating holes on the other section. Wood paddles rely on a brass or stainless collar to fit the two pieces together.

Whatever the material, salt and fine sand build up around the joint, at times effectively gluing the sections together if left unattended. Regularly rinse the joint with fresh water, then wipe down the fittings and hardware with silicone lubricant. If your paddle seems hopelessly stuck, try saliva at the joint. You might also let it soak in fresh water (tethered) overnight, or spritz TriFlow into the

Once you've cleaned up the joint, check it for roundness; splits or fissures may be causing fit difficulty.

joint and snap-lock. Once separated, inspect for roundness; splits or fissures may be causing fit difficulty.

PFDs

See also Zippers: The Full Discolsure, beginning on page 10; and chapter 2, Fabrics and Insulations

THE TEST

Holding up the tattered, bleached web of fabric that somehow holds an old flotation device together, Dave looks resolutely skeptical. Yet he manages to zip the vest shut and jump into the lake with a yowl. Surprisingly, a moment later he's bobbing with nose and mouth above the water. Trouble is, there are blocks of foam floating alongside, blown out of tattered sun-rotted fabric by the impact. Old Orange, his original piece of techy paddle gear, is finally retired.

All your PFDs (personal flotation devices) should be subjected to this annual dunk test, since

the sun cooks the life right out of both shell fabrics and flotation fillings. And even if you float, the fabric may be so rotted from sunny fun in the salt sea that it's ready to give up the ship.

Rinse your PFD with fresh water after every outing. Salt water is the obvious enemy, but so are body salts from perspiration, plus other unknown contaminants found in our less-than-pristine lakes and streams. An excellent way to delay UV damage is to coat your PFD fabric with 303 Protectant at least twice a season; store it out of the sun when not in use.

Treat life-vest zippers as recommended on pages 10–15, keeping in mind that the flotation device only works as well as its fastener.

CHAPTER 21

Dry Storage and Flotation

I must tie up the letters in oil-cloth. That is something to do first—else they will get all sweated. . . . He bound them into a neat packet, swedging down the stiff, sticky oilcloth at the corners, for his roving life had made him as methodical as an old hunter in the matter of the road.

Rudyard Kipling, *Kim*

See also Fabric Patching, beginning on page 10

Flotation and dry bags are made with one of two synthetic materials: vinyl or coated nylon (usually urethane-coated). Since each type of bag is designed to be airtight and ostensibly waterproof, maintenance means preserving the fabric, while repair means sealing leaks.

Coated-nylon bags hold many advantages over vinyl bags. Although pricier at the outset, woven nylon fabric has more structural integrity and is less likely to puncture than vinyl. Coated fabrics don't need to be as thick as vinyl to achieve the same durability; the lighter nylon therefore folds more tightly and seals out water better than vinyl. When it comes to seams, the adhesion and burst strength of urethane-coated fabrics are much greater than those of vinyl. Finally, nylon offers a lower friction coefficient; that means it's easier to stuff into a kayak hatch (think what it's like wearing shorts and unpeeling yourself from a vinyl car seat on a hot day).

Patching

Finding a pesky leak can be tough. You can seal the bag, empty it, and listen closely for the hiss while you exert pressure. Or do the same thing and spritz water on the surface, looking for escaping air bubbles. Another method is the "thousand points of light" technique: place the bag over your head and look for spots where the light shines through.

If the bag is cracked or torn at the seal area, you're pretty much hosed, since this is a structural problem. Clearly label the bag in big fat letters "SEMI-DRY" and back it up by lining it with a big plastic trash bag.

When patching any bag, patch both the inside and the outside to ensure a watertight seal. A urethane patch alone will not be as effective as a glued patch. We recently discovered a great nylon-reinforced repair tape developed specifically to

Down & dirty dry bag fashioned from any waterproof material.

Twist the open end & secure as shown.

solve waterproofing problems. Barrier Tape is clear, stretchy, and fast to use, with a very aggressive glue flexible to –40°F.

Whatever patch you apply, make sure the adhesive is allowed to fully cure before using the bag. Of course, duct tape is the preeminent field solution (applied to both sides of the puncture or tear).

Most manufacturers offer a guarantee against seam leakage. Once a welded seam springs a leak, you'll have a hard time correcting the problem. It's worth pursuing the warranty.

Dry Bag Tips

- Damage to dry bags often comes from the inside out, when a hard or pointed object inside the bag (like a tuna can, boot heel, or cracker box) concentrates abrasion in one area.
- Never store sunscreen or insect repellent containing DEET inside a dry bag (or any synthetic bag). DEET will literally melt the material.
- When opening a dry bag that's wet on the outside, avoid pouring water onto your dry gear. Open the bag so its mouth points down and allow the water to run off.
- When packing for an expedition, *do not* stuff your dry bags to the max, nor should you seal them, prior to shipping. We once did this, thinking we'd be ready that much sooner at the put-in; our big duffle came down the luggage belt full of abrasion holes, and three loaded dry bags suffered similarly. We had a patching party right in the airport lounge, where at least it wasn't raining.
- If your dry bag has a zipper, store with coil or plastic zippers securely shut; metal zippers should be stored in the open position.
- Clean and dry bags thoroughly after—or even during—each trip. Once, Mary Gorman's elegant fruit salad fermented and exploded in her dry bag, saturating the lining and contents with sticky goo. Turn bags inside outt, rinse with fresh water, and sponge with a mild soap (Dr.

Bronner's, Ivory Flakes) if necessary. Don't use solvents, which may damage waterproof fabric coatings. Make sure there's no salt or sand trapped in seams or under fasteners.
- Annie usually lines her dry bags with a clear plastic trash bag just to be on the safe side. If carrying liquids like cooking oil, she double-bags them in zippered plastic bags before committing them to the dry bag.
- Make sure the bag is completely dry before folding and storing it in a cool, dry place.
- Occasionally apply 303 Protectant to keep vinyl or coatings supple and to protect against UV exposure.
- Don't keep your camera or other delicate gadgets in a dry bag, which does not protect against impact (and is not usually completely watertight anyway). Condensation inside the dry bag can also cause damage to lenses or electronics. Use a hard dry box with O-ring seals.

Flotation Bag Tips

- Don't overinflate the bags, which stresses seams and coatings, making the bags more susceptible to abrasion or pinhole punctures. If you cannot depress the surface 3 or 4 inches, the bags are overinflated.
- Monitor bag pressure throughout the day. Sunlight can overheat float bags even through the deck of a kayak. Heating causes the air inside the bags to expand and can easily blow a seam. Excess pressure can also pop bags by forcing them against rough spots or protruding hull hardware.
- Release air and remove the flotation bags from the boat for transporting. Not only are road grime and the constant flapping from rooftop air turbulence hard on the material but you're less likely to lose bags (basically giant balloons) along the highway.
- Rig your bags with a quick-release system so

Inflate the bag and close the valve, or close air into the empty dry bag and seal. Immerse the bag in a tub of water and watch for a telltale stream of bubbles. Another way to pinpoint a leak is to spray an inflated bag with a mist of water and watch for bubbles on the water-saturated fabric surface.

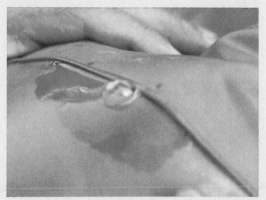

A little moisture, and a telltale bubble.

they're easier to remove for transport. Remember not to use cord stronger than 500-pound breaking strength for lashing so the flotation rigging will be less likely to hang up your boat midstream.

- Clean bags with mild soap and water but no solvents.
- Canoe flotation bags catch a lot more sun than kayak bags, so periodic use of 303 Protectant is a good idea.

- Flotation bags must be patched on the exterior, so it is especially important to use compatible adhesives. For vinyl, use Vynabond; for urethane coatings, use a urethane adhesive. As with dry bags, a fabric patch will last longer.
- If you absolutely can't find a slow leak, try a can of Fix-a-Flat, available at auto parts stores. Shoot a can of the stuff into the inflated bag and shake the bag until the interior is well coated. This should seal any elusive pinholes. This is pretty much a last-resort solution.
- Like dry bags, most flotation bags are backed by a solid manufacturer's warranty.

Dry Boxes

Though dry boxes are pretty simple, it's important to practice mindful use. When closing, always make sure the carrying straps and other debris are not pinched in the lid or contaminating the O-ring seal. After each use, empty the box of its padding and use a water jet to clean the hinges of sand, salt, and grit. If you notice that the hinges or closures are stiff and hard to close, it probably means they're packed full of grime. If you don't irrigate these moving parts, they're likely to snap. Peel O-rings out of their channels and clean them with soap and water. Use 303 Protectant or silicone to keep the O-rings supple and prevent cracking.

APPENDIX A

Adhesives

THE MONTREAL PROTOCOL

First signed in 1985, the Montreal Protocol is a treaty among developed nations that aims to reduce production of ozone-depleting chemicals. Many times expanded, ratified, amended, and side-stepped, the agreement requires participating countries to first eliminate production of chlorofluorocarbons (CFCs), then reduce the use of halons and other solvents containing chlorine, like methyl chloroform, carbon tetrachloride, and methyl bromide, all of which hasten global warming.

The response? Some of the more environmentally enlightened countries have aggressively begun essential research to create ozone-friendlier alternatives. Many big U.S. companies have yet to embrace "green" solutions and have focused on a stopgap use of hydrochlorofluorocarbons (HCFCs) to replace CFCs, which still contribute to our thinning atmosphere. Loopholes notwithstanding, HCFCs will be phased out too, though probably not in this lifetime.

Many "second-world" nations, including India and China, are not bound by terms of the Montreal Protocol and use cheaper, more toxic chemicals to create foams, insulations, propellants, and other products that eventually enter other markets as "cheap imports."

But what does the Montreal Protocol have to do with a book about outdoor gear repair? Ask any maker of outdoor equipment, and you'll hear a lot about how increased environmental regulations have decreased solvent options, particularly solvent-based adhesives, and complicated shipping procedures, thereby affecting operations. In many cases a manufacturer would willingly switch to a less toxic binder if one were available.

"Until recently, nobody's really had to *try* to develop good, flexible, water-based adhesives," says Paul Hebert, of Ascension Enterprises, a manufacturer of climbing skins for skis. When his preferred adhesive was phased out of production, he was forced to switch to a highly flammable alternative. This unattractive situation in turn forced him to reconsider his manufacturing process, and he's now busy developing a heat applicator system for less toxic and less flammable bonds.

"The way footwear is made today, adhesives are everything," says Dave Page, a Seattle cobbler who gets his water-based glues from Germany. Since his shop runs twelve hours a day, six days a week, using solvent-based adhesives and inhaling their carcinogenic fumes would be just plain bad for business.

This gap between phasing out solvent-based adhesives and developing environmentally friendly alternatives is beginning to touch the home user too, as favorite standby products are quietly removed from the market. Unfortunately, most of the glues represented in this book are solvent-based, primarily because of their superior function and flexibility. Currently, the main drawbacks to water-based glues are that they're difficult to handle in cold weather and good ones just aren't yet available to the average person. As restrictions increase, perhaps a powdered form (just add water!) will be developed.

DON'T KNOW MUCH ABOUT CHEMISTRY

Adhesives are pretty simple to understand, even for those who dozed through Chem 101. Adhesives cure in one of two ways: by evaporation of the solvent constituents, leaving the desired hardened material; or by a chemical reaction between two materials that produces a third substance.

Set versus Cure

If you break a leg, you first set the bone and then allow time for it to heal. Adhesives work the same way: the bonded material must first set up, or harden, before it begins to cure and reach maximum strength. Even though many adhesives set up in minutes (like some epoxies), actual curing time may take days. Curing time is hugely affected by the external variables of temperature and humidity. The best adhesion occurs when there's little moisture and the ambient temperature is a consistent 55° to 70°F. Ideally, a glued repair should not be put to use until full curing has occurred.

Instant setup (as with Superglue or contact cement) is desirable if you can't clamp the two surfaces together and won't need to make adjustments. Instant setup does not necessarily mean instant cure—read the label.

Chemical versus Mechanical Bonding

Like butlers, the best adhesives are basically invisible. That is, the bond created should be chemical rather than mechanical, penetrating surfaces rather than sitting on top and forming yet another layer of material. There are certainly situations where a mechanical bond is desirable; it's important to recognize the difference.

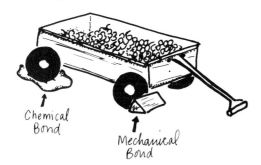

Chemical Bond

Mechanical Bond

GENERAL GLUE TYPES
Contact Cement

Contact cement works well with foams and most plastics. Highly water-resistant, this is a favorite in the boat shop. Glue both surfaces with a thin layer and allow to sit until the material appears dry and is tacky but not glossy. Solvent: acetone, nail polish remover. When contact cement has not fully

evaporated before surfaces are joined, the leftover solvent trapped in the bond can cause damage to the original surface material. **Caution:** Like the name suggests, this stuff bonds upon contact—you only get *one* chance to position your repair. If you blow it, you must start all over again.

Epoxy

Epoxy is a two-part structural adhesive mixed just before application. Different brands offer different viscosity and setting times. A puttylike consistency is most desirable for repairing small holes or binding nonsimilar materials because it sets up in as little as five minutes (curing overnight) to provide a bombproof, waterproof fill. Solvent: acetone while the material is still soft. Epoxy is difficult to sand, so experienced users sand during the "green" phase, when the material is set but not fully cured.

Hot-Melt

Normally used in special glue guns, hot glue is popular for its quick setting and curing capabilities, though it is not nearly as strong as other types. A stick or cartridge of solid adhesive is ideal in the repair kit—melted with a candle, hot-melt glue sticks to fabric and leather, fills holes, and cures instantly. It is waterproof and fairly flexible. Solvent: acetone, nail polish remover.

Peanut Butter

A particularly popular adhesive in the backcountry repair kit, P.B. effectively bonds porous surfaces like week-old bagels. While excellent filling for belly holes, peanut butter has a long cure time and is difficult to work with in cold temperatures. Choking hazards exist. Solvent: lemonade, whiskey, creek water.

Polyester Resin

This resin is activated with a small amount of liquid catalyst just before application and is normally used to bind fiberglass fabric layers to a fiberglass or Kevlar surface. Setup occurs within an hour; curing takes at least 24 hours. Hardened polyester is rigid and waterproof. Solvent: acetone while the material is still soft, or Res-Away, a commercially available, more environmentally friendly alternative. Sanding is also very easy, but wear a respirator mask and eye protection.

Silicone

Silicone is not really an adhesive but a sealant, producing a strictly mechanical yet waterproof bond. The hardened material can be peeled or scraped for removal.

Superglue

Superglue and other cyanoacrylate adhesives work on nonporous materials. Superglue is very rigid, with no tensile strength or flexibility. It works well in cold weather and is water-resistant. It is best suited to small repair jobs, like repairing a stripped binding screw. Superglue sets almost instantly and cures in less than an hour under ideal conditions. Climbers use it on big walls to hold split fingers together, but this is not doctor-recommended. Create a Superglue filler by mixing with talcum powder (ideal for filling chips in a knife housing). Solvent: acetone, nail polish remover. Direct heat also loosens glue. **Caution:** Avoid use on polyethylene, and avoid contact with skin, face, or eyes. This stuff can stick a finger to your eyelid in a heartbeat, which, take it from Dave, is *not* funny.

Urethane

Urethane forms the base for the most flexible adhesives, making this the repair material of choice for large and small fixes. Urethane rubber adhesives usually take about 24 hours to fully cure, but once hard, they are virtually indestructible. Many urethane adhesives will shrink as they dry, causing fabrics to pucker; a higher rubber-to-solvent ratio is desirable. To find out the content, you'll have to

contact the manufacturer. Solvent: toluene, acetone while still soft. Direct heat for removal.

Vinyl

Used like contact cement, vinyl adhesive bonds PVC, vinyl, foam, and wood without clamping. It sets up in under 20 minutes and cures overnight. Solvent: methyl-ethyl-ketone (MEK). Nasty! Best breathed by people you do not like.

Vinylester

Similar to polyester, yet this is the most flexible thermoset resin used in boat layups. Because of its short shelf life and other mitigating factors, vinylester is rarely available in small quantities for home-repair purposes.

GLUE RULES

As Dave Page noted above, adhesives are everything to modern outdoor gear manufacture and repair, but they are usually toxic to living creatures. Many techniques in this book, from sealing seams to patching to filling gouges, depend upon a successful chemical bond. No matter what material you use, the same general rules apply.

Safety Precautions

- Always work in a well-ventilated area. Generally, the toxic ingredients are heavier than air, so low-level ventilation is important (like a fan on the floor blowing away from the repair area).
- Work away from any heat source.
- Wear eye goggles and a respirator mask to filter fumes. Make sure your respirator has been approved by OSHA for filtering the toxics in question. If you wear glasses, be aware that some solvents and adhesives can potentially alter plastic lenses and frames upon contact.
- Avoid working directly over, or with your face close to, the repair. If you're working with your head inside a kayak, come up for air every few minutes.

- Use gloves. If you do a fair amount of gluing or painting, spring for a pair of heavy-duty rubber gloves (not dishwashing or surgical gloves) for gunky jobs. For jobs in which greater sensibility is desired, you may want to use thinner surgical latex gloves. Watch out! Thin gloves stick to many glues. Barrier creams are an option.
- Keep kids and pets away from the repair area until the adhesive has cured. Errant Labrador retriever hair will flat ruin a neat gelcoat repair.
- Wash hands immediately after using any adhesive or solvent.
- Allow any unused, activated adhesives to harden fully before proper disposal. Most community fire departments and transfer stations sponsor an annual household toxics roundup—call your town office to find out if there's one in your area.
- *Never* pour toxics down the drain.

Avoid Junk Bonds

A bad glue job is a hassle, particularly if you don't realize it until the material has hardened. It's easy to create a permanent mess instead of a first-rate repair. Take every precaution and allow plenty of space and time when working with adhesives.

1. Actually read all pertinent instructions. Twice. Three times. Plan your steps, lay out the needed materials, and generally get organized. Allow twice as much time as you think you'll need.
2. Use as little glue as possible—more is not better!
3. Wait for ideal conditions before starting your repair. The two critical factors for a good bond are a moderate temperature and low humidity.

PREPARATION IS EVERYTHING

1. Remove any dirt, grease, or sticky residue with mild soap and water.
2. Clean with alcohol or other solvent.
3. Buff or roughen the area with sandpaper, emery cloth, a wire brush, beach sand, or a stone.
4. Wipe again with alcohol or solvent.
5. Apply adhesive.

(If conditions are less than ideal, you can try to accelerate a cure by setting the object in direct sun or heating with a hair dryer or heat gun, using a circular motion to keep the air moving.)

4. After sanding large areas (as on a boat), vacuum, sweep, or wipe away any dust or shavings with a tack cloth, then wait a few minutes before final prepping to allow airborne particles to settle.
5. Carefully clean and prep the surfaces to be glued.
6. After applying adhesives and joining surfaces, clean up any drips or slops with a lint-free cloth dipped in the appropriate solvent or alcohol.
7. Contact cement or vinyl adhesive should be slightly tacky, not dry, to the touch before bonding. If you think your glue is too dry, swab a little of the appropriate solvent on both surfaces. Wait for the sheen to disappear, then mate.
8. As you clean up the repair area, be careful not to stir up any dust that may stick to curing glues.

Low-Tox Cleaning Solutions

IS IT GREEN TO BE CLEAN?

Though keeping gear clean and cootie-free is the mainstay of preservation, there's no need to employ harsh chemical cleaners. Not only can these damage both natural and synthetic materials but average household cleaning products represent real environmental hazards on many levels—during manufacture, promotion, distribution, consumption, storage, and, ultimately, substance and container disposal.

Researchers estimate that more than 13 tons of liquid household cleaners are discharged into U.S. drains each month, not including the volume of hazardous waste discharged into septic systems or tossed into the backyard. Improper disposal stems less from malice than from ignorance. Most people simply don't realize that scouring the sink with an ammonia-based abrasive is both corrosive and toxic to creatures and groundwater.

Most household paints, solvents, and cleaners affect humans and their ecosystems in one or more of the following ways:

Irritants can cause sore or inflamed tissue or mucous membranes.

Toxics can cause injury or death upon ingestion, inhalation, or absorption.

Flammables can be ignited at most temperatures.

Corrosives (substances or vapors) can irreversibly alter or deteriorate tissue or material at the contact site.

HOME-BREWED LOW-TOX ALTERNATIVES

The following low-tox recipes and recommendations approximate the effectiveness of popular commercial mixes. Granted, there are times when you may resort to more potent measures, but for everyday use these simple solutions are easier on your health, the environment, your budget, your gear, and your peace of mind, especially in a home with kids or pets. (Think of all the cupboard space you gain!)

Alternatives to . . .

Abrasive cleaners—Baking soda or borax. For tough spots, rub the area with half a lemon dipped in borax or presoak with citrus solvent.

Ammonia cleaners—Undiluted white vinegar in a spray bottle. Annie's Mom's personal favorite: 1 part vinegar, 1 part liquid soap, 1 part water.

Bleach cleaners—Try ½ cup white vinegar, baking soda, or borax in the laundry. At the very least, seek out a nonchlorine bleach (basically hydrogen peroxide and water), available at natural-foods stores.

Disinfectants—Add ½ cup borax to 1 gallon boiling water; try white vinegar or citrus solvent to kill mildew, pet odors, and other slimy stuff.

Metal cleaner—For cleaning copper or brass, dissolve 1 tablespoon salt in ½ cup vinegar. Apply and allow to sit a few minutes before rubbing, rinsing, and buffing. Amaze your friends by slathering ketchup on a tarnished brass surface, rub briskly, then rinse, and presto! Shiny stuff, and permanently turned-off ketchup eaters.

Moth balls—Cedar blocks, chips, or essential oils in a pomander. Try other astringent herbal deterrents like tansy, rosemary, artemesia, lavender (also effective against fleas).

Oven cleaner—Apply a mixture of 2 tablespoons liquid castile soap, 2 tablespoons borax, and 2 cups water. Allow it to set for about 30 minutes, then scrub with baking soda and salt.

Stain remover—For greasy or oily stains, mix 1 tablespoon liquid castile soap, 1 tablespoon glycerin (available from drugstores or natural-foods stores), and 1 cup water. Work into the stain, then launder or flush with water.

STAIN REMOVAL

There are two basic types of stains: protein (from food, plants, blood) and grease (from oil); to remove the stain you must use a like substance that will penetrate the material. However, the real secret to stain removal is to attack the spot as soon as possible. Don't expect to get a big glob of grease off your ski pants after storing them for the summer. Remember too that you may scrub the material to death—sometimes it's better to accept the mark.

Protein Stains

Blood—Salt, milk, and 3 percent hydrogen peroxide are all common remedies. A commercial enzyme such as one recommended for drain cleaning is also effective (available at natural-foods stores). Annie's favorite secret weapon is a bar of seaweed soap (from a natural-foods store or kitchen shop), scrubbed directly on the stain with cool water. If the stain persists, bathe it in lemon juice and sunshine, then wash normally.

Food—For miscellaneous food stains like fruit juice, spritz with a solution of vinegar, soap, and water, then pour boiling water through the stretched fabric.

Grass—Try denatured alcohol or a solution of vinegar, soap, and water (ammonia substitute). An enzyme cleaner will also work.

Gum—Freeze the garment, then chip off the gum. Slather the remaining sticky stuff with peanut butter to remove as much as possible—seriously, boys, this actually works—then wash as usual. Peanut butter or cooking oil works well in the field.

Ink—Dab on or soak in denatured alcohol or try a short soak in citrus solvent at the recommended dilution.

Good Old Grease Stains

If the spot is fresh, dust with a little cornmeal or other absorbent material (talcum powder, cornstarch). Let it sit, then brush off and treat the grease spot with glycerin or clear glycerin soap. If the stain is persistent or has had time to set, apply citrus solvent, then rinse thoroughly before laundering. Another option is to soak in homemade oven cleaner (*described above*).

PAINTS AND THINNERS

Just about everyone knows by now that lead-based paints are bad juju, but oil-based paints are also flammable and toxic. Whenever possible, employ latex or water-based paints (which in turn contain their own hazards). Rustproof coatings are wicked too, but as yet there are no viable alternatives. Purchase a handheld, refillable sprayer (at an auto parts or hardware store) to reduce packaging waste.

Paint thinners and strippers are rife with acetone, esters, ketones, and other heinous petroleum distillates—a case where the cure is worse than the disease. Use latex paint! Scrapers, heat guns, or sanders (used with a respirator mask) are the best paint-removal tools. If you use thinner, maximize it by storing used thinner in a tightly capped jar until the contaminants settle out. Strain the thinner through a screen, store the solid contaminants for later collection, and reuse the thinner.

CITRUS CLEANERS AND SOLVENTS

The best all-around alternative cleaners for household use are concentrated, citrus-based cleaners like CitraSolv, also sold as Citru-Solv-It (this and other brands are available through coops or from auto parts or hardware stores). Citrus solvents are made with D-limeone, a byproduct of the juice industry, instead of with petroleum distillates.

You can use varying strengths (dilute with water) of a citrus oil cleaner to penetrate and dissolve most sticky stuff like grease, tar, wax, gum, and adhesives,

HARBORING HOUSEHOLD HAZARDS:
A FEW GOOD RULES OF THUMB

Johnny was a chemist
but Johnny is no more
What he thought was H_2O
was H_2SO_4

- Keep substances in their original containers.
- Store in a cool, dry place inaccessible to children or pets. A locked outbuilding is ideal.
- Keep incompatible chemical products separated.
- Periodically inspect containers for deterioration.
- Read product literature and instructions before each use, following manufacturers' recommendations.
- Use products at their recommended strength and do not mix different chemicals.

- Completely use all substances before disposing of containers. Buy what you need, or share the remainder with someone who will use it.
- Follow local disposal requirements—you may need to store spent containers for an annual toxics collection at your dump or recycling center.

air enters spout

Pour with spout at top to avoid splashing toxics.

not to mention stains and general grime. Although most citrus solvents are biodegradable and cruelty-free concoctions, they are still irritants and combustible to some degree, so they are not recommended for use on silk, wool, or any styrene plastics. (Contact Citru-Solv-It, Chempoint Products, P.O. Box 2597, Danbury, CT 06813, 800-343-6588.)

FIND OUT MORE
Your library, town office, and local transfer station (that's p.c. for "dump") can provide you with more literature about toxics. Tell your family and friends about the alternatives highlighted here.

The Environmental Hazards Management Institute, a nonprofit environmental organization, publishes unique *Waste Wheels*, easy-to-use guides that help citizens and businesses identify and modify sources of toxics and waste in their daily lives. (Contact Environmental Hazards Management Institute, P.O. Box 932, Durham, NH 03824, 603-868-1496.)

Kit Suggestions

There's a thin line between preparedness and retentiveness. If you tried to accommodate every possible emergency, you'd need a Sherpa just to carry your kit. In fact, most world travelers head confidently into the void with little more than a roll of duct tape and a Swiss Army knife. If you take exceptional care of your equipment or are of an innovative nature, the duct tape program should suffice.

However, during long, committing expeditions, cold-weather travel, or trips with large groups, you're likely to encounter many problems calling for minor repairs, like a broken zipper or a clogged stove. And you'll need to be ready for catastrophes, like getting bumped by a whale or losing your sole 10 miles from the trailhead.

The first edition of this book helped goad the outdoor industry into recognizing and capitalizing on the concept of repair kits as profit centers. Now you can find nicely detailed, prepackaged field kits tailored to every activity, from backpacking to mountain biking to river rafting. The selection is great, but as *Backpacker* magazine's gear editor, Kristin Hostetter, points out, "it's a lot more fun to whip up your own special repair kit."

The following kit guidelines are culled from various resources and experiences, to be mixed and matched according to travel style.

FRITA'S EVERYDAY KIT FOR ACCRUING FABULOUS FAVORS

This is the lightweight contingency bag Annie carries in her purse, engendering countless snide comments—until someone else on the trip inevitably weasels some obscure widget out of the bag. The palm-sized packet slips into a pack or complements other repair kits as needed. Remember Aesop's fable about the lion with the thorn in his paw? With this kit one may accrue many favors.

- Swiss Army knife with corkscrew, screwdriver accessory, and scissors
- Old Chouinard sewing kit, including several sizes of safety pins, needles, assorted threads, two buttons, heavy-duty nylon thread, collapsible awl
- dental floss
- alcohol swab
- one 3- by 7-inch strip of self-adhesive nylon tape

Fix a boat, tent, knife, flesh wound, or sagging spirit with your own special kit.

Annie's Official Alaska Solo Kayak Trip kit: everything she could possibly need stuffed into a package the size and weight of a loaf of good German bread.

- superfine nylon cord
- butane lighter (small)
- assorted rubber bands
- silk handkerchief
- box of wooden matches with several winds of duct tape wrapped around the box

ESSENTIAL TENT REPAIR KIT

Stash these items in your tent stake bag:
- large piece (about 1 foot square) of ripstop nylon cloth
- self-adhesive nylon repair tape
- alcohol swab
- pole splint wrapped with duct tape
- extra nylon cord

STOVE REPAIR KIT

Depending on your preferred boiler, carry in your stove bag
- jet-cleaning tool
- spare jet
- scratchy cleaning pad (such as 3M Scotch-Brite)
- spare O-rings
- spare pump cup
- operating instructions

MURPHY'S LAW BACKCOUNTRY KIT

Michael Jay Coe wanted to start a very small business that would fill a niche in the outdoor industry, provide a service, and remain affordable at his one-man level. After three summers as a wilderness ranger around Mount Hood, Coe saw more broken gear and heard more hikers' epic horror stories than he cared to count. The Murphy's Law Backcountry Repair Kit is his answer to both self-employment and disaster deployment. With this 4-by 6-inch, 3.5-ounce kit you're completely covered. It contains twenty-five-plus essentials plus straightforward instructions to get you out of a jam. Commercially available at your favorite outdoor store for $14.95. Contact: Outdoor Essentials, 7276 SW Beaverton Highway, Suite 230, Portland, OR 97225, 503-233-1911.

DAVID "THE DOCTOR" GOODMAN'S SKI REPAIR KIT

Professional powder lunatic and backcountry luminary David Goodman is the author of *Classic Backcountry Skiing: A Guide to the Best Ski Tours in New England* (AMC Books, 1998). In his kit:
- Essential: screwdriver (Pozi-Drive or No. 3 Phillips head)
- duct tape
- small sharpening stone
- predrilled scraper (for tip repairs)
- spare binding parts (cables, bails, etc.)
- extra binding screws
- steel wool (for packing in binding screw holes)
- galvanized wire
- assorted hose clamps (to splint poles or skis)
- aluminum flashing or empty soda can (for splints)
- curved tent stake (for pole splint)
- suitable spare parts for ski boot buckles
- small blister pack of quick-set epoxy sealed in a plastic bag
- Superglue (sticks better than epoxy in really cold conditions)
- spare pole basket, expander plug, and replacement tip
- wooden matches (for packing holes)
- small Vise-Grips
- small bungee cord
- nylon cord

Note: A multitool with adjustable heads (so you can place a No. 3 screwdriver or Pozi-Drive bit), knife, pliers, and awl is ideal for a backcountry ski kit.

PADDLERS' REPAIR KIT

Depending on type of craft and materials, a group should have:
- duct tape, kept easily accessible in the cockpit

- alcohol swab
- appropriate hull-repair material, e.g., epoxy, packaged in a resealable plastic bag with accouterments (rubber gloves, waxed-paper mixing cup, squeegee, or patch and rivets)
- small spool of galvanized wire
- knife with awl
- multitool, small Vise-Grips, or pliers
- saw blade for wood (or hacksaw blade for metal if using a folding boat)—a pocket chain saw is an excellent lightweight option
- 50 feet of nylon cord
- spare hardware or fittings
- rubber gaskets or one-size-larger screws to block enlarged fittings
- spare rudder cables and swages, and something to cut them with (multitool or pliers)
- tube of urethane adhesive or sealant
- large square of coated nylon
- bungee cord
- condom

FOLDING BOAT REPAIR KIT, À LA BAIDARKA BOATS

This kit comes in a wide-mouth Nalgene bottle and can fix just about any foldable boat malady known to man or babe. You tell kayak guru Larry Edwards what brand of boat you have, and he'll customize the kit with the appropriate hull and deck material, cold-cure epoxy, air tube patches, and clear, concise instructions. Everything you need, including his own Super Duct Tape. (Contact Baidarka Boats, Box 6001, Sitka, AK 99835, 907-747-8996, <http://www.kayaksite.com>.)

CASCADE OUTFITTERS' RIVER AMBASSADOR INFLATABLES KIT

All you need to save your own wilderness raft trip, and anyone else you meet out there. Everything is contained inside a "Special Weapons" ammo can: PVC and Hypalon repair kits, five kinds of raft valves, esoteric tools, glues, and sewing awl. The cool part is that if you save someone else's hiney out there and tell Cascade Outfitters the story, they'll replace the material you used—for free. (Contact Cascade Outfitters, 604 East 45th St., Boise, ID 83714, 800-223-RAFT/800-223-7238, <http://www.cascadeoutfitters.com>.)

CASCADE DESIGNS THERM-A-REST REPAIR KIT

If you own a Therm-a-Rest or dry bag, you'll need this handy kit. It includes various precut patches of compatible urethane-coated fabric, a tube of Seam Grip, and clear instructions for use. Available at your favorite outdoor store for under $5. (Contact Cascade Designs, 4000 1st Avenue South, Seattle, WA 98134, 206-583-0583, <http://www. cascadedesigns.com>.)

ESSENTIAL MISCELLANY

Aside from items mentioned in the above kits and throughout the book, you might wish you had

- a spare zipper slider
- extra nylon cord
- spare fasteners: hipbelt buckles, ladderlocks, and sliders in assorted widths
- spare cordlocks
- tweezers
- monofilament line
- tie-wraps in various sizes
- hose clamps or Flex Clamps
- glue (Superglue or hot-glue stick)
- urethane adhesive
- cork (fuel bottle cap, instant plug, good fire-starter)
- alcohol swab
- butane lighter and matches

(continued next page)

THE ULTIMATE REPAIR KIT

In the highlands of Guinea in the heart of West Africa a tent pole broke. A seemingly small matter in most places, but we were camped in suffocatingly dense sword grass with buzzing bugs blackening the air. All interstices were thick with carnivorie. To spend a night outside the tent (or with the mosquito netting flat against your body, allowing bugs to shove their proboscises through the nylon) was to wake up the next morning with malaria. But duct tape and a small aluminum sleeve put the tent right and possibly saved our lives.

In the high peaks of Tibet in the heart of Asia a stove stopped. No stove means no water, which means slow, thick blood and frostbite and hypothermia and death at altitude. Here every precious drop of water must be obtained by melting snow. A gasket in the stove's pump had to be replaced, but we didn't have a spare. With a tiny pair of scissors we fashioned a new one from a piece of leather clipped from the tongue of a hiking boot.

My grandmother used to say, "It's the little things in life that matter." In the backcountry, nothing could be more true. The backcountry is abusive; what is made in civilization will break in the wilderness. And it's always the little things that break. The only way to keep going, or sometimes simply to stay alive, is to fix those things yourself. In the wilderness you must be your own mechanic.

To do so, you need a bag of tricks. What follows are the contents of just such a bag. My bag. It's time-tested and has proved its worth on so many occasions I can't remember all the emergencies and all the continents. It weighs about 2 pounds, or 910 grams. (The weight of each item is in parentheses, for you gram counters.) And, like my grandmother used to say, "two pounds of cure are worth a ton of misadventure," or something like that.

- Spare AA batteries (2) for the flashlight (55 grams)
- Buckle, 1 inch, plastic, for ones that break on your pack (5 grams)
- Spare flashlight bulb (5 grams)
- Buttons (5), assorted sizes and colors (5 grams)
- Candle, a squatty one for melting the glue stick and ends of cord to prevent fraying when making repairs; also better than matches for fire-building in survival situations (35 grams)
- Tube of Barge Cement, a multipurpose, heavy-duty glue strong enough to glue soles onto boots, available at shoe-repair stores (70 grams)
- Butane lighter, works better than matches (25 grams)
- Hose clamp, large enough to splint a broken frame pack (25 grams)
- Clevis pins (2) with wire rings, for external-frame pack repair (10 grams)
- Spare compass, very small, in case you lose your big one and your way at the same time (15 grams)
- Cord, 30 feet of the 2 mm thickness, for var-

- webbing pack strap
- pair of 36-inch rawhide laces
- fishing swivel (fixes eyeglass hinges)
- 50-pound-test fishing leader (use for anything)

ZIPPER RESCUE KIT

Any repair service will tell you that nearly a third of its income is zipper-related, and most of those jobs take about 15 minutes to fix. During his tenure in the canvas business, Mike McCabe, of

ious duties like lashing pack parts together when zippers or straps fail (40 grams)

- Cordlocks, replacements for when those on your sleeping bag, pack, or jacket fail (10 grams)
- Duct tape, minimum of a half a roll of the highly adhesive, reinforced kind; uses are innumerable (60 grams)
- Glue, one stick of the heat-gun type which, when held over a candle, can be used for such things as sealing a tiny hole in a self-inflating sleeping pad, or a cracked water bottle (15 grams); you can opt for a tiny tube of Superglue
- Mosquito netting, 5- by 5-inch piece, for patching holes in the tent's bug shield (5 grams)
- Paper and pencil, for emergency messages (20 grams)
- Nylon packcloth patch, 5- by 5-inch piece, for tent, pack, or jacket repair (5 grams)
- Leather patch, 5- by 5-inch piece, for heavy-duty patching needs (wears better than nylon) (20 grams)
- Diaper pins (5), largest and strongest you can find (10 grams)
- Pliers, 4-inch, for zipper repair and removing teeth and stray bullets (150 grams)
- Pole sleeve, 3-inch aluminum tube that slips over broken tent poles (15 grams)
- Razor blades (2), single-edged (15 grams)
- Rubber bands, assortment, heavy gauge (15 grams)

- Sandpaper, 5-inch by 5-inch piece, medium grade (10 grams)
- Scissors, sturdy, high-quality, collapsible (40 grams)
- Stove parts: filter, filter wire, plugs, stove wrench, gaskets, spare jet, and any other miscellaneous pieces your model might need (30 grams)
- Strap, 10 feet, 1-inch flat nylon with buckle, for replacing those that inevitably pop off your pack (100 grams)
- Thread, needle, and a metal thimble. Thread should be thin and waxed (or use dental floss). You'll need one large, one medium, and two leather needles (3-sided, that can penetrate thick material like leather and webbing). All should have large eyes (20 grams).
- Velcro, 5 inches of a 1-inch-wide strip with the sticky stuff on both sides, for jacket or sleeping bag repair when the zippers are shot (10 grams)
- Wire, 5 feet of high-quality braided steel, flexible and resistant to snapping (25 grams)
- Zippered plastic bags (5), assorted sizes (10 grams)
- Zipper heads and sliders, set each for tent, jacket, and pack zipper (20 grams)
- Small Swiss Army knife with bottle opener, blade, and screwdriver
  Carry it all in a well-stitched nylon stuff sack.

Reprinted from *Backpacker* magazine, October 1992, with permission of author and adventurer Mark Jenkins.

McCall, Idaho, realized that what most people didn't know about zippers would fill a book. Mike's superb booklet serves as a manual to his various Zipper Rescue Kits, complete little zipper tackle boxes. The kits include zipper sizes most commonly used in outdoor gear, plus stops, thread and needle for home and field repair. Find them in your outdoor shop or contact Z.R.K. Enterprises, P.O. Box 1213, McCall, ID 83638, 208-634-4851, <*http://www.mccall.net/zippers*>.

Tools and Supplies for the Trail and Shop

Awl A punch for creating stitch holes in beefy materials, like leather or vinyl.

Buffer Orbital, auto-waxer type for spiffing up fiberglass or aluminum boats.

Bungee Elastic cord with hooked ends useful for temporary fastening; make your own from old inner tubes.

Candy Helps keep blood sugar and spirits up during late-night-before-the-trip repair jobs.

Caulk Urethane adhesive type or silicone comes in handy for filling holes or sealing joints.

C-clamp A size range of C-clamps are useful when gluing anything from boot soles to canoe rails. Vise-Grips also serve the purpose.

Chamois Ideal for cleaning optics or buffing glass boats.

Closed-cell foam *See* Minicell foam.

Corrugator Small roller that gives even distribution of adhesive or resin.

C-clamp

Dragonskin Cheese-grater-like sanding sheets originally designed for sheetrock; a popular sculpting tool for minicell foam blocks.

Drill Cordless is ideal for driving or removing screws, sanding, or buffing.

Eyedropper For intricate cleaning or priming your Optimus stove.

power drill

Fan May be required when working with flammable or toxic adhesives and resins to ventilate a space; usually placed low to blow away heavy toxic fumes.

File For sharpening skis, knives, and climbing hardware;

mill bastard file

a 10- to 12-inch mill bastard file gives best all-around results. For field use, break the file in half to make it more compact. You might want a round chain-saw file to touch up damaged ice screws.

Flex clamp This modern, lightweight alternative to lashing and hose clamps eliminates the need for tools, so it is especially useful in the backcountry repair kit. Nylon flex clamps are reusable and don't rust. (Contact P.D.S. International, P.O. Box 381, New Milford, CT 06776.)

Gloves Several types, including thin leather, heavy-duty rubber, nitrile, and surgical latex.

Grommet setter Home users can purchase a small grommet kit, including a setter, at a sewing supply or hardware store.

Hose clamps Like the name implies, hose clamps are designed to secure auto hoses to ports; they

hose clamp

come in zillions of sizes and adjust to fit any diameter with a screwdriver and wrench. Hose clamps are useful for splinting skis and poles of any type.

Inner tubes Save old bicycle tubes for roof-rack tie-downs or any job requiring elastic bungee action. For recycled straps rigged with Fastex buckles, contact Tube Ties/Resource Revival, 2342 NW Marshall, Portland, OR 97210, 503-226-6001, 800-866-9923.

Lubricants Various types for different tasks; i.e., silicone, dry graphite, waterproof bike grease, household oil.

Minicell foam Super as padding, blocking, or filler—custom-shape with Dragonskin. Use as disposable applicator for adhesives or as squeegee.

Multitool, a.k.a. Leatherman Collapsible multitools are a pioneer's dream, with everything on a Swiss Army knife plus the torque of full-sized pliers. Definitely worth the price.

PakTowl Cut up one of these viscose fiber camp towels to use like chamois cloth for a zillion tasks.

Superabsorbent, easy to clean and dry.

Paracord Trust us, you will never have enough of this repair commodity. Buy it by the mile.

Pozi-driver An obscure but important tool for setting ski binding screws; may be purchased as a stout screwdriver or as drill bits (ask at a ski shop). A No. 3 Phillips head may be substituted.

Preval sprayer Refillable cartridge sprayer for painting, sealing, or thin gelcoat applications.

Quick Grip Miniclamp available at hardware or auto parts stores; like a ratcheting Vise-Grip for awkward jobs when you need an adjustable third hand.

Respirator mask For use anytime you glue or sand to avoid inhaling fumes or particles.

Rivet gun Basically a specialized stapler, a rivet gun saves a lot of extra dings and dents caused by hammering a rivet into position.

Safety goggles Protect your eyes from metal, wood, or glass particles whenever filing, sanding, scraping, or cutting. Also essential for safety when using adhesives or thermoset resins.

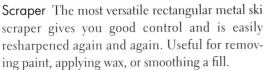

wear safety goggles

Scraper The most versatile rectangular metal ski scraper gives you good control and is easily resharpened again and again. Useful for removing paint, applying wax, or smoothing a fill.

Seam sealer Myriad uses, from filling to caulking to patching.

Silica gel packets To absorb moisture in electronics bags.

Sharpening stone Palm-sized for a winter kit to smooth burrs on ski edges and of course for sharpening.

Ski vises Different from a regular bench vise, ski vises are sold by the pair and are designed to accommodate ski widths for efficient tuning.

Snap setter Like a grommet setter, snap setters are usually procured as part of a kit at a sewing supply or hardware store.

Squeegee For spreading adhesives or scraping up messes.

Surform A raspy file that looks like a cheese grater, this is the tool for trimming and shaping green epoxy, C4 rubber, and the like.

Sweater Stone A square-cut pumice that scrapes cooties and fuzz balls off wool and synthetic fabric. From yarn shops or sweater boutiques. (Contact Sweater Stone, Box 467, Issaquah, WA 98027.)

surform tool

Swiss Army knife The original red essential can be all things to all people. Remember, a knife that's also a saw that's really a magnifying glass may be too cumbersome to actually carry.

Syringe Irrigating type without needle (also used to dispense baby aspirin) is ideal for fine seamsealing work.

Tack cloth Lint-free, solvent-impregnated cloth used to remove fine dust particles immediately prior to gluing or painting.

Tape Duct tape, nylon repair tape, electrical tape, and white adhesive tape are all considered essentials.

Tie-Wraps Good for restraining hostages. Nah, get these in several sizes; they save you from having to learn how to lash things the old-fashioned way.

Tool dip Plastic grip material for recoating handles; useful for finishing raw edges and rope ends.

TriFlow Penetrating lubricant with Teflon available at auto or bicycle shops.

Tweezers A tiny precision tweezer will come in handy for stitch removal, splinter extraction, or when rebuilding watches. Use those on your Swiss Army knife or look for the superb handling pinpoint type manufactured by El Mar (43 Cody Street, West Hartford, CT 06110).

Twist ties Coated wire (gardener's tye), a litter nuisance cured by Ziplocs but very useful for eyeglass hinge, zipper pull, etc.

Utility knife For cutting or trimming rubber, ABS, you name it.

utility knife

Vise-Grips The third hand. Available in various sizes, adjustable, locking Vise-Grips are used as a clamp or pliers.

Waxing iron Usually a yard-sale score, a waxing iron is used to apply or remove waxes from ski bases and occasionally to remove adhesives. Don't use an iron set higher than "wool" on any synthetic, or you risk altering the material. Commer-

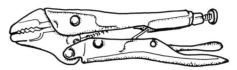

ViseGrips -- locking pliers -- essential "third hand"

cial waxing irons (available at ski shops) allow you to control temperature settings more accurately.

Woodburning pencil Useful when held in a vise to heat-seal edges of synthetic fabrics.

Useful Knots

Learning a few knots so well you can tie them upside down in the dark is an important aspect of repair. You may need to join two lines of different sizes or lash splintered parts together; with the basic knot repertoire suggested here, you'll be well equipped.

Bowline Fast and supersecure, a bowline is favored for anchoring, hauling, and many other jobs because the knot is essentially slip-proof, making a fixed loop.

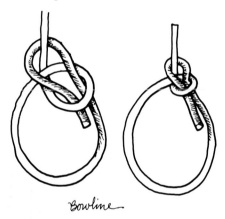

Bowline

Clove hitch Two stacked loops attach a line to a bar or post. A clove hitch is easily tied with one hand, is adjustable after tying, and is the start of most lashings.

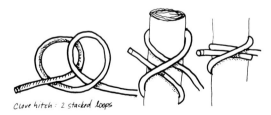

Clove hitch : 2 stacked loops

Figure 8 Symmetrical and strong, the figure-8 is popular for fastening loops because it's easy to check for accuracy.

Figure Eight

Figure 8 on a bight One of the simplest methods to create a fastening link, an eight on a bight is fast and strong. Finish with an overhand knot.

Figure Eight on a Bight

SUSAN MANNING, KNOTWRIGHT

A sharp, round, homespun woman, Susan Howard Manning somehow gives the sense of being old and young at the same time. One moment she is a pigtailed girl in a pirate blouse with the laugh of a loon; then she is of another age entirely, one that preferred buttons to zippers. She reminds us of an outspoken Victorian naturalist: she is frank when she chooses to speak and enjoys the clarification of all things—shells, bedrock, flora, moods, birds, the weather. Annie likes what they talk about together, the questions she asks, the questions she makes Annie ask. She's gifted with her hands, can make something out of nothing with soft, earthy material like clay, canvas, or string. She attributes her passion for found objects to a piratical nature—Susan's mercurial father claimed Blackbeard as a distant progenitor.

Susan's vocation as a knotwright became apparent when she was a 10-year-old mate on her father's Danish sailboat. "My father taught me how to whip and splice rope: the Matthew Walker knot, the wall and crown. He had a copy of *The Ashley Book of Knots*. I wasn't a good reader, so I followed the drawings." *Ashley's* is found on every nautophile's shelf, so it's no surprise that Susan's canvas-covered book looks like a careworn family Bible. As Annie leafs through it, the elegant patterns and intricate labyrinths make her eyes blur; she recalls the spirograph set she had as a kid.

There are about 4,000 known and recorded knots, and given enough time, Susan could do them all. "I will do those that have a use," she explains. Susan sees beauty in necessary things. Annie and Susan talk about the lost art of knot-tying, eclipsed by much stronger, modern casted or molded parts and fittings. Ever the pragmatist, Susan sternly diffuses our romantic notions about her craft. "The seamen who made knots like this had nowhere to go but down. They couldn't read, couldn't write; sailing—with its tropical diseases and accidents—ruined their health, and they died friendless in foreign ports. . . . I don't want to do that."

Well, we're still impressed. If you paw around in her handworked canvas sack, you'll find the arcane tools of the knotwright's trade. Contents: needlenose pliers; assorted needles and awls for working canvas and leather; 25-year-old sailor's palm; lump of wax; assorted brass hollow fids for threading; tiny knotted doll for good luck. Open a spice tin and find dozens of neatly coiled bits of thread—the proverbial box of string too short to save.

Susan takes time for things most people never bother with. It's not that Susan and her husband, Sam, reject our cellular age; they just

Fisherman's knot (grapevine) Used to join two ropes of equal diameter, this knot is bombproof but difficult to untie. Basically formed by tying an overhand knot over

fisherman's knot

Susan Manning, knotwright.

The knotwright's arcane tools include various marlin-spikes, awls, hooks, clamps, hollow fids, wax, thread, an antique bone seam-flattener, and a whole lot of know-how.

don't set their clocks by it. What may seem to some as anachronicity is authenticity; what appears utilitarian becomes high art. Austerity is rich, economy is Zen. Their thrift is essentially efficient, with no more or no less effort than is necessary to accomplish a task. There's a right way to do things, and that's what they do. Annie seeks them out when she's disillusioned and brings some mending along. They talk about birds and books and boats, and she leaves feeling something like belief, or maybe faith. Both hard to come by, harder to pass up.

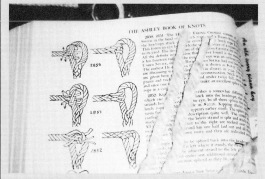

The Ashley Book of Knots *is every sailor's Bible.*

another line, then repeating the step with the opposite line. A double grapevine is stronger than a single.

Double Fisherman's Knot a k a Grapevine

Lashing Successful lashing relies on a secure start (the clove hitch) plus equal and opposite tension on the objects you are trying to lash.

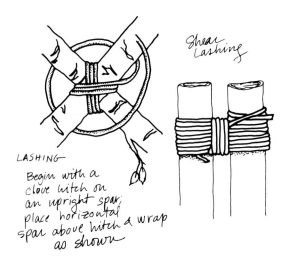

Square knot Join lines of equal diameter with a square knot. Be aware that this knot is a little *too* easy to untie.

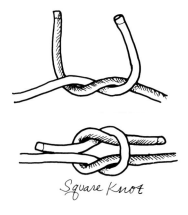

Shear Lashing

LASHING

Begin with a clove hitch on an upright spar; place horizontal spar above hitch & wrap as shown

Square Knot

Overhand knot The simplest knot is most commonly used to finish another knot.

overhand knot

Sheet bend Lines of unequal diameter are united with a sheet bend; use the larger-size line to form the bight. This is the classic jury-rigging knot, and it's easy to untie.

Tautline hitch Take up slack or maintain tension on a guyline with a tautline hitch; this knot works best with larger ropes (about ¼-inch diameter or greater).

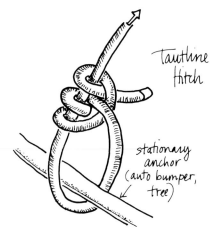

Tautline hitch

stationary anchor (auto bumper, tree)

sheet Bend

Trucker's hitch A must-know knot for roof-racking, the trucker's hitch provides strong cinching power for tent guylines and boat tie-downs.

Whipping Finish the end of a natural-fiber rope by tightly whipping with a length of string.

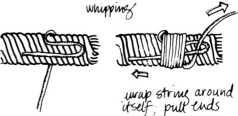

whipping

wrap string around itself; pull ends

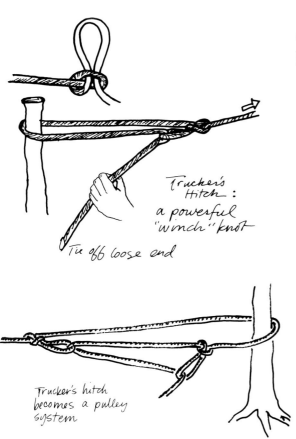

Trucker's Hitch : a powerful "winch" knot

Tie off loose end

Trucker's hitch becomes a pulley system

Directory of Repair Services

There are always times when repair solutions are better left to an expert. Those listed here have long experience revitalizing worn equipment and know the ins and outs of fabric, boot, or stove construction better than anyone. Manufacturers, retailers, and consumers alike rely on the accumulated expertise of repair centers—many are actually factory-certified "outreach" clinics. For the best and most efficient service possible, it pays to follow a few simple rules of etiquette.

1. **Call first.** Find out the preferred method and exact location for shipping your gear, and what minimum charges and turnaround time may be. Do not expect a cost estimate over the telephone (although you can request one before any work is begun).

2. **Clean the gear prior to shipping.** Imagine the fumes in a cobbler shop with several dozen climbing boots waiting for resoles! If you do send in grungy gear, you'll be charged for cleaning—especially if you fail to remove a "temporary" duct tape patch. Remove laces from boots, check pockets, shake out tents, and detach any removable appendages.

3. **Clearly label your gear.** Provide a note with instructions or further information about the prospective repair.

4. **Send only the item to be repaired.** If a tent needs new zippers, don't send the fly and poles, too.

5. **Allow plenty of time** for repairs, or expect to pay a rush charge.

SOFT GOODS/SEWING REPAIR SERVICES

Cascade Designs
Warranty & Repair
4000 1st Ave. South
Seattle WA 98134
800-527-1527, fax 206-467-9421
http://www.cascadedesigns.com
Warranty service on all Therm-a-Rest mattresses; field kits available.

Cyrex Accessories & Mountaineering Products
Andrew Mysyk
#9 4412 Manilla Rd. SE
Calgary AB
T2G-4B7 CANADA
403-243-7086
Complete sewing repairs and cleaning of packs, garments, tents and bags, including zippers and tent poles. Custom design and modifications a specialty. Gore-Tex authorized.

Mountain Gear, Inc.
Paul Fish
2002 North Division
Spokane WA 99207
509-325-9000, 800-829-2009
http://www.mgear.com
General sewing and zipper repair to tents, packs, bags. Also provides general stove service and repairs to MSR and Optimus brands.

Needle Mountain Designs
Peggy Quinn & Laura Pierce
P.O. Box 3578
28261 Main St.
Evergreen CO 80439
303-674-2941, 800-795-2941
General sewing and repair of tents, bags, packs, zippers, including structural repairs, custom designs, and modifications for disabled athletes. Refilling of down bags and garments.

Patty Spiro Sewing
264 Tanasee Gap Road
Balsam Grove NC 28708
704-862-3278

PSEWING@citcom.net
General sewing and outdoor gear repair for bags, packs, and tents.

Ragged Mountain Equipment
P.O. Box 130
Rte 16/302
Intervale NH 03845
603-356-3042
Fabrics, notions, and patterns available. General sewing and repair, plus custom packmaking. Climbing runners bartacked; also reslinging of cam units.

Rainy Pass Repair
5307 Roosevelt Way NE
Seattle WA 98105
888-747-7867
http://www.rainypass.com
Authorized Gore-Tex repair specialist, plus factory authorization from myriad manufacturers and retailers. Repairs and alterations, custom sewing, down re-filling, zipper repairs, plus cleaning service. Also service on Coleman camp stoves.

Seattle Fabrics
3876 Bridge Way North
Seattle WA 98103
206-632-6022
Though not a repair service, this is fabric Mecca for outdoor enthusiasts. Fabrics, notions, patterns, accessories galore, plus sound advice. Call for listing of current inventory and prices.

Sport Sewing Shop
Karen Abbot
1931 Gerrard St. East
Toronto ON
M4L 2C2 CANADA
416-690-4669, fax 416-690-4987
sportsewing@sprint.ca
Fabrics and notions supplier. General sewing/repair and alterations on packs, tents, bags, zippers, garments. Authorized Gore-Tex service, Suter waterproof testing, and factory-like finished repairs.

Super Stitches
Terry Sheban
904 Tod Ave.
Youngstown OH 44502
216-743-6865
Sewing and zipper repair to packs, tents, bags. No garments, please.

ZRK Enterprises
258 A St. #16B
Ashland OR 97520
800-735-4620
http://www.mccall.net/zippers
Factory-authorized by YKK to minister to all zipperheads. Repair on all softgoods, plus great kits.

STOVE REPAIR

Consult your local outfitter for parts, and ask if they'll service your stove.

A & H Enterprises
1582 Parkway Loop G
Tustin CA 92680
888-456-0748
http://www.packstoves.com
Cleaning and repair of Optimus, Svea, Primus, Camping Gaz, Coleman camp stoves. Spare parts available.

Coleman Products
Consumer Repair Information
800-835-3278
Don't expect to get through to an actual person when you call this national number. Instead, run down to your local outfitter and purchase the well-distributed replacement parts there.

Mountain Safety Research
Warranty & Repair
4225 2nd Ave. South
Seattle WA 98134
800-245-2992, fax 206-682-4184
http://www.msrcorp.com
If you simply can't work out the quirks on your stove, MSR's excellent service department can revive it.

TENT POLE REPAIR

Consult your local outfitter or tent manufacturer—your pole problem may be covered under warranty.

Ralph's Tent & Tarp
Ralph Powell
10253 Mississippi Blvd.
Coon Rapids MN 55433
612-421-7053
General tent repairs including sewing, zippers and tent poles fixed or replaced. Also general sewing and zipper repairs to packs and bags.

Sunshine Tent Pole Specialists
23679 Calabasas Rd. Unit 162
Calabasas CA 91302
818-222-5217
polerepair@aol.com
Factory authorized by most major manufacturers and retailers.

TA Enterprises
8212 NE 99th Circle
Vancouver WA 98662
800-266-9527
http://www.alcasoft.com/TA-enterprises
Repair or replacement of any tent poles using Easton aluminum tubes and accessories.

Tent Repair Services (formerly Moss Tent Repair)
Pendra Legasse
P.O. Box 577
20½ Sea St.
Camden ME 04843
207-236-0997
Besides warranty repairs to Moss tents, repairs on tents, zippers, and other outdoor gear.

BOOTS

Most of these superb cobblers can provide you with factory-original replacement soles and several varieties of climbing rubber; just ask what brands they specialize in. Many also offer varying midsole stiffnesses for a custom fit. Not all have deep-cavity presses to rebuild molded-sole boots.

Cobbler & Cordwainer
David Yulan
73 Crescent Ave.
New Rochelle NY 10801
800-788-2668
Resoling of hiking boots; telemark boots rebuilt, resoled; rock climbing shoes resoled. Can resole molded soles.

Dave Page, Cobbler
3509 Evanston Avenue North
Seattle WA 98103
206-632-8686, 800-252-1229
Repairs and resoles for climbing, hiking, telemark boots. Besides restoring to original quality "every mountain or hiking boot sold in North America for the last twenty-five years," including plastic mountain boots and supergaiters, Dave Page is also the place to get your Birkenstocks or sport sandals attended to. Deep-cavity presses for molded soles.

Komito Boots
Steve Komito
P.O. Box 2106
235 West Riverside
Estes Park CO 80517
800-422-2668
303-586-5391
General repairs and resoles of climbing, hiking, and telemark boots. Custom fitting a specialty; also conversion of leather hiking boots or old leather downhill boots to telemark.

L.L. Bean Boot Repair Center
Casco St.
Freeport ME 04032
800-341-4341
Reconditioning and rebottoming of the classic gum rubber and leather boots.

Mekan Boot
Gary Mekan
2070 E. 3900 South
Salt Lake City UT 84124
800-657-2884

General repairs and resoles on hiking, climbing, and telemark boots. Birkenstock and sport sandal resoles. Custom boots made to order.

Morin Custom Boots & Repair
P.O. Box 3277
1446 Miner St.
Idaho Springs CO 80452
800-228-BOOT/800-228-2668, 303-567-4686
Custom boot construction plus repair and resoling to all types of boots, featuring a proprietary "Morin" midsole. Custom footbeds and orthotics fitted. Molded soles resoled.

Mountain Soles
Bill McKinney
P.O. Box 28
Trout Lake WA 98650
509-395-2844
bimkin@linkport.com
Call for shipping address. Climbing, mountain, and telemark repair and resoles, including leatherwork on telemark boots. Conversion of hiking/ski boots to telemark a specialty. Birkenstocks and sport sandal resoles.

Progressive Outdoor Footwear Repair
John Southward
8235 La Mesa Blvd.
La Mesa CA 91941
619-469-0567, 800-783-7764
General repairs and resoles of climbing, hiking, and telemark boots; sport sandals and Birkenstocks a specialty.

Wilson's Eastside Sports
224 N. Main St.
Bishop CA 93514
760-873-7520
http://www.eastsidesports.com
Full boot service: resoling rock, hiking, telemark, and double boots. Supergaiter rands rebuilt. Also pack, tent, and stove repair.

CANOES AND KAYAKS

Consult your manufacturer for the recommended repair resource closest to you. The manufacturer is also your best source for repair kits and parts suited to your exact hull.

Baidarka Boats
Larry Edwards
Box 6001
201 Lincoln St.
Sitka AK 99835
907-747-8996, fax 907-747-4801
http://www.kayaksite.com
Unsurpassed folding boat experts. Larry Edwards knows every part and widget on every skin boat ever sold in North America. Great stock of obscure, specialized hardware for all makes, plus fine outfitting gear for discerning paddlers.

Jack's Plastic Welding
Jack Kloepfer
115 South Main
Aztec NM 87410
505-334-8748, fax 505-334-1901
jacks@frontier.net
Although Jack's is a wholesale supplier of plastic welding supplies, they do offer a kayak repair video that demonstrates the process. Additionally, they may be able to refer you to someone in your area who is experienced and equipped for welding polyethylene hulls.

Klepper Service Center–North America
Mark Eckhart
2526 South Adams
Denver CO 80210
303-782-9743
Full repair service for Kleppers of all vintages. Replacement parts available.

(See also appendix G, Materials Resources, Canoe and Kayak Outfitting and Supplies, beginning on page 237.)

Materials Resources

This listing groups suppliers of materials referenced in the text—some are manufacturers or distributors, others are mail-order retailers. Consult your nearest outfitter first and buy locally if possible (especially when purchasing adhesives, often hazardous to ship). Manufacturers or distributors may choose to refer you to a dealer in your area.

SEAMSEALERS, FABRIC TREATMENTS, AND REPAIR ADHESIVES

(See also appendix F for purveyors of fabrics and notions.)

Kenyon Consumer Products
P.O. Box 3715
Peace Dale RI 02883
800-537-0024
kcp@kenyonconsumer.com
Manufacturer of the ubiquitous K-Tape nylon repair tape available at most outfitters; K-Kote seamsealer and recoating products; some water-based formulas also available. Spray and wash-cycle fabric treatments and cleaners for down. Compact sewing kit.

McNett Corporation
1405 Fraser Street
P.O. Box 996
Bellingham WA 98227
800-221-7325
office@mcnett.com
Superior urethane adhesive products designed for watersports but transcending to any outdoor fabrics that require waterproofing—Seam Grip, Freesole, etc.

Nikwax USA
P.O. Box 1572
Everett WA 98206
800-577-2700, fax 425-303-1242
http://www.nikwax-usa.com
Ask your local outfitter to carry these fine water-based fabric and leather treatments. High-performance and long-wearing DWR treatments are state-of-the-industry, with formulations for leathers, cotton, down, waterproof-breathable, and coated fabrics.

Tectron
4445 E. Fremont St.
Stockton CA 95215
800-289-2583, fax 209-465-5896
http://www.bluemagic.com
Tectron family of waterproofing treatments include products for every type of fabric and leather. Its DWR formula contains UV-inhibitors—ideal for tents or tarps.

ROCK SHOE RESOLE KITS
Five Ten
P.O. Box 1185
Redlands CA 92373
909-798-4222, fax 909-798-5272
Various types of sticky rubber for do-it-yourself resoles.

BOOTFITTING
Superfeet
800-634-6618, fax 360-384-2724
http://www.superfeet.com

ALPINE AND WINTER GEAR RESOURCES
Ascension Enterprises
Box 159
Ridgway CO 81432
970-626-5612, fax 970-626-5107
ascension@ascensiongear.com
Climbing skin manufacturer provides regluing service and proprietary adhesive for at-home repairs.

Custom tip and tail kits available. Skin regluing service using proprietary hot-melt process.

Mountain Tools
140 Calle del Oaks
Monterey CA 93940
408-393-1000
Excellent catalog offers top-quality mountain gear and care accessories, including boot-fitting supplies, resole kits, rope cleansers, webbing, more.

Ramer Products
1803 S. Foothills Hwy.
Boulder CO 80403
303-499-4466
State-of-the-art backcountry ski technology includes climbing skin accessories and adhesives, plus high-tech adhesive laminate process for skins that have not seen silicone. Ask about the unique Ramer Pole Patch, ideal for any aluminum tube repair.

Stowe Canoe & Snowshoe Company
Box 207 River Road
Stowe VT 05672
800-882-2748, fax 802-253-9982
http://www.tubbssnowshoes.com
Repair parts, accessories, and terrific step-by-step instructions for reweaving traditional wooden snowshoes with rawhide or neoprene lacing.

CANOE AND KAYAK OUTFITTING AND SUPPLIES

Baidarka Boats
Box 6001
201 Lincoln Street
Sitka AK 99835
907-747-8996, fax 907-747-4801
http://www.kayaksite.com
Great stock of obscure, specialized hardware for all folding boats; fine outfitting gear for discerning paddlers.

Cascade Outfitters
604 E. 45th St.
Boise ID 83714
800-223-7238
http://www.cascadeoutfitters.com
Resource nonpareil for all inflatable supplies, including glues and field kits.

Dyson Baidarka & Co.
435 W. Holly
Bellingham WA 98225
360-734-9226
Skin-boat visionary Dyson offers plans and materials.

H.H. Perkins Company
10 South Bridge St.
Woodbridge CT 06525
800-462-6600
Since 1917. Caning supplies and instructions for repairing canoe seats. Small quantities available.

Headwaters
P.O. Box 1356
Route 8, Box 204
Harriman TN 37748
615-882-8757
Canoe and kayak outfitting supplies and accessories. Check out their E-Z UV Cure fiberglass patch kit, a wilderness tripper's dream.

Mad River Canoe/Confluence
P.O. Box 610
Waitsfield VT 05673
802-496-3127, fax 802-496-6247
http://www.madrivercanoe.com
Mad River spends about as much time educating about care and repair of their fine boats as they do designing and paddling them. Repair kits plus a full range of outfitting adhesives and supplies available, including the sometimes-hard-to-find 303 Protectant.

Nantahala Outdoor Center
41 Hwy. 19 West
Bryson City NC 28713
800-367-3521
If you're stumped for a boat-fixing solution, chances are somebody at NOC has already been there, done that. Great catalog with full range of adhesives, foams, outfitting supplies, and ideas.

Northwoods Canoe Company
RFD 3 Box 118-A2
Dover-Foxcroft ME 04426
207-564-3667
Home of wood-and-canvas gurus Stelmok and Thurlow. Find literature, supplies, and a l-o-o-ong waiting list for one of their signature canoes.

Northwest River Supply
2009 South Main St.
Moscow ID 83843
800-635-5202
Another fine regional resource for watersports out-fitting and repair accessories and adhesives.

OS Systems
33550 SE Santosh
Scappoose OR 97056
503-543-3126
Drysuit seals par excellence, including proprietary adhesive and suggestions for home repair. Gasket replacement service.

Under Cover
P.O. Box 609
Hyannis MA 02601
800-275-2580
Canoe and kayak covers for indoor-outdoor storage and transport.

Recommended Reading

BOOKS

Barry, John. *Snow and Ice Climbing*. Seattle: Cloudcap, 1987.

Beckett, Samuel. *Waiting for Godot: With a Revised Text*. Ed. Dougald McMillan and James Knowlson. New York: Grove Press, 1994.

Benuzzi, Felice. *No Picnic on Mount Kenya*. New York: Lyons Press, 1999.

Bloch, Arthur. *Murphy's Law, and Other Reasons Why Things Go Wrong*. Los Angeles: Price/Stern/Sloan, 1977.

Burch, Monte. *Outdoorsman's Fix-It Book*. New York: Harper & Row, 1971.

Campbell, Charles. *The Backpacker's Photography Handbook*. New York: Amphoto, Watson-Guptill Publications, 1994.

Conover, Garrett, and Alexandra Conover. *A Snow Walker's Companion*. Camden ME: Ragged Mountain Press, 1995.

Daffern, Tony. *Avalanche Safety for Skiers and Climbers*. Seattle WA: Cloudcap, 1983.

Davidson, James W., and John Rugge. *Complete Wilderness Paddler*. New York: Random House, 1982.

Diaz, Ralph. *Complete Folding Kayaker*. Camden ME: Ragged Mountain Press, 1994.

Dowd, John. *Sea Kayaking, A Manual for Long-Distance Touring*, 3rd ed. Seattle: University of Washington Press, 1988.

Dunn, John M. *Winterwise, a Backpacker's Guide*. Lake George NY: Adirondack Mountain Club, 1989.

Gillette, Ned, and John Dostal. *Cross-Country Skiing*, 3rd ed. Seattle: Mountaineers, 1988.

Goodman, David. *Classic Backcountry Skiing: A Guide to the Best Ski Tours in New England*, 2nd ed. Boston: AMC Books, 1998.

Graydon, Don, ed. *Mountaineering: Freedom of the Hills*, 5th ed. Seattle: Mountaineers, 1992.

Haban, Melanie, ed. *Field Manual for the U.S. Antarctic Program*. Englewood CO: Antarctic Support Associates, 1994.

Jacobson, Cliff. *Canoeing Wild Rivers*, 2nd ed. Merrillville IN: ICS Books, 1989.

Juster, Norton. *The Phantom Tollbooth*. New York: Random House, 1996.

Kline, Rich, and the editors of Stackpole Books. *Taking Care of Outdoor Gear*. Harrisburg: Stackpole Books, 1983.

Long, John. *How to Rock Climb!*, 2nd ed. Evergreen CO: Chockstone Press, 1993.

Osgood, William E., and Leslie J. Hurley. *The Snowshoe Book*. New York: Viking Penguin, 1983.

Parker, Paul. *Free-Heel Skiing: The Secrets of Telemark and Parallel Techniques—In All Conditions*. Post Mills VT: Chelsea Green, 1988.

Putz, George. *Wood and Canvas Kayak Building*. Camden ME: International Marine, 1990.

Riviere, William, and the staff of L.L. Bean. *The L.L. Bean Guide to the Outdoors*. New York: Random House, 1981.

Sports Afield, editors of. *Outdoor Skills: An Almanac with Thousands of Helpful Ideas for Better Hiking, Fishing, Camping, and Other Outdoor Activities*. New York: Hearst Books, 1991.

Stelmok, Jerry, and Rollin Thurlow. *The Wood and Canvas Canoe: A Complete Guide to Its History, Construction, Restoration, and Maintenance.* Gardiner ME: Tilbury House, 1987.

Sumner, Louise L. *Sew and Repair Your Own Outdoor Gear.* Seattle: Mountaineers, 1988.

Townsend, Chris. *The Backpacker's Handbook.* Camden ME: Ragged Mountain Press, 1992.

Vaillancourt, Henri. *Making the Attikamek Snowshoe.* Greenville NH: Trust for Native American Cultures and Crafts, 1987.

Washburne, Randel. *The Coastal Kayaker's Manual: A Complete Guide to Skills, Gear, and Sea Sense.* Old Saybrook CT: Globe Pequot, 1989.

PERIODICALS

Backpacker
33 E. Minor Street
Emmaus PA 18098
http://www.bpbasecamp.com

Canoe & Kayak
P.O. Box 3146
Kirkland WA 98083
http://www.canoekayak.com

Climbing
P.O. Box 339
Carbondale CO 81623
http://www.climbing.com

Sea Kayaker
P.O. Box 17170
Seattle WA 98107

HELPFUL WEBSITES

http://www.altrec.com
http://www.backpacker.com
http://www.gorp.com
http://www.npca.org
http://www.nps.gov
http://www.tia.org/discover/getallstos.asp (travel and tourism offices for the 50 states)
http://www.usfs.gov

touring skis. *See* skis, cross-country
Trango USA, 132
TriFlow, uses of, 17, 115, 126,
    175
trucker's hitch knot, **231**
Tubbs, snowshoe repair kits, 150
tumplines, **74**
tweezers, 225
twist ties, 225

U

umbrellas, use of, **119**
underlayers, 28
Upton, Bob (Rainy Pass Repair), 9
urethane adhesives, 214
    fabric patches, 8–9, 36, 38, 39,
        41
    hull patches, 173
    on telemark boots, 86
UV degradation, 37–38, 44–45

V

valves (sleeping pads), 61
vapor barrier liners (VBLs), 56,
    80
Varathane, 174
varnish, 204, 205
Velcro, 16, 35
vents
    in clothing, 32
    in tents, 45, 47, 48
vinegar, 173
vinyl, patching with, 63–64, 214
vinylester resins, 161, 214
Vynabond, 63, 189

W

waders, neoprene, 38
water filters, care and use of, **104**–6
water-repellency. *See also* seam-
    sealing
    boots, 77–80
    cotton, 26
    drysuits, 39–40
    DWR (durable water repellent),
        26, 31–33
    gloves, 42
    restoring
        in fabric, 26, 31–33, 36
        in tents, 26, 47, 49
    ropes, 128
    synthetics, 36
    tents, 26, 47, 49–50
    water-based polymer coatings, 79
wax, ski, 140, 141–42
waxes
    on boots, 78
    as cotton waterproofing, 26
    for zippers, 15
webbing, **20**
websites, recommended, 240
WEST System kits, 177
wetsuits. *See also* neoprene
    care of, **37**–39
    patching, 38–39
    storage of, 38
    zippers, 15
whipping, **231**
wind, tents and, 46
wine bladders, uses of, 155
winter gear

care and repair, 137–53
materials and resources, 236–37
wood and canvas boats, 190
    adhesives/resins/fillers, 158, 160
    books on, 190
    hull properties, 158
    storage, 158
    UV protection, 158
Wood and Canvas Canoe, The
    (Stelmok and Thurlow), 190
wood ash, cleaning with, 108
wood rails, on canoes, 191–**92**, 193
wool
    care and cleaning, 27

Z

zippers
    care and Zen of, 14–15
    coil, 11–**12**, 13, 57
    drysuit, 39
    lubrication, 14–15
    nonseparating, **12**
    on packs, 66
    parts of, 12
    repairing, **13**, 14, 57, 66,
        222–23
    replacing, 14
        sliders, 12–13, 66
    sizes, 12–13
    sleeping bag, 57–58
    toothed, 11, **12**
    troubleshooting problems,
        13–14
    types of, 10–**12**
    wetsuits, 15